Bulbs of North America

BULBS
of
North America

Jane McGary

EDITOR

Timber Press
and
North American Rock Garden Society

Mention of trademark, proprietary product, or vendor does not constitute a
guarantee or warranty to the product by the publishers or authors and does
not imply its approval to the exclusion of other products or vendors.

Printed in Singapore

Published in 2001 by
Timber Press, Inc.
The Haseltine Building
133 S.W. Second Avenue, Suite 450
Portland, Oregon 97204, U.S.A.

Reprinted 2002

Library of Congress Cataloging-in-Publication Data

Bulbs of North America / Jane McGary, editor.
      p.   cm.
    Includes bibliographical references (p.   ).
    ISBN 0-88192-511-X
    1. Bulbs—United States. 2. Bulbs—Canada. I. McGary, Mary Jane.
  II. Title.

SB425 .B89 2001
635.9′4′097—dc21

2001025348

This volume is dedicated to

WAYNE RODERICK

who has spent nearly eight decades in the study,
conservation, and cultivation of the bulbs of the American West,
and in tirelessly and generously introducing them
to plant-lovers from around the world.

Contents

Color plates follow page 176

Foreword

I regard it as a great honor, as an "outsider," to have been invited to write the foreword to this most exciting book. It is, surprisingly, the first comprehensive work on the North American bulbs and, as such, fills a great gap in the available literature on the world's bulbous plants. Those from the Mediterranean and Middle East, such as the tulips, crocuses, and hyacinths, have been grown for nearly 500 years, and many volumes are devoted to their study and cultivation. To a large extent their equally fascinating relatives from North America were overlooked by gardeners until the end of the nineteenth century, when they began to appear more generally in bulb catalogs. Now a great range is available, and they are more popular than ever before with growers, both in their native lands and in Europe.

Coupled with the fact that here, in this book, the enthusiast is presented with a refreshingly "new" range of bulbs, comes the excitement that, in this vast continent, especially west of the Rockies, new species and variations are still being discovered. These are not just minor variations on a theme; whole new species of, for example, *Erythronium* and *Calochortus* were discovered during the last decade! They are all here, from the bulbs that were familiar and useful to the indigenous people to those that excited the early explorers on arrival in the New World, and through to the recent innovations.

North America has provided the gardener with an interesting and very diverse array of bulbs, some of them belonging to genera which are familiar to all and with a wide distribution around the Northern Hemisphere, while others are confined to the continent. Most "bulbous" genera of Europe and the Middle East are distributed in an east–west direction and occur in fairly uniform latitudes. One reason for the great diversity in North America is that there are very strong climatic differences in a north–south direction, the result being that the bulbs range from indestructibly hardy *Fritillaria* and *Erythronium* species in the north to subtropical *Hymenocallis* and *Crinum* species in the south. In addition, the east–west element is there too, with marked differences in climate and geological history. This has given rise to separate eastern and western endemics like the weird *Arisaema* species of the east and the bizarre, sumptuous *Calochortus* of the western ranges.

Instigated by the North American Rock Garden Society, this is no trivial book on the subject. Authors for each genus have been chosen because they know their plants, both in the field and in the garden. Some are professional taxonomists with a love and understanding of the living plant, and most are knowledgeable enthusiasts who have hiked the country in search of their chosen specialties. With so many different authors, the generic treatments vary somewhat in their approach to content—adding to the appeal of the book—but the work has been skillfully brought together under the editorial eye of Jane McGary, herself a bulb enthusiast with a considerable knowledge of the subject. I have no doubt that botanists, gardeners, and bulb connoisseurs will find much to enjoy and inform in this exciting publication.

Brian Mathew
Editor, *Curtis's Botanical Magazine*

Introduction

JANE McGARY

This volume was born out of a desire by the board of the North American Rock Garden Society (NARGS) to support the publication of new works pertaining to rock gardening and appropriate plant introductions in the United States and Canada. It is the first book devoted entirely to bulbous plants native to this continent and the first detailed presentation of these plants primarily by American authors with a view to informing an international audience of sophisticated gardeners.

It was our hope to solicit articles from authors who observe wild plants and garden in the areas where their subjects are native. We are happy to have been successful in this aim: every contributor is a skilled and enthusiastic gardener, and among them they have covered many thousands of miles in the mountains, deserts, and forests to study their subjects. Only one genus, *Fritillaria*, has a nonnative author, and David King's many field seasons in the American West will surely serve readers well. Three of the contributors (Meerow, Callahan, and Sanderson) are academic botanists; the others—some of them professionals in other sciences—have studied botany to enhance their avocation.

The chapters in this volume are not botanical monographs. No new taxa are published here, though some authors have taken this opportunity to discuss taxonomic problems and express their opinions on which authority's viewpoint best represents the reality of the plants as they have been observed in nature. Nonetheless, familiarity with botanical terms—which are defined in most regional floras and in standard horticultural reference works—is essential to the reader who wishes to use these descriptions to verify the identity of plants in the garden. Most terms are defined upon their first use in a chapter; genera for which specialized terminology is in use (for example, *Calochortus*) feature explanatory text and drawings.

One important goal of this volume is to enable gardeners who have grown plants from seed to verify their identity before distributing seed or other material obtained in cultivation. It is sometimes difficult to identify bulbous plants in the wild from their dry, leafless stems and seed capsules, and so misnamed seed often gets into exchanges and even commercial collectors' lists. Visiting your calochortus or allium collection with this book in hand at the proper season should clear up some questions.

Scope and Contents

A fundamental problem in constructing a manual of bulbs is defining the scope of that category. The coverage here is limited to monocotyledonous (monocot) genera, although many American dicots are tuberous or rhizomatous geophytes (plants that spend part of their annual cycle underground as enlarged storage organs). Significant geophytic dicots are found, for example, in *Anemone, Claytonia, Corydalis, Delphinium, Dicentra, Lewisia, Talinum*, and *Trientalis*. Moreover, we have not addressed liliaceous genera with extensive rhizomatous root systems, such as *Polygonatum* and *Disporum*, though the authors of the miscellaneous articles have commented on a few such plants.

Two genera that might be expected to appear here—*Iris* and *Trillium*—were omitted because both are the subjects of contemporary monographs of great quality, Brian Mathew's *The Iris* (1990) and Fred and Roberta Case's *Trilliums* (1997). Moreover, no American irises are bulbous, though some (such as Louisiana irises) have enlarged rhizomes.

Finally, this volume—like most manuals of bulbs—does not venture into the vastness of the Orchidaceae. Its many genera and species and their specialized requirements are best treated separately, as they are by Philip Keenan in *Wild Orchids across America* (1998).

The chapters of this book mention all members of the major genera covered and describe most of them. Special attention has been paid to identifying the distinguishing features of the species so that those growing them from seed or viewing them in the wild can identify what they have before them. Geographical ranges and descriptions of the soils, moisture regimes, and exposures preferred by each species will guide the gardener as well as the hiker seeking photographs in nature.

The authors' different specializations have led them to focus on slightly different aspects of their subjects. Thus, Alan Meerow uses his experience in horticultural extension work to recommend suitable commercial subjects among the southeastern amaryllids; Cole Burrell, a garden designer and writer, recommends visually and ecologically pleasing companion plantings; and Edward McRae reflects on his forty years of growing American lilies and using them in hybridizing. Frank Callahan's work in environmental assessment is apparent in his focus on the conservation aspects of *Calochortus*, and that indefatigable hiker Loren Russell has obviously met all his subjects in many wild places.

Viewing and Purchasing American Bulbs

Gardeners are usually unable to read about choice plants without wanting to see and grow them. Obviously, the best way to see American bulbs in flower is to travel through their native territories at the proper time, and the habitat and flowering descriptions here will help toward that goal. Most states have native plant societies which offer information and tours. The annual meetings of the NARGS, especially those held in the West, are good opportunities to see excellent plant sites on guided hikes. Back issues of the NARGS journal, the *Rock Garden Quarterly* (formerly *ARGS Bulletin*), and the *Bulletin of the Alpine Garden Society* offer plenty of suggestions for visitors.

In captivity, good collections are maintained at several botanic gardens. Notable in the Far West are the University of California Botanic Garden, Berkeley, and Tilden Park, Oakland, California. The Denver Botanic Gardens in Colorado has collections of American alliums, arisaemas, brodiaeas, camassias (*camases* is the usual plural form in the West), calochortus, fritillaries, and lilies, as well as the rarely cultivated genera *Nemastylis* and *Leucocrinum*. Shows sponsored by alpine and rock garden societies in various countries usually include some container-grown American bulbs.

An appendix lists some reputable suppliers of nursery-propagated bulbs and of seeds. At this writing, few nurseries offer a wide selection of native American bulbs, many of which cannot be reproduced vegetatively in large quantities. Growing from seed is likely to remain the best way to obtain most of these plants, so this is a pursuit for the patient.

Conservation

Bulbous plants, unfortunately, are well represented on lists of threatened and endangered species. In 2000 the U.S. federal government listed the following as threatened or endangered: *Allium munzii, Brodiaea filifolia, B. pallida, Calochortus tiburonensis, Chlorogalum purpureum, Erythronium propullans, Fritillaria gentneri, Helonias bullata, Iris lacustris, Lilium occidentale, L. pardalinum* subsp. *pitkinense, Trillium persistens,* and *T. reliquum.*

In addition to federal listing, most states maintain programs that designate numerous other species as rare, threatened, sensitive, or endangered within the state. Not all plants so designated are in danger of extinction. For example, a plant that is rare in Oregon may be common in adjacent California; a rare or sensitive species may be a narrow endemic, perhaps a relict population (for example, *Erythronium elegans*), that is numerous within its small range. The term *sensitive* means that the plant's long-term survival depends on the continuing availability of suitable habitat, and perhaps protection from grazing and other activities. The U.S. Forest Service maintains a separate list of plants that are sensitive to logging and other forest management practices.

Conservation listing presents an interesting interface between taxonomy and politics. Listing a plant species may provide grounds for protecting its habitat from development, logging, or other disturbance. For this reason, species that are not firmly established in the botanical sense sometimes appear on lists, especially state ones. This explains such anomalies as California's listing of *Fritillaria roderickii*, a form of *F. biflora*.

It is unwise to dig bulbs from the wild, and in the case of endangered species, it is illegal as well. Bulbous plants moved in growth—the only phase of their life cycle when novices are likely to notice them—are not likely to survive. At this stage, their reserves are depleted and their bulbs are tender and fragile. It is fortunate that many American bulbs grow readily from seed, and our contributors have given detailed instructions for their management.

Hardiness

Probably the first question most gardeners ask about a plant is whether it is hardy. This ill-defined adjective is especially problematic in the context of bulbous plants. Readers east of the Rocky Mountains often rely on U.S. Department of Agriculture hardiness zones, the familiar zones 1 through 10 based on annual minimum temperatures (see Plate 102), but these zones are difficult to apply in other regions or in relation to plants native to the West. The bulb grower must understand two critical climatic factors.

First, many geophytes grow well only where the timing and amount of moisture resemble what they experience in the habitat where they evolved. Plants from summer-rainfall areas like the Atlantic states and prairies dwindle away in the sodden winters and arid summers of the West, and western plants rot while trying to lie dormant in the humid Midwest and East Coast summers. These are not inevitable results, of course; every region has produced a few species that are more adaptable, perhaps because they frequent moist habitats in a generally arid zone, or very well drained sites in a wet area. Managing growing conditions with irrigation and drainage helps; sensitive species may need to be covered where there is rain when they don't want it. Many species of the dry-summer parts of the West (not all of it is dry then, as Mary Irish points out in her chapter on the Southwest) do best elsewhere in a bulb frame, which is simply a raised bed covered with a cold frame.

Second, it is not the absolute temperature that affects bulb hardiness but rather the timing of cold periods. Many bulbs can grow in climates much colder than their native ones provided they do not receive moisture or warming periods that stimulate them into emerging before the danger of severe frost is past. In contrast, bulbs that are normally unproblematic to grow in a moderate climate, like that of the Pacific Northwest states, may be killed by a sudden deep freeze without snow cover after they have sent up their flowering stems. This principle is important in relation to the Mediterranean-climate bulbs of the low-elevation Pacific Coast, which may need frost protection simply because they emerge in January in response to fall rains.

What American bulbs, then, should gardeners in colder climates plant? We can only suggest trials of as wide a selection as the grower can obtain. It is difficult to predict what will succeed in a given garden with its individual soils, slopes, and microclimates—not to mention the skills of its proprietor. The serious collector will benefit from having a bulb frame or alpine house where some plants of a stock can be kept safe under controlled conditions while others are planted out experimentally. Raising one's plants from seed improves the chance of obtaining healthy, well-adapted clones. Good drainage, as provided in a scree or gritty raised bed, is beneficial to many species, but it should be remembered that sandy, gravelly soil is not very effective at insulating bulbs against severe cold without snow cover. When sudden cold snaps threaten bulbs in growth, they can be protected for a few days with an agricultural row cover (such as Reemay), or even with a few loose sheets of newspaper where these will not blow away.

Climate

The climatic regions of North America are complex and varied, but an understanding of them is indispensable to success in growing the plants discussed in this volume. Even U.S. and Canadian gardeners and horticultural writers tend to be parochial in their approach to climate-related topics. For many years, almost all popular American garden books and magazines were written from the perspective of the Northeast and either ignored or misinterpreted the climates west of the Central Plains. This problem was addressed by the editors of the *Sunset Western Garden Book*, which presents 24 climate zones based on temperature and moisture regimes; it is a useful reference for those growing western American bulbs.

It must be remembered that the kinds of generalizations that can be made in a discussion like this one do not apply to every plant species within a large region. A plant of the humid Southeast may specialize in high, well-drained, rocky habitats, while one of the arid West may live in moist seeps and streamsides. Therefore, the authors in this volume have given habitat information for every species, and some (for example, McDonough, McRae) have organized their discussions around habitat types.

The Pacific Coast—the home of the majority of North American bulbous species—is separated from the rest of the continent by a series of high north–south mountain ranges. These ranges intercept precipitation from storms that sweep in from the Pacific Ocean and experience heavy snowfall at higher elevations. As far north as the Columbia River, a parallel mountain chain, the Coast Ranges, forms a lower barrier directly adjacent to the shoreline; snow lies here only intermittently except on the higher summits. Transverse ranges join the two chains, and in these geologically complex regions we find a wonderful diversity of bulbs.

Almost all precipitation in the region from southern California to northern Oregon falls from October through May; farther north, rain in summer is somewhat more common but by no means as heavy as in winter. This is sometimes called a Mediterranean climate. Frost is rare in the far south and immediately along the Pacific shore, and winter-growing bulbs from this zone need protection from frost. Winter extremes drop with increasing elevation, but winters are much warmer here than in the Rocky Mountains. High-elevation Pacific Coast bulbs, depending on elevation and latitude, come into growth as snow melts and flower from late spring to midsummer. Their cultivation presents the usual problem of growing alpine plants at lower elevations—intolerance of winter wet—and in addition, most of them require a dry period after flowering.

Between the Sierra-Cascade ranges and the Rocky Mountains lie the regions known as the Intermountain West and the Southwest. Here, too, we find many bulbs. Those that grow at high elevations in the region's many small mountain ranges can be considered alpine in their growth cycle and cultural requirements. The rest are adapted to drier conditions: semiarid steppe in the north, and true desert in the south. The desert Southwest environment is described in Mary Irish's article in this volume.

The semiarid steppe of the Columbia Plateau and much of the Great Basin experience cold winters (extremes usually around −20°F [−29°C]) and very hot summers. Precipitation is low and falls as light snow in winter; the ground is really moist only in spring. Summer thunderstorms occur but rarely saturate the soil. Most gardeners outside this region find its plants the most difficult of North American groups in cultivation. Their seed also tends to be more recalcitrant in germination than that of related species from the Pacific Coast region.

The Rocky Mountains extend from near the U.S.–Mexico border to the Canadian Arctic. Precipitation is moderate to the north and lower to the south. Frost and snow are the rule in winter, even at the southern end of the range. Summer thunderstorms are frequent. The Rockies are relatively poor in bulbous species. Those that occur fall into various habitat categories, and each must be considered from the perspective of its individual adaptations.

Very few bulbous plants are native to the prairie provinces of Canada and the northern Central Plains of the United States. Here, winters are bitterly cold. Moderate snow cover usually insulates the ground surface, and dormant plants remain chilled and rather dry from mid-autumn until the spring thaw. The average frost-free period along the U.S.–Canada border is about 90 days. June is the wettest month. Annual precipitation is lowest in the rain shadow just east of the Rocky Mountains and increases as one moves eastward. In the United States the western precipitation extreme is about 12 inches (300 millimeters) annually, and the eastern (just west of the Appalachian Mountains) is about 50 inches (1250 millimeters). Summers are very hot, broken from time to time by rainfall in the form of brief, often violent thunderstorms. Severe summer droughts are not uncommon. The Great Lakes, a cluster of huge freshwater bodies at the U.S.–Canada border, exert a modifying influence on the climate of that region. Snowfall is greater than in other lowland areas, and summers are wetter.

Along the Atlantic Coast, annual precipitation generally ranges from 50 to 70 inches (1250 to 1750 millimeters). Snow may fall as far south as Florida in exceptionally cold winters, and northern New England has a long winter with extensive snow cover. Rain may occur in any season; the hurricane season (late June through October) often brings torrential rains interspersed with dry periods. Summers are hot and usually humid, so the area does not experience the sharp night cooling common in equally hot parts of the drier West. Bulbs native here include woodland, meadow, and wetland species that require some moisture throughout the summer, and a few plants of rocky slopes that can be allowed to dry out, though not to the extent that western bulbs tolerate. The chapters by C. Colston Burrell, Michael Chelednik, and Alan Meerow address plants adapted to this region.

Acknowledgments

Funding for the development of this volume was provided by the North American Rock Garden Society through its publications program. Thanks are due to Patricia Bender, who as president of NARGS was instrumental in conceiving and promoting this project. Successive Publications Committee chairpersons, Louise Parsons and Bobby Ward, provided efficient support throughout the project, as did Neal Maillet of Timber Press.

Many expert gardeners and botanists have helped with information and suggestions. In addition to the writers and photographers who con-

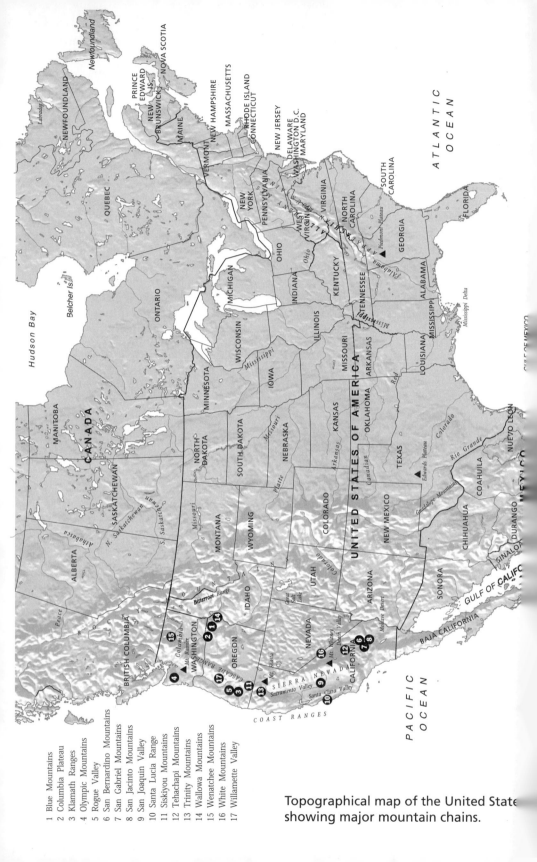

1 Blue Mountains
2 Columbia Plateau
3 Klamath Ranges
4 Olympic Mountains
5 Rogue Valley
6 San Bernardino Mountains
7 San Gabriel Mountains
8 San Jacinto Mountains
9 San Joaquin Valley
10 Santa Lucia Range
11 Siskiyou Mountains
12 Tehachapi Mountains
13 Trinity Mountains
14 Wallowa Mountains
15 Wenatchee Mountains
16 White Mountains
17 Willamette Valley

Topographical map of the United States
showing major mountain chains.

tributed, I would like to thank Jim and Jenny Archibald, Wim de Goede, Phyllis Gustafson, David Hale, Sean Hogan, Antoine Hoog, Panayoti Kelaidis, Jay Lunn, Wayne Roderick, and James Waddick.

Further Reading

Each chapter includes a bibliography of works cited and otherwise useful to the student of its particular genus or region. I would like to recommend the following works of a more general nature for the library of anyone seriously interested in American bulbs.

Beckett, Kenneth, ed. 1993. *Alpine Garden Society Encyclopaedia of Alpines*. 2 vols. Pershore, United Kingdom: AGS Publications. Contributions on individual genera are uneven but indispensable for *Fritillaria* (by Martyn Rix), and for suggestions for cultivation.

Brenzel, Kathleen N., ed. 1995. *Sunset Western Garden Book*. Rev. ed. Menlo Park, California: Sunset. Indispensable for gardeners in western North America and useful elsewhere for its clear explanations of the climate and geography where many American bulbs have evolved.

Bryan, John, and Mark Griffiths, eds. 1995. *The New Royal Horticultural Society Dictionary Manual of Bulbs*. Portland: Timber Press. Collects the entries on bulbs from the four-volume *RHS Dictionary of Gardening* in a compact, affordable volume.

Case, Frederick W., and Roberta B. Case. 1997. *Trilliums*. Portland: Timber Press. Very thorough treatment of a genus not covered in the present volume.

Hickman, James C., ed. 1993. *The Jepson Manual: Higher Plants of California*. Berkeley: University of California Press. The most prestigious manual of the flora of California, the premier North American region for bulbs.

Kartesz, John T. 1994. *A Synonymized Checklist of the Vascular Flora of the United States, Canada, and Greenland*. 2nd ed. 2 vols. Portland: Timber Press. Useful as a handy reference to synonymy and for conceptions of American genera, though not all taxa presented as current are uncontroversial.

Keenan, Philip E. 1998. *Wild Orchids across America: A Botanical Travelogue*. Portland: Timber Press.

Mathew, Brian. 1990. *The Iris*. Rev. ed. Portland: Timber Press. A complete treatment of a genus not treated in the present volume but often considered together with bulbous plants.

Mathew, Brian. 1997. *Growing Bulbs: The Complete Practical Guide*. London: Batsford. Good introductory manual with sensible information from the bulb world's most eclectic and knowledgeable botanist-gardener.

McGary, Jane, ed. 1996. *Rock Garden Plants of North America: An Anthology from the Bulletin of the North American Rock Garden Society*. Portland: Timber Press. "Liliaceous Bulbs" by Wayne Roderick and "Calochortus: Why Not Try Them?" by Boyd Kline are valuable adjuncts to the present volume.

Ogden, Scott. 1994. *Garden Bulbs for the South*. Dallas: Taylor.

Phillips, Roger, and Martyn Rix. 1989. *Bulbs*. New York: Random House; London: Pan. This inexpensive large-format paperback is the reference book many bulb enthusiasts use most constantly for its brief but informative descriptions and superb array of clear color photographs.

Rix, Martyn. 1983. *Growing Bulbs*. London: Christopher Helm; Portland: Timber Press. Thorough, accessible scientific explanations of bulb growth cycles, climate geography, and morphology.

− 1 −

The Genus *Allium*

MARK McDONOUGH, JIM ROBINETT,
AND GEORGIE ROBINETT

The genus *Allium* is familiar to even the botanically challenged in the form of common vegetables like onion (*A. cepa*), garlic, leeks, shallots, scallions, and chives. In all parts of the Northern Hemisphere where alliums are found, including North America, native peoples have eaten wild species. The genus also has a nonculinary persona, and the ornamental onions are grown solely for their floral beauty.

All but the dedicated *Allium* aficionados derive their impression of the genus from just a handful of species. Nevertheless, the genus contains between 600 and 1000 species worldwide, placing it among the largest monocotyledonous genera in the plant kingdom. (The broad discrepancy in species count results from both the great geographical range and the division of taxonomists into "lumpers" and "splitters.") The genus holds a vast, barely tapped reservoir of gardening potential.

In North America, the genus is represented by more than 130 taxa. Only one species, *Allium schoenoprasum* (chives), is native to both North America and Eurasia. The American onions present a fascinating and diverse group of small bulbous plants found in a wide variety of habitats, with at least a few species suitable to cultivate in almost any locale. Only two American species—*A. cernuum* and *A. unifolium*—enjoy widespread cultivation at this time. Except for chives, the North American alliums stand unequivocally separate from the Old World species and pose their own taxonomic difficulties and cultural challenges. In areas of botanical controversy we have erred on the side of firsthand experience rather than simply repeating conventional answers.

In the nineteenth century George Don and later E. A. von Regel named a modest number of species. The first significant delineation of American species was Sereno Watson's "Revision of the North American Liliaceae" (1879); most species described there are still valid. We, however, lack a single comprehensive treatment of the genus in North America. An understanding of American alliums can only be gleaned from a stack of obscure botanical works, state and regional floras (many out of print), dissertations, individual species published here and there, firsthand experience, and Internet resources. It is harder still to make sense of these piecemeal works, many of which are confused, incomplete, contradictory, and regionally confined or lacking context. The present chapter probably represents the first complete discussion in print of the genus *Allium* as it occurs in North America.

The single most important contribution to understanding American alliums was a series of studies by Marion Ownbey in the mid-twentieth century. Ownbey aligned groups of similar species into alliances, a concept without true botanical standing, but a convenient way to organize the many species. In California, where nearly half the American species reside, Dale McNeal has built on the work of predecessors (including Ownbey) to bring a semblance of order and clarity to the species of that state. Hamilton Traub, with assistance from Thaddeus Howard, identified and published most of the Mexican species, a distinct group of bulbous alliums which still remain in relative obscurity; many new species may await discovery in the vast, isolated, and largely unexplored Mexican territories.

The genus *Allium* was considered part of the large family Liliaceae, but it is now segregated into its own family, Alliaceae, which also includes such familiar western American genera as *Brodiaea* and *Triteleia*. Only very recent publications are likely to cite Alliaceae; older botanical references, such as those listed in the accompanying bibliography, assign *Allium* to the Liliaceae.

Discussing the broad scope of North American alliums is difficult on several counts. First, there is no single comprehensive treatment of the genus, and none of the taxonomic alignments can be considered complete, although a number of good regional floras help fill in the puzzle. Second, so many species grow in such remote and diverse habitats that it would require a lifetime to study them all at first hand. Third, there are recognized series of related species, or alliances, but there are other alliances which are not fully understood or perhaps even yet proposed. In the sections that follow we will highlight a few species to typify a general look of a series of onions, then briefly list those species that share a set of common physical characteristics. This grouping for purposes of discussion does not imply any actual taxonomic relationships; it is merely a convenience to help sort through the many names.

The main part of this chapter, by McDonough, first describes the species that are found outside California. It is followed by a separate section, written by Robinett and Robinett, devoted to the many species which have their ranges entirely or primarily in that bulb-rich state. We have chosen to arrange the species in groups reflecting morphology and habitat, as follows: *Allium cernuum* and *A. stellatum*; rhizomatous, moisture-loving species; alliums of the eastern United States; alliums of the

Southwest, Texas, and Mexico; alliums of the western United States, excluding California; western alliums with a single leaf; western alliums with broad, falcate leaves; western dwarf alliums; California alliums; and nonnative alliums.

The Plant

Alliums usually have true concentric bulbs (the culinary onion is a common example of a true bulb), though a few have elongated rhizomes. The basal roots wither away annually in dryland species, but wet-growers (for example, common chives) may have persistent roots. Directly from the bulb rise one to many leaves; these may be flattened, channeled, or terete (cylindrical) in cross section; straight, longitudinally or spirally twisted, or falcate (sickle-shaped); dark to bright green, glaucous, or grayish. In some species, especially drylanders, the leaves wither during or before anthesis (flowering).

Each bulb typically produces a single flowering stalk (scape), always unbranched. The scape is technically leafless, but the leaves often clasp the scape and appear to the casual eye to be attached to it above the bulb. The flowers, few to many, are borne in an umbel atop the scape; the inflorescence is enclosed before the flowers open by a spathe (a membranous or papery sheath) with one or more bracts. There are six stamens. The ovary has three locules (chambers). The seed capsules of American species are often crested. The seeds are usually dark and angular. The perianth—the showy part of the flower—has three petals and three sepals which are very similar in appearance, and so are loosely all called tepals. The individual floret may be campanulate (bell-shaped), urceolate (urn-shaped with a constricted mouth), or widely open to flat and starlike. Worldwide the genus displays almost every floral hue, but American alliums are mostly white, pink, or reddish purple; there is only one yellow-flowered species, and no true blue.

Allium cernuum and *A. stellatum*

Allium cernuum and *A. stellatum* are closely allied and can easily be confused. The basic distinction is the posture of the flowers: those of *A. cernuum* are permanently nodding, whereas in *A. stellatum* the nodding buds rise to an erect position as the flowers open. The bulbs of *A. stellatum* are ovoid, in contrast to the elongated bulbs of *A. cernuum*, and the flowers of the former are more stellate (starry), while those of the latter are bell- or cup-shaped. Ownbey (1950b) concludes that these distinctions between *A. cernuum* and *A. stellatum* don't always hold true, making certain identification of some specimens difficult. This is borne out in material of *A. cernuum* I have collected from various regions of the United States in which the flowers are starry, and the heads turn sideways or almost erect, blurring the line between the two species. Hybrids between the two species are likely and may account for these anomalies.

Allium cernuum Roth

North America contains a rich assortment of ornamental onions native to a variety of habitats; at least one or two species are found in every U.S. state. It is therefore surprising that so few American onions are common in gardens, with the notable exception of *Allium cernuum*, the nodding onion, which is the best-known American onion and among the most easily grown alliums (Plate 1).

The nodding onion inhabits much of North America, from the Pacific Northwest to the Atlantic coast of Massachusetts, and from Canada to northern Mexico. Thus, it is not surprising that the species varies considerably; however, it is always unmistakable with its crook-necked nodding flower clusters. Its habitat varies, too: it can be seen on the prairie, in open woodland, or on forested mountains, preferring higher elevations in hot southern and western regions. In Washington State it has a few sites along the shore of Whidbey Island by the Strait of Juan de Fuca, where myriad nodding onions grow among rounded beach stones just above the high-tide level.

The nodding onion's popularity is due to its indestructibility, tolerance of almost any growing conditions, and ease of propagation, as well as the dangling showers of small white, pink, or bright rosy-purple bells produced in early to midsummer. The plant grows from an elongated bulb attached to a short stipitate (stalked) rhizome; the rhizome is obvious only during some parts of its growth cycle. In some forms the bulb tunic (the outer coat, or skin) is shiny blood-red, while in others it is pink or whitish.

Marion Ownbey, who was responsible for much of our understanding of the genus *Allium* in North America, early in his studies delineated two varieties of *A. cernuum*—var. *obtusum* and var. *neomexicanum*—based largely on the color of the bulb tunic, but also on minor leaf characteristics. Ownbey's later publications rescinded the status of both varieties, putting them in synonymy with the type species; unfortunately, these names persist (for example, they were published in an online project, the Biota of North America Program). The invalid variety "obtusum" should not be confused with the valid Californian species *A. obtusum*. Other synonyms for *A. cernuum* include *A. recurvatum*, *A. alleghieniense*, and *A. oxyphilum*. The plant's long popularity in gardens results in the frequent appearance of these synonyms among donations to seed exchanges.

Edgar T. Wherry in 1925 described a southeastern plant under the name *Allium oxyphilum*, separating it from *A. cernuum* because of its preference for acidic soils, white flower color, and very long pedicels. The first two characteristics can easily be dismissed as normal variability, but the long pedicel is unique. Wherry admitted that he had not seen any material from western collections; if he had, he might have come to a different conclusion. In the context of the entire range, I concur with authorities who claim that this is merely a form of *A. cernuum*, albeit a distinctive one, found in the woods of West Virginia and adjacent Virginia. To distinguish this fine garden plant, however, I have provided the name *A. cernuum* 'Oxy White'. It grows admirably in good garden soil in full sun, making clumps of slender leaves and 50-centimeter flowering stems. The arching pedicels lend an airy grace to the symmetrical flower bursts. Pink-flowered garden hybrids between this and colored forms of *A. cernuum* are not uncommon.

The handsomest garden forms of *Allium cernuum* are stalwart plants that form bold clumps of fleshy, glaucous straplike foliage and stout 60- to 75-centimeter stems in June and July. Luminous, waxen-textured rosy-purple flowers are suspended with geometric precision on thick, arched pedicels tinted gray to near black. Yellow anthers light up each urn-shaped flower. Deep-colored forms can be grown from seed offered under such invalid names as *A. alleghaniense*, *A. cernuum* var. *neomexicanum*, and *A.* 'Major', or they may arise by chance.

On the opposite end of the spectrum is a small form discovered on Rich Mountain, North Carolina, and named *Allium cernuum* 'Rich Mountain' (Plate 2). The few-flowered heads of small purple flowers just top the tidy clumps of narrow grayish foliage on 15- to 20-centimeter stems from July into August, later than most other forms. This cultivar appears to be sterile.

The most common types encountered in cultivation are those with tall, slender stems and unremarkable, rather small heads of pale pink or white flowers. Though pleasing in a quiet way, they can be overshadowed by more substantial plants. After collecting and growing numerous forms of *Allium cernuum*, I have named a few that warrant identity in the horticultural trade.

A large, stocky white-flowered form from near Monarch, Wyoming, which I dubbed *Allium cernuum* 'Monarch White,' grew magnificently in my garden near Seattle. It had large, compact flower heads, not as open as the typical form, which made a real statement in the border. In my New England garden, sadly, the plant exhibited a poor constitution and seemed unwilling to increase, eventually dying out.

Perhaps to compensate for my loss, I then chanced on another superior clone in a local nursery, where it was misidentified as *Allium cuthbertii*. Subsequently named *A. cernuum* 'Leo' in honor of nurseryman Leo Blanchette, who brought the plant to my attention, this white-flowered cultivar is distinct on several accounts. The leaves are light green and remain in short basal tufts, from which spring naked 75-centimeter stems topped with a tightly crooked cluster of crisp white flowers, faintly tinted pink in cool weather. The plant does not bloom until late July and lasts into August.

Another invalid epithet sometimes encountered in seed lists is *Allium cernuum* 'Minor'. Plants grown from seed I received under this name from Joseph Halinar, an allium aficionado in Oregon, yielded small *A. cernuum* plants with unusual threadlike foliage. I named the one with the narrowest leaves and most compact growth 'Little Joe'. The bulbs, also slender, increase to produce tidy, leafy clumps of arching foliage and a profusion of petite pink flower clusters atop 40-centimeter stems in June to July.

Cultivation of all *Allium cernuum* forms is easy in almost any sunny to partially shaded spot, but sun seems better. The plant does not need the cool, moist conditions many writers recommend: it prospers under dry sandy conditions with equal fervor. I have always seen it in the wild (mostly in the West) in rather dry situations. Plants can flower the second year from seed. In fact, the seed germinates all too readily, and unwanted seedlings will abound unless the seed heads are cut off before they ripen. Separate the closely set bulbs and rhizomes at almost any time of the year for quick increase.

Allium stellatum Nuttall ex Ker-Gawler

Allium stellatum is a valid species and generally easy to recognize. It is also a very ornamental one, valuable for its late flowering. This is a plant of the plains in Canada and the central United States, with sporadic distribution as far south as Texas and east to North Carolina. There appear to be several races that vary considerably: some flower in midsummer, and others in late summer and fall—some, I am told, not until October, even in the South. Appearance varies, too: short to tall, few-flowered to densely flowered, and white to deep rose pink, with all sorts of intermediate characteristics.

Allium stellatum tends to be a solitary grower, less inclined to build into large clumps like *A. cernuum*. Individuals having rich pink flowers with yellow anthers, held in sidewise sprays atop 45-centimeter stems in September, are among the most attractive American onions (Plate 3). A tall variety with white and pale pink flowers carries dense heads atop 75-centimeter stems in July. Plants are hard to find in nurseries, but seed often appears in seed exchanges. As effortless to grow from seed as *A. cernuum*, this one is less inclined to seed about indiscriminately in the garden. Because they tend to shed their leaves at anthesis, the plants look best poking through a light ground cover as vertical accents.

When sorting through plants received as *Allium cernuum* and *A. stellatum*, it becomes clear that some specimens are intermediate between the two species. One apparent hybrid, sent to me labeled *A. drummondii*, looks like a narrow-leaved *A. cernuum* until the blooms appear atop the

40-centimeter stems. The nodding buds become semi-erect and open in side-facing sprays of medium pink star-cups. The lateral stance and the starry flowers clearly indicate *A. stellatum* influence. The airy, spokelike arrangement of the lovely inflorescence led me to name it 'Ferris Wheel'.

Rhizomatous, Moisture-loving Species

Most American alliums have true bulbs; only a few are rhizomatous. These, however, are not rhizomatous in the same way as those in *Allium* section *Rhizirideum*. Some American species have short, stipitate vestigial rhizomes that are apparent only during certain phases of the growth cycle, as described for *A. cernuum*. Others have offset bulblets that are attached to the parent bulb for a brief period by thin, stolonlike rhizomes which later wither and break off. Some species exhibit this characteristic even though it is not reported in their current descriptions. In only a few American species—*A. validum*, *A. brevistylum*, and *A. gooddingii*—is the rhizome more highly developed. Like Asian and European rhizomatous alliums, these species prefer moist soils and grow in ditches and swamps. A fourth species, *A. eurotophilum* from Baja California, rounds out the group, although this narrow endemic grows on dry rocky slopes. A few other species with distinct rhizomes—*A. glandulosum*, *A. howardii*, and *A. kunthii*—are discussed below with alliums of the Southwest, Texas, and Mexico.

Allium validum S. Watson

Allium validum is found in high, wet mountain meadows and seeps in a number of western mountain ranges, from California to British Columbia, Idaho, and Nevada, at elevations from 4,000 to 11,300 feet (1200 to 3400 meters). It is the tallest American wild onion, with stems reaching 100 centimeters. Umbels to 7 centimeters in diameter are densely packed with pink to white flowers having prominently exserted (protruding) stamens. A form from near Sonora Pass, California, at 9700 feet (2900 meters), is described as "cerise." The three to six leaves are generally a little shorter than the scape and may remain green throughout the summer. Bloom time is early to midsummer. Seed germination can be slow and erratic; the seeds may require cold stratification, although low-elevation forms germinate without chilling. Often seeds planted in fall begin to germinate in early spring and are still germinating sporadically in midsummer. (This may be an adaptation to uncertain climate: if the early seedlings are killed by frost, the later ones still have a chance.) This species likes full sun and copious water, at least through midsummer if not year-round.

Allium brevistylum S. Watson

Allium brevistylum resembles a reduced *A. validum*, generally smaller in all its parts, but differentiated in having stamens and style that are not exserted (that is, they are shorter than the tepals). This species essentially replaces *A. validum* east of the latter's range, in the Rocky Mountains from Montana south into Utah and Colorado, with a couple of disjunct outposts in Nevada and California. In Idaho I frequently found this plant growing in swampy meadows or along small streams. In cultivation the plant withstands all but the most parched or sun-blasted positions, although filtered shade in moist soil suits it best. The vinous purple-red flowers are produced in few-flowered heads atop 45-centimeter stems. After flowering, plants die down to resting buds that poke up just above the soil surface, vulnerable to attack from slugs. Their positions need to be marked carefully to prevent inadvertent damage.

Allium gooddingii Ownbey

Allium gooddingii (frequently misspelled with a single *d*) is a lovely plant with a very limited distribution in Arizona and a few sites in New Mexico. It has attractive glaucous gray foliage and upright few-flowered umbels of shiny deep purple flowers above 50-centimeter stems. In some forms the flowers are medium to light pink and less attractive. Like *A. brevistylum*, it dies down to a resting bud after flowering, although short leaf tips may emerge in late summer or fall. It is easy to grow from seed under average garden conditions but benefits from a moist soil.

Allium plummerae S. Watson

Another specialized moisture-loving species, this one has a restricted range in southeastern Arizona and adjacent northern Mexico, growing at high elevations in swampy meadows, along streambanks, and occasionally on rocky slopes. Given good garden soil and average irrigation, it ranks among the finest American onions. Plants make strong growth to 45 centimeters, rising from elongate bulbs connected by short, stipitate rhizomes. The strongly keeled gray leaves grow vertically and remain in good condition throughout the growing season, a garden statement in their own right. Thick, ribbed stems, as tall as the foliage, support showy upright umbels of large white flowers. Each flat, starry floret has conspicuous pinkish nerves (veins) and a central ovary that changes from pale yellow to reddish brown when the flowers are fertilized (Plate 4). The species blooms for a long period from June to August. It is easy to grow from seed but can skip flowering for a season if it does not get enough moisture.

Allium schoenoprasum Linnaeus

Believe it or not, common chives is the only *Allium* species that is native to both the Old World and the New. This rhizomatous onion prefers moist soils in colder regions throughout the Northern Hemisphere. It can also be found in most northern U.S. states and in Canada, all the way to Maine, Newfoundland, and Alaska. The race found in North America is sometimes called *A. schoenoprasum* var. *sibiricum* (Linnaeus) Hartman, but many authors do not accept this varietal epithet. There are some peculiar forms of *A. schoenoprasum*; one collected in northern Maine grew in solitary form and did not build into the usual thick clump, and its 30- to 40-centimeter stems were topped with dingy gray flowers.

Alliums of the Eastern United States

There are relatively few *Allium* species in the eastern United States. Previously discussed were the ubiquitous nodding onion (*A. cernuum*) and chives (*A. schoenoprasum*), both common in the West and East. *Allium stellatum* is really a Central Plains species, but it has a few outposts in the Southeast. One allium that most eastern gardeners know and despise is *A. canadense*, common throughout the eastern half of the United States and north into Canada. The form typically encountered is var. *canadense* (synonym *A. mutabile*), in which bulbils are produced in the inflorescence, sometimes replacing the flowers entirely. These drop off to scatter new plants through the garden. Fortunately, there are at least a couple of good wild onions in the east.

Allium tricoccum Aitken

Allium tricoccum, known as ramps or wild leek, occurs in moist woodlands from New Brunswick, west to Michigan and Iowa, and is common in the southeastern states as far south as Georgia. In spring two broad leaves appear, resembling those of lily-of-the-valley (*Convallaria majalis*). These die down before the flowering stalk appears in summer. The stem rises 15 to 30 centimeters, with a small spherical head of whitish flowers. My woodland may be too dry for this species, since it rarely blooms for me. In the Southeast this plant is locally abundant and is the subject of considerable folklore; some communities hold "ramp festivals" where the bulbs are eaten, reputedly inducing powerful halitosis. *Allium tricoccum* var. *burdickii* Hanes is a distinct race from Michigan with reddish leaf petioles and scape. The elevation of this minor variant to species status as *A. burdickii* seems questionable, given that *A. tricoccum* stands quite alone, without affiliation or resemblance to any other American onion.

Allium speculae Ownbey & Aase

An eastern onion for which there is barely any published information is the rare flatrock onion, *Allium speculae*, a species of the Piedmont Plateau found in a few counties in Georgia and adjacent Alabama. Though not included in the federal list of threatened and endangered species, it has been assigned threatened status by the state of Georgia. It is genetically isolated from other American alliums, but its closest relatives are *A. cuthbertii* and *A. plummerae*. This is a small plant, flowering in May with upright, few-flowered umbels of spreading, pinkish blooms on stems 20 to 30 centimeters tall. This species is probably not known in cultivation.

Allium cuthbertii Small

Among the best garden onions of the American species, and certainly the best in the East, is this little-known species. It is found growing in sandy soil in Florida, Alabama, Georgia, and the Carolinas. Despite its southerly distribution, it is perfectly happy in a northern garden (USDA Zone 5), where it has grown outdoors for years without protection. Though it reportedly resembles *Allium canadense, A. cuthbertii* is immediately recognizable. It seems to have no clear affinity to any other species, though it has been dubiously placed within the "*canadense* alliance." Ownbey (1956) astutely points out that *A. cuthbertii* is the only member of the alliance that has crested ovaries, similar to those of *A. cernuum*; Ownbey also suggests that, in some characteristics, *A. cuthbertii* is closer to *A. plummerae*.

In spring *Allium cuthbertii* produces a few flat leaves, ruddy purple as they emerge. It is generally described as having only two leaves, but there can be more, though only two persist at anthesis. In June, stems rise to 45 centimeters, sporting upright, domed clusters of stellate flowers. The flowers open flat and have a diffuse lavender-pink stripe down the center of each tepal on a paler pink ground, giving a lovely two-toned effect and hence the common name, striped garlic. I have found this plant long-lived but very slow to increase in sandy soil in full sun. Seed is reliably set but reluctant to germinate. These factors make it difficult to locate in cultivation; moreover, *A. cernuum* is often sent out misidentified under this name.

Alliums of the Southwest, Texas, and Mexico

Our impression of the genus *Allium* as it occurs in Texas is based largely on the work of Ownbey (1950b). Unfortunately, his studies were incomplete, possibly resulting in oversimplification of this complex group of species. Numerous subsequent studies have helped to clarify the difficult taxonomic relationships, but these seem to have been largely ignored by modern authors dealing with the general flora of the area, who clearly have drawn their information only from Ownbey's early work.

The most significant advance in southwestern *Allium* taxonomy is the work of Hamilton P. Traub and Thaddeus M. Howard. Many of their revisions have been published in *Herbertia*, a journal of the International Bulb Society (formerly the American Plant Life Society). I have also been able to observe living material of many of these taxa, sent to me by Thad Howard. Howard has spent a lifetime studying the bulbous flora of Texas, Mexico, and South America and is personally responsible for the discovery and subsequent publication of numerous taxa. He has collected and studied populations of *Allium* with exacting detail and critical observation. Correspondence with Ownbey and Traub helped Howard to offer an insightful, if not radical, view of the genus in Texas. In the following discussion I follow his progressive view of the species of the U.S. Southwest and Mexico. (This section excludes a few species that occur in Texas but are widespread elsewhere and are discussed in other sections.)

The large and taxonomically difficult group of species in Texas contains some highly ornamental onions. Many have proven winter hardy in USDA Zone 5. Others present a challenge in finding just the right spot, with the right combination of springtime moisture and summer dryness.

The border with Mexico spans four U.S. states, and plant communities don't stop at political boundaries: a dozen or more "American" alliums cross into Mexico. The Mexican ranges are not specified in the discussion below because they are inadequately documented. The following are the presently known species endemic to Mexico, many of which were discovered, named, and published by Howard and Traub: *A. californicum, A. durangoense, A. eurotophilum, A. fantasmosense, A. glandulosum* (sensu Howard), *A. guatemalense, A. huntiae, A. kunthii* (sensu Howard), *A. mannii, A. melliferum, A. mexicanum, A. michoacanum, A. ownbeyi, A. potosiense, A. pueblanum, A. stoloniferum, A. telaponense, A. traubii,* and *A. traubii* f. *liberflorens.*

My only experience growing Mexican alliums is with *Allium traubii*, a fall bloomer. Each bulb has several channeled, gray-green, minutely scabrid (rough) leaves which appear in late summer. Every few years, buds are produced very late in fall—but too late in my New England garden to open. Recent arrivals to my collection from Mexican material include *A. potosiense*, with squat, plump bulbs and two or three 30-centimeter stems arising from each bulb, and an open inflorescence of small, starry, white flowers; *A. mannii*, with clustered bulbs, white flowers, and 30-centimeter tall green leaves, said to grow in standing water but hardy and easy in normal garden conditions; *A. glandulosum* in the true type form from central Mexico with maroon-red flowers; and an unidentified rhizomatous species, said to be tall-growing with white, purple-tinged flowers, and to inhabit wet soil. Perhaps someday the Mexican alliums will be better understood and grown in gardens. Since at least a couple bloom in fall, they would be welcome additions, even if they prove so tender that they have to be kept in frames or alpine houses.

Allium canadense Linnaeus

Having moved to Texas and the Central Plains, we are now in a position to discuss *Allium canadense*, an important element of this geographic group. All forms of this species with bulbils in the inflorescence are conveniently referable to *A. canadense* var. *canadense* (synonyms *A. continuum*, *A. mutabile*; *A. acetabulum* is wrongly cited as a synonym in some books), though several geographical races are involved. I grow a robust Texas form with novel flower heads comprised of fat whitish, red-tinged bulbils that sprout green shoots 5 to 7 centimeters long. From among the congested bulbils sputter a few pure white starry flowers in pleasing contrast. To avoid unwanted increase, cut the stems, being careful to pick up every bulbil that drops off—and don't discard them in the compost pile.

Allium canadense var. *lavandulare* Bates is a distinct race of robust plants with lavender-pink flowers. It occurs in Missouri, Arkansas, Oklahoma, Nebraska, Kansas, and South Dakota. This attractive variety has densely packed flower heads with as many as 175 individual blooms on strong 60-centimeter stems. Like many American prairie plants, it seems to have been ignored by gardeners. It has been suggested, though not yet validly published, that this race should be elevated to species status as *A. lavandulare*.

Allium canadense var. *florosum* is a name proposed by Thad Howard, but not yet published, for a floriferous form he found in several locations growing among large populations of typically bulbiliferous *A. canadense* in north central Texas. Though perhaps regarded as a forma at most (or simply under a cultivar name, for example, 'White Queen', proposed by Howard), it deserves recognition and segregation from *A. canadense*. Growing to 60 centimeters high, this selection blooms in June with large, showy heads of up to 120 clean white flowers in 7.5-centimeter wide hemispherical heads. Some bloom heads lack bulbils altogether, and others have only three to eight small bulbils, inconspicuously sessile in the center of the umbel. The plant remains stable in cultivation.

Ownbey recognized a number of distinct yet allied races and described them all as subspecies of *Allium canadense*. Later studies vigorously dispute Ownbey's broad approach, and from the taxonomic muddle several good species have been delineated, along with new taxonomic combinations. The *"fraseri* alliance" is one such group of four species emerging from Ownbey's definition of *A. canadense* var. *fraseri*. The alliance includes *A. eulae*, *A. fraseri*, *A. pseudofraseri*, and *A. texanum*, discussed below. I have seen living specimens of all of these, and they are clearly distinct when viewed side by side. *Allium texanum* and *A. eulae* have proven hardy and ornamental in my northern garden.

Allium eulae Howard

Allium eulae (synonym *A. fraseri* var. *eulae*) is native to central Texas; according to Thad Howard (personal communication), it "grows in seepy places" and is "endemic to the granite hills of the Texas Highland Lake region." The species is unmistakable in cultivation, with upright, twisted, light green leaves to 20 centimeters tall, narrow and firm. The dome-shaped clusters of creamy white flowers on 45-centimeter stems make an attractive display in June (Plate 5). The flat, stellate flowers have propeller-shaped tepals which thicken at the base and become noticeably reflective. The stamens and ovary are also white. The membranous-coated (or faintly reticulated) bulbs go dormant after flowering and re-emerge in the autumn. The plant is easy to grow from seed, flowering the second year.

Allium texanum Howard

Following *Allium eulae* by three weeks and flowering in July is this robust white-flowered species. It hails from central Texas and the Wichita Mountains of Oklahoma, growing in wet swales and river bottoms. The handsome leaves are much broader and more substantial than those of *A. eulae*, and are glaucous gray and spirally twisted. Large, showy, many-flowered umbels of stellate white flowers clear the foliage on 60- to 75-centimeter stems. Greenish ovaries diminish the clarity of flower color, but it is nonetheless a first-rate garden plant that can be seen as an American version of garlic chives (*A. tuberosum*). Much like *A. eulae*, the bulbs of *A. texanum* go dormant after flowering; the plant sets plenty of viable seed and resprouts in autumn. The bulb coats are membranous or obscurely reticulated.

Allium fraseri Shinners

Howard (1954) defines *Allium fraseri* as an endemic species of central and southwestern Texas, and distinguishes it from *A. eulae* and *A. texanum* on the basis of its heavily reticulated, burlaplike bulb coats—no doubt an adaptation to dry, well-drained soils. The dark green foliage is much narrower and appears in early spring, without any early sprouting in fall. Inflorescences with 20 to 90 slightly fragrant flowers appear in spring; the individual flowers are broadly campanulate to stellate and white or rarely pinkish. The bulbs are sensitive to rot in cultivation, probably because of the thick tunic.

Allium pseudofraseri Howard

In the "*fraseri* alliance," *Allium pseudofraseri* is closest to *A. fraseri*. It grows in Texas, Oklahoma, and Kansas, extending north to Nebraska and South Dakota. This entity can be assigned in part to Ownbey's *A. canadense* var. *fraseri*. Flowering several weeks earlier than *A. fraseri*, it differs from that species in its urceolate flowers with pink or yellowish anthers, greenish ovary, and thinner pedicels. The flowers are sweetly scented like hyacinths, a characteristic shared with *A. elmendorfii*, *A. hyacinthoides*, and *A. perdulce*. I manage to keep both *A. fraseri* and *A. pseudofraseri* alive in the garden, but they have not been as satisfactory as *A. eulae* and *A. texanum*.

Allium mobilense Regel

Allium mobilense (synonyms *A. arenicola*, *A. canadense* var. *mobilense*, *A. microscordion*, *A. mutabile*) has narrow, glossy green leaves and pink, thin-textured flowers on stems about 30 centimeters tall. The small bulbs, which have fibrous, reticulated coats, increase by dividing in half and do not produce offsets. *Allium canadense* var. *mobilense*, as proposed by Ownbey, represented a sexual or nonbulbiliferous race of *A. canadense* occurring primarily in the southern coastal plain from eastern Texas east to Georgia and Florida, and also found in other habitats north to Missouri. The type plant is distinctive on account of its narrow, glossy green rushlike foliage and small, densely flowered, nearly spherical heads of lavender-pink flowers. The name *A. mobilense* var. *parksii* has been proposed (but not published) for a rare bulbiliferous form of *A. mobilense* found in east central Texas; it is a small plant with filiform (threadlike) leaves and pink flowers and bulbils, distinct from *A. canadense*.

Allium zenobiae Cory

Ownbey (1950b) quietly dismissed *Allium zenobiae* and put it in synonymy with his *A. canadense* var. *mobilense* without any discussion. Victor L. Cory (personal communication), who has done valuable work on southwestern alliums, discovered this robust race growing in mud or shallow water alongside a rivulet. The umbels bear as many as 175 lavender (or rarely white) florets on 60-centimeter stems (Plate 6). The species differs from *A. mobilense* in that it has basally attached bulblets around the parent bulb, whereas *A. mobilense* increases by dividing. *Allium zenobiae* also has larger flower heads that appear later. Endemic to east central Texas, it is a hardy garden plant, though perhaps a little fussier to grow than *A. texanum* is.

Allium ecristatum M. E. Jones

The distinctive *Allium ecristatum* (synonyms *A. canadense* var. *ecristatum*, *A. reticulatum* var. *ecristatum*) is endemic to the central coastal plain of Texas, growing in prairie and river bottomland. It has a coarsely reticulated bulb coat. The few-flowered (5 to 10) umbels of upright, urceolate, thick-textured lavender-pink flowers are very attractive. The flowers, atop 30-centimeter stems, are mildly fragrant. Thad Howard (1954) reports a second race of this species, overlooked by Ownbey, that is much more robust, with larger, many-flowered (20 to 40) umbels and a sweet fragrance. *Allium ecristatum* is reportedly as good a garden plant as *A. texanum* and *A. eulae*.

Allium hyacinthoides Bush

Allium hyacinthoides (synonym *A. canadense* var. *hyacinthoides*) has a narrow distribution in the prairies of north central Texas and nearby Oklahoma, generally on sandy soils. It is named for its strong fragrance, much like that of hyacinths. It has many-flowered umbels of pink (rarely white) urceolate flowers, quite unlike the white stellate flowers of *A. canadense*. Its bulb coat is strongly reticulated. The species grows to 30 centimeters or more.

Allium elmendorfii M. E. Jones ex Ownbey
Allium runyonii Ownbey

The rare endemic *Allium elmendorfii* has a small range in southern Texas, where it grows in sandy soils. Another of the *"canadense* alliance," this species is distinct enough to have been accepted even by Ownbey. It has a very thick, coarsely reticulated bulb coat and bears tiny basal bulblets on short stalks. The leaves are few and narrow, the stems about 30 centimeters tall; the inflorescence is a compact umbel of 10 to 30 urceolate, pink or whitish flowers. This species too has a powerful hyacinth-like fragrance. Reputedly difficult to grow, it must be given full sun and sand, and water should be withheld after flowering.

Allium runyonii was named by Ownbey, but other authorities, including Howard, have concluded that this plant is identical to *A. elmendorfii* and should be regarded as a synonym or at best a variety of that species. The only real difference appears to be that the former's bulb coats are even heavier and more persistent than those of the latter.

Allium glandulosum Link & Otto
Allium howardii Traub

The type plant of *Allium glandulosum* is from Mexico, where the flowers are deep red. Howard (1960) describes the plants as having "loose, starry, mahogany-red flowers, with a tiny, shiny gland at the base of each petal, an unusual species." This small species (15 to 30 centimeters tall) is also unusual in that it flowers late summer or autumn (August to October) in its native habitat of moist slopes, meadows, and mountains. It is reported to occur as far south as Honduras.

Ownbey (1950b) states that *Allium glandulosum* occurs north to Texas and Arizona, where it has paler flowers with color restricted to the midrib. According to Howard (1960), however, *A. glandulosum* is a strictly Mexican species, and the pale-flowered race found in Texas and Arizona is really *A. howardii* (named by Traub). Howard reports that *A. howardii* has starry, whitish flowers with pink midribs, flowers in late summer, and occurs in Texas, Arizona, and south into Mexico. *Allium howardii* resembles *A. kunthii* and the Mexican *A. potosiense*.

Allium kunthii G. Don

Another pair of confused yet related species is *Allium kunthii* (synonym *A. scaposum*) and *A. glandulosum* (synonym *A. rhizomatum*), with a third species, *A. howardii*, emerging from the confusion. Both of the former two have basal bulblets—short stipitate in *A. kunthii*, long and slender in *A. glandulosum* (so that the plant becomes stoloniferous). The bulb coats are membranous and not reticulated. The fourth member of the "*kunthi* alliance" is *A. stoloniferum*.

Allium kunthii has a range similar to that of the true *A. glandulosum* (sensu Howard) in Mexico, but it grows on dry hillsides and outcrops in the mountains rather than in moist soils. It is similar in appearance to *A. glandulosum*, but it has smaller flowers, white or pale pink, which appear from July to September; it lacks the long rhizomes characteristic of *A. glandulosum*.

Allium stoloniferum Ownbey & Jacobsen

Allium stoloniferum is a Mexican member of the "*kunthii* alliance." It has a few white, red-nerved flowers that are mostly replaced by bulbils—not a great beauty.

Allium drummondii Regel

This species and *Allium coryi* are another similar pair. *Allium drummondii* (synonyms *A. helleri*, *A. nuttallii*) occurs in northern Mexico, is widespread in Texas and Oklahoma, and reaches Kansas, Nebraska, and New Mexico. It is a small (15-centimeter), spring-blooming plant with white, pink, purplish, or fuchsia-red starry flowers, growing from small bulbs with tightly reticulated coats. Howard (1960) reports that the flower color is often muddy pinkish to whitish, but very attractive pure color forms can be selected. I have seen some deep color forms and, if these plants were more amenable to cultivation, they would be very desirable. I manage to keep them alive for a year or two, but invariably they dwindle in my garden. Ownbey (1950b) noted that under cultivation, *A. drummondii* had the ability to flower successively with two to three scapes from the same bulb. Gardeners should strive to find the right cultural conditions for this attractive little onion.

Allium coryi M. E. Jones

Allium coryi has the distinction of being the only yellow-flowered onion native to North America. It is a rare endemic of the mountains of western Texas, with a spotty distribution. It looks very similar to *A. drummondii*, except that its flowers are bright yellow, sometimes tinged red. I grew it outdoors for a couple of years in a raised sandy bed, where it overwintered and flowered with a handsome head of full-petaled florets on a 15-centimeter stem. I was struck by the floral resemblance to the Spanish species *A. scorzonerifolium*, which was growing near it in my garden. Howard has documented numerous hybrids (both natural and artificial) between *A. drummondii* and *A. coryi*, with startling results, including bicolors of red and gold, or pink and yellow. *Allium coryi* is available from specialist lists, and it is hoped that this charming species will gain wider popularity in the bulb world.

Allium perdulce S. V. Fraser

The Central Plains species *Allium perdulce* ranges from South Dakota and Iowa to northern Texas and eastern New Mexico. This is another of America's treasures—a delightful small, slow-growing onion with a floral fragrance that mingles hyacinth with a spicy scent near *Dianthus* (pinks). (I find it curious that so many southwestern American species have evolved this wonderful trait, flying in the face of the common notion that alliums are stinky!) The bulb coats are heavily reticulated, and after flowering the plants retreat into dormancy until the next spring. The plant is easily recognizable by its few spreading leaves, which are terete; the scapes are 10 to 15 centimeters tall, bearing few-flowered clusters of waxy, urceolate, deep rose flowers (Plate 7). The plant is frustratingly slow to propagate, and the few seeds I have obtained have resulted in very few flowering plants.

Allium perdulce var. *sperryi* Ownbey, from the mountains of western Texas, is stouter and with more numerous and larger florets, white to pale pink flowers with a lighter fragrance. Howard (1954) reports that this variety occasionally produces a large single bulbil in the inflorescence, and it generally is not as attractive as the typical species. It is also more difficult to grow because it resents too much watering—it grows in near-desert conditions.

Alliums of the Western United States, Excluding California

Everywhere one travels in the western states, one is likely to encounter flowering onions. In this section we first meet some widespread and variable species; then I discuss several alliances, or complexes, of similar species.

Allium geyeri S. Watson

This common species of meadows, streambanks, and other moist locations, mainly in the mountains, has a peculiarly disjunct though wide distribution that has perplexed botanists, resulting in a swarm of synonyms: *Allium dictyotum, A. arenicola, A. fibrosum, A. pikeanum, A. rubrum,*

A. rydbergii, and *A. sabulicola*. It can be found in the Pacific Northwest, including outposts in southern Alberta, and as far south as the Guadalupe Mountains of western Texas. It is a pleasant allium with a reticulated bulb coat, a few narrow green leaves, and stems 30 to 45 centimeters tall; the upright clusters of narrow-tubed pink flowers appear in June and July. Superficially this species resembles the European *A. angulosum*, with which it is sometimes confused in cultivation. A good doer in part shade in any decent soil, it prefers moisture but tolerates hot sun and dryness.

A dwarf form of the species found on Pike's Peak, Colorado, was named *Allium pikeanum* by Per Axel Rydberg but has been reduced to synonymy with *A. geyeri*. At very high elevations the plant is tiny, with little fans of green foliage flat against the ground. In cultivation it grows taller and more upright but still small in stature. The small bundles of pink flowers are produced on 15-centimeter stems. *Allium geyeri* var. *tenerum* M. E. Jones is the form in which the flowers are mostly replaced by small reddish bulbils. This is one of the few bulbiliferous onions that I allow in the garden, because in my experience the bulbils do not pose an invasion threat. Named in 1993, *A. geyeri* var. *chatterleyi* Welsh is a rare endemic of the Abajo Mountains in Utah, with persistent, many-layered bulb coats.

Allium textile A. Nelson & J. F. Macbride

Another ubiquitous onion of the West, found growing in dry soils or heavy clay that is vernally moist but bakes during the summer, is *Allium textile* (synonyms *A. aridum*, *A. geyeri* var. *textile*, *A. reticulatum*). It appears not to be amenable to cultivation, but it is not missed: it is not showy. *Allium textile* has a pair of basal green leaves and a small head of starry whitish flowers with reddish-brown midribs on a 15-centimeter stem. In Idaho it forms expansive colonies, growing thickly enough to create an alliaceous ground cover. It can be found from southern Canada to New Mexico, with a few outlying stations as far east as Minnesota (Plate 8).

Allium macropetalum Rydberg

Similar to *Allium textile*, *A. macropetalum* is separated from it on account of its larger, pink or white flowers, a number of more minor differences, and its more southerly distribution: to Texas and possibly just across the Mexican border. In Colorado I've only found the white-flowered phase of *A. macropetalum*, which is not very showy.

Allium douglasii Hooker

Allium douglasii presents taxonomic complexities; some varieties have small, narrow leaves, while others have broad, falcate (sickle-shaped) leaves. The species and its varieties are native to Washington and northeastern Oregon. Ownbey (1950a) describes four varieties: *douglasii*, *co-*

lumbianum (which extends the range to western Idaho), *constrictum*, and *nevii*. (The latter, found along the eastern slope of the Cascade Range, is the westernmost representative of the complex.)

I had the good fortune to study extensive populations of *Allium douglasii* on several trips to the Wenatchee Mountains, an eastern spur of the Cascade Range in Kittitas County, Washington (Plate 9). I first met this species alongside logging roads at elevations to 5000 feet (1500 meters). The dry area supported a scattered population of small *A. douglasii* plants that were not very impressive: narrow channeled leaves and poor heads of light pink flowers on 20- to 30-centimeter stems. These fit the picture of variety *nevii*. Later I discovered a beautiful, flowery meadow filled with many thousands of onion plants. After closely examining numerous individuals, I concluded that Ownbey's subdivision of *A. douglasii* was quite meaningless. The plants showed great diversity that encompassed all his varieties in a single population, with the possible exception of variety *constrictum*, which has a conspicuous swelling of the flower stem just below the inflorescence, a trait I did not observe in the study populations.

It was clear that many characteristics of an individual plant—size, breadth, and shape of foliage as well as size and number of flowers in the inflorescence—were directly attributable to the bulb's maturity and habitat. This species prefers vernally wet soil in shallow depressions or on moist slopes. In the center of a moist depression filled with a colony of *Allium douglasii*, the plants were remarkably variable, with a high percentage of robust plants, some with wide, falcate leaves and others with heavy channeled leaves, and most with showy, spherical heads of pink flowers. These could be assigned to varieties *douglasii* and *columbianum*. They grew alongside obviously younger plants with much narrower foliage and smaller heads which fit the description of variety *nevii*. At the periphery of the depression, in much drier soil, grew depauperate plants that also fit variety *nevii*.

An amazing colony of *Allium douglasii* exists in an area west of Colockum Pass in the Wenatchee Mountains. I visited it to see onions growing by the millions, coloring whole hillsides pink, filling the air with an intoxicatingly sweet yet mild oniony aroma, and buzzing with myriad bees. The soil was very wet with snowmelt. In some places the alliums grew in running water along with magenta *Dodecatheon*, the yellow thimbles of *Fritillaria pudica* (yellow fritillary), and the rich rose-red *Olsynium douglasii* (grass widow). Once again great variability was in evidence, although most plants were robust with glossy green, falcate to channeled leaves and perfect balls of candy-pink flowers. There were some deeper pinks, many light pinks—and one plant out of millions that was pure white. When I returned to the same spot a few weeks later, the soil was baked rock-hard, and the alliums and other little geophytes had completely disappeared into dormancy.

Had Ownbey studied a larger cross section of living material, or inspected remarkable colonies like those in the Wenatchee Mountains, he might not have split *Allium douglasii* into varieties. More disturbing is the fact that the Biota of North America Program has elevated the varieties to species status, yielding *A. columbianum*, *A. constrictum*, and *A. nevii*, a taxonomic change I cannot endorse.

In my Seattle garden *Allium douglasii* responded well when planted in a peat-sand mix in full sun, but it was harder to please in New England, probably because of my failure to provide proper moisture and drainage conditions. Plants can be raised from seed, but like most western alliums that have a short spring season of growth and a long period of dormancy, it takes four to five years to reach flowering size.

Allium macrum S. Watson

Confusing the concept of *Allium douglasii* even more is the fact some plants have bumpy purple anthers, agreeing with the description of *A. macrum*, a species that occurs in the same area. In fact, very little separates *A. macrum* from *A. douglasii* var. *nevii* except for the differing anthers. In Ownbey's (1950a) words, "*Allium macrum* is almost *Allium douglasii* in miniature." *Allium macrum* (synonym *A. equicaeleste*) may well come to be regarded, after further study, as a synonym of *A. douglasii*. This allied species has white to pale pink flowers, prefers arid hillsides and gravelly soil, and has a range similar to that of *A. douglasii*. The growth habit of *A. macrum*, with a pair of narrow, upright, often channeled leaves, a short stem usually under 30 centimeters tall, and an open cluster of small star-cup flowers, can be used as a convenient baseline for describing a number of similar-looking species, although each has its own distinguishing characteristics. Among these are *A. madidum* and *A. bisceptrum*.

Allium madidum S. Watson

This species, from seasonally wet meadows in eastern Oregon and western Idaho, grows 10 to 20 centimeters tall and has white or pinkish flowers. It is related to *A. bisceptrum* and *A. macrum*.

Allium bisceptrum S. Watson

Allium bisceptrum inhabits meadows and slopes in Oregon, California, Nevada, Idaho, and Utah. It grows to 30 centimeters or more and has open, spherical heads of white, pink, or lavender flowers; robust specimens may produce two flowering scapes per bulb. *Allium bisceptrum* var. *palmeri* (S. Watson) Cronquist (synonym *A. palmeri*) has a more southern distribution in New Mexico and Arizona. It is surprising that Arthur Cronquist and Noel Holmgren sank *A. palmeri* as a variety of *A. bisceptrum*; they differ in several important features. In variety *palmeri* the basal bulblets are produced on long slender rhizomes, whereas the bulblets are sessile in *A. bisceptrum*. Variety *palmeri* is a smaller plant, with flower tips becoming involute, a pronounced keel along the midrib of the tepal, and deeper color range of rich purple to pink. *Allium bisceptrum* is related to *A. macrum* and *A. madidum*.

Allium dictuon St. John

Rather similar to the widespread *Allium acuminatum* (discussed in the section on California species) is *A. dictuon* from eastern Washington and Oregon. The flowers are bright pink with long pointed tepals and are held in an open, hemispherical head. Once on the endangered species list, it has now been removed.

Allium fibrillum M. E. Jones

Allium fibrillum (synonym *A. collinum*) is a modest little onion ranging from eastern Washington and Oregon east to Idaho and Montana. The pair of channeled leaves rises above the 5- to 15-centimeter stems and heads of white flowers (sometimes pink) with greenish midribs.

Allium bigelovii S. Watson

This species from Arizona and New Mexico has stems only 5 to 10 centimeters tall, a pair of leaves that exceed the scape, and few-flowered heads of pinkish flowers.

Western Alliums with a Single Leaf

Only a few species produce a single leaf per bulb. Note that the number of leaves in a species description is often based on the plant in flower, without considering leaves that withered away before flowering. Under favorable conditions, many species may produce more leaves than the botanical description specifies; however, single-leaved species with terete foliage appear *never* to produce more than one leaf. (Other single-leaved species are discussed in the section on California alliums.)

Allium nevadense S. Watson

Widespread in desert environments in many western states, *Allium nevadense* grows in sandy, gravelly, or clay soils. It has a solitary, terete, rat-tail leaf, which may coil at the end; the flower stalk pokes out from the leaf partway up, reaching just a few centimeters in height. The flowers are white or pink, with deep pink midribs.

Allium atrorubens S. Watson

Allied to *Allium nevadense*, *A. atrorubens* is endemic to Nevada and grows a little taller (to 15 centimeters). Two varieties are identified: *A. atrorubens* var. *atrorubens* with deep reddish-purple stellate flowers, and *A.*

atrorubens var. *inyoensis* (M. E. Jones) Ownbey & Aase with pale flowers and pink midribs, extending the range of the species into California. McNeal (1922b) put *A. atrorubens* var. *inyoensis* and the Californian *A. cristatum* in synonymy under the name *A. atrorubens* var. *cristatum*.

Allium parishii S. Watson

The third member of this single-leaved group grows up to 15 centimeters tall, with a few-flowered to many-flowered head of pale pink flowers with long tepals. It occurs in the desert mountains of western Arizona and southeastern California.

Western Alliums with Broad, Falcate Leaves

Species with falcate leaves are often pleasing for the foliage alone.

Allium pleianthum S. Watson

This rather specialized onion with falcate leaves is a beautiful species endemic to Oregon. At one time it was listed as an endangered species, but it has been removed from the list. It can be successfully cultivated in various soil types, including sand, but the most luxuriant plants grow in rich, heavy soils that are allowed to dry out after flowering. In spring, several ribbonlike, glossy leaves, undulating flat on the ground, are attractive in their own right. By June, several large, spherical bloom heads appear, up to 8 centimeters across. The inflorescence is dense-flowered and appears spiky on account of the long, reflexed beige-pink to lavender-pink blooms (Plate 10). This species seldom sets seed in cultivation.

Allium anceps Kellogg

Allium anceps is a handsome species with shuttlecock-shaped heads of white to deep rose on 10- to 15-centimeter stems. Found in Nevada and adjacent Oregon and California, it has a fragrance reported as carnation-like but also oniony.

Allium lemmonii S. Watson

Allium lemmonii (synonyms *A. incisum*, *A. scissum*) grows on clay soils in Oregon, Idaho, Nevada, and adjacent California. Akin to *A. anceps*, it has a pair of slender but fleshy leaves that sweep in one direction (mildly falcate) and slightly exceed the 5- to 15-centimeter flowering stems. The flowers are white to pink, with thickened midribs of pink or green.

Allium platycaule S. Watson

Allium platycaule is a beautiful and distinctive species with exceptionally broad falcate leaves and a large, dense head of pink to deep rose flowers atop 10- to 15-centimeter stems. The tepals are very long and narrow, with the stamens well exserted, giving the inflorescence a spidery look.

Allium passeyi N. & A. Holmgren

Allium passeyi, endemic to Utah, has two or three broad leaves and large, upright heads of pink flowers that just top the leaves.

Allium tolmiei (Hooker) Baker ex S. Watson

This variable onion, though falcate, is somewhat similar to *Allium douglasii* and has as one of its many synonyms *A. douglasii* var. *tolmiei*. It is divided into three varieties, *A. tolmiei* var. *tolmiei* (synonym *A. cusickii*), *A. tolmiei* var. *platyphyllum* (Tidestrom) Ownbey (synonym *A. platyphyllum* Tidestrom, non Diels), and *A. tolmiei* var. *persimile* Ownbey, collectively found in eastern Washington and Oregon, northeastern California, and west to Idaho, growing in rocky or clay soil among sparse vegetation. The species grows 15 to 30 centimeters tall, with broad, variably falcate leaves and heads of pinkish flowers.

Western Dwarf Alliums

In this section, I single out a few particularly attractive dwarf species that are suitable for the rock garden or cultivation in pots and troughs. Many of those already described are equally suitable, but these are especially small and pleasing. Several are sessile-flowering (the inflorescence is at ground level).

Allium simillimum Henderson

Perhaps the smallest American onion is *Allium simillimum*, a diminutive plant that grows in basaltic screes and sandy soils at high elevation in the mountains of Idaho, just crossing into Montana. I've only found it growing on black basalt screes, with fine silty soil below the coarse stone layer. Each bulb has a pair of leaves just 1 to 2 millimeters wide, and a nearly stemless bundle of small white flowers with green or reddish midribs. The plant is amenable to careful cultivation but is easily lost if overgrown by neighboring plants.

Allium aaseae Ownbey

A rather rare onion endemic to Idaho, *Allium aaseae* is a beautiful little sessile species with ample, deep pink flowers that fade to white and with a pair of narrow, channeled leaves that are much longer than the scape and tend to lie on the ground. It has an extremely restricted distribution in southwestern Idaho on sparsely vegetated sandy foothills near Boise. It is closely related to *A. simillimum*, but it prefers lower elevations and has pink rather than white flowers. At one time *A. aaseae* was listed as an endangered species, but it has since been removed from federal candidate status, though it remains a sensitive species, monitored by several agencies. Finding significant information on highly local native flora—especially our native onions—is almost as hard as finding the plants themselves, so it is encouraging to find that the state of Idaho and several other organizations maintain an exemplary web page on *A. aaseae*, including photos.

Allium scilloides Douglas ex S. Watson

Favoring arid, gravelly soils in eastern Washington, *Allium scilloides* (synonym *A. fragile*) is another species with a pair of falcate leaves that exceed the short bloom stalk. It is easily recognized because the few-flowered inflorescence is congested at first, rather than spreading as it is in many other American onions. The flowers are white to pinkish, and are said to fade to red; I've never seen it in the fruiting phase to verify this unusual color transition. All the plants I have seen were white-flowered, growing among sagebrush (*Artemisia*) in good company with the lovely blue and purple *Viola trinervata*, gnarled bonsai shrubs of *Eriogonum thymoides* with hot red and orange flowers, and golden-yellow *Ranunculus glaberrimus*. In cultivation, bulbs of *A. scilloides* require a long, dry summer rest.

Allium brandegei S. Watson

A few species I know only from herbarium specimens and drawings. *Allium brandegei* (synonyms *A. diehlii, A. minimum, A. tribracteatum* var. *diehlii*) has a wide distribution from Colorado, Wyoming, and Montana to Idaho, Oregon, Utah, and Nevada. The two leaves surpass the flowering stem, which is only a few centimeters tall. The rounded head contains white flowers with green or reddish midribs, another common theme in pale-flowered American onions.

Allium parvum Kellogg

Allium parvum and *A. punctum* are similar. *Allium parvum* (synonyms *A. modocense, A. tribracteatum* var. *andersonii*) is a better-known and more widespread species from Idaho, Oregon, and adjacent California south to Utah and Nevada, growing on stony clay slopes. It is slightly larger than *A. punctum* and has rose to purple flowers, or sometimes white with pink midribs.

Allium punctum Henderson

Allium punctum (synonym *A. miser*), known only from Oregon, has a pair of leaves which coil at the end, a scape only 2 to 5 centimeters tall, and a head of deep rose-purple flowers.

Allium crenulatum Wiegand

Moving up to alpine heights, *Allium crenulatum* (synonyms *A. cascadense, A. vancouverense, A. watsonii*) is a delightful small plant that should be attempted in a pot, trough, or choice niche in the scree garden. It's a variable species with small populations in a disjunct distribution from Vancouver Island in British Columbia through the mountains of Washington (where it is common) and south to Oregon; it grows in gravelly soils at high elevations and on rocky summits. From a pair of narrow leaves lying on the ground sprout short, stout, winged stems a few centimeters high. The spreading umbels of flowers range from white to pink—deep rose red in the best forms. I have grown only white-flowered plants from the Cascades, which persist in the garden in sandy soil but never flourish and only occasionally flower. In a bulb frame they do much better.

Allium robinsonii Henderson

Of all the small American onions, I unequivocally vote *Allium robinsonii* my favorite. After searching in vain for this rare onion in its type locality at the confluence of Oregon's John Day River with the mighty Columbia, I later learned that it is considered extinct in Oregon, now found only in Washington. Its habitat is highly specific: it grows on sand "benches" just a few feet above the river's high-water level and does not venture onto the high, steep banks. Numerous hydroelectric dams have been built along the river, raising the water level and destroying the habitat of this onion. It is therefore surprising that it has been removed as a candidate for threatened status in the federal register.

The populations I observed were growing along one of the last remaining free-flowing stretches of the Columbia River. Here *Allium robinsonii* grew in pure sand among occasional outcrops of black basalt, perilously close to the water's edge. It was not particularly abundant but only sporadic, sometimes out in the open but most often under the protection of a handsome purple-flowered shrub, *Salvia dorrii* var. *carnosa*. Digging into the sand revealed that just inches down it was cool and barely moist, with a trace of organic matter—clues to this allium's requirements in cultivation.

What struck me most about finding this elusive onion was that the stark, look-alike drawings and inert botanical descriptions in published floras do not prepare one for the thrill of the real plants, which invariably have more liveliness and character than one could imagine from the descriptions. This is certainly true of the delightful *Allium robinsonii* (Plate 11). Two basal, ribbonlike leaves grow to 12 centimeters and are strongly falcate in more mature, robust specimens. The umbels contain 10 to 35 flowers in rather tight, upright heads atop 2- to 8-centimeter stems that are noticeably winged. The reddish-purple spathe segments split into two and persist during flowering. The tepals are fairly long and of a warm flesh pink with deeper midribs, accented with black-red anthers. The flowers age to a deep rosy red as they become papery and loosely surround the crested ovary and developing seed. The plants retreat into dormancy immediately after flowering until the following spring.

In Seattle *Allium robinsonii* grew well in raised sand beds and in large pots of pure sand with a bit of organic matter added. I do not grow it in New England, but I sent bulbs and seeds to the Royal Botanic Gardens, Kew. Perhaps they still cultivate this desirable species, and one day seed will become available for allium aficionados.

California Alliums

It may seem odd to single out the California alliums, but this separation is well justified. The comprehensive taxonomic treatment of alliums in California in the *Jepson Manual* (Hickman 1993) lists 59 native species and subspecies—more or less half of those native to North America (depending on who is counting). Many of these are almost unknown outside California. Botanists and field workers have struggled for many years to organize this wealth of material. Dale W. McNeal of the University of the Pacific in Stockton is responsible for bringing order to the California species.

The geographic area covered here is centered on what botanists call the California Floristic Province, a construct based not on state borders but on geography and climate, and thus on plant communities. It is one of three floristic provinces in California. The Desert Province includes the Mohave and Sonoran deserts and extends east into Arizona and New Mexico and south into Mexico. The Great Basin Province includes the areas east of the Sierra Nevada and Cascade Range that are too moist to be considered true desert; it extends into Oregon, Idaho, and Nevada. The California Floristic Province comprises the rest of California; it has extensions in southwestern Oregon, Baja California, and the parts of Nevada around Lake Tahoe and between Reno and Carson City.

Most Californian alliums bloom fairly early in the year, in mid to late spring or early summer at the latest, no doubt an adaptation to California's Mediterranean climate, with mild, wet winters (except at high elevations), and long, hot, dry summers. Many of these plants may be difficult in gardens in other climates. Some of them, however, are attractive enough to be worth the effort to give them the conditions they must have. A few—notably *Allium campanulatum*, *A. hyalinum*, and *A. unifolium*—are widely cultivated and are sold inexpensively in commercial bulb catalogs.

The following discussion is organized around co-occurring traits by which we recognize the many species. Some of these groups have been designated alliances or complexes by botanists. The term *alliance* denotes a (usually large) group of distantly related species, while a *complex* is a smaller group of very closely related ones; thus, an alliance may include several complexes.

Allium sanbornii Alliance

McNeal (1989) contrasts the *Allium sanbornii* alliance with other North American species, all of which have either two or more leaves per scape, or a single leaf which is flattened or broadly channeled. The *A. sanbornii* alliance, by contrast, is characterized by a single, erect leaf which is terete. This alliance includes two complexes of very closely related species as well as several more distantly related ones, as follows:

Allium sanbornii complex
  A. *tuolumnense*
  A. *sanbornii* var. *sanbornii* and var. *congdonii*
  A. *jepsonii*
Allium fimbriatum complex
  A. *fimbriatum* var. *fimbriatum*, var. *mohavense*, and var. *purdyi*
  A. *sharsmithae*
  A. *parryi*
  A. *munzii*
  A. *diabloense*
  A. *denticulatum*
  A. *abramsii*
A. *shevockii*
A. *monticola*
A. *atrorubens*
A. *nevadense*
A. *parishii*
A. *howellii* var. *howellii*, var. *sanbenitense*, and var. *clokeyi*

Allium tuolumnense (Ownbey & Aase) S. Denison & McNeal

This is a very narrow endemic, known from only a few scattered locations in the central Sierra Nevada foothills, where it grows on serpentine soils, blooming from late March to early May. It is listed as rare and endangered by the California Native Plant Society (CNPS), and as a Level 1 candidate species by the U.S. Fish and Wildlife Service; however, it is not so listed by the state of California. McNeal describes it as a loose umbel of 20 to 60 white flowers on a 25- to 50-centimeter stem, sometimes flushed pink, with spreading perianth segments and prominent ovary crests, and notes that its single terete leaf is withering from the tip by anthesis. Because of its status, we have not collected seed or tried to grow it.

Allium sanbornii Wood

This species is among the latest-blooming Californian onions. Variety *sanbornii* is a tall, pretty plant, with a tight umbel of as many as 150 florets, usually hot pink, with erect perianth segments, on a 15- to 30-centimeter stem (Plate 12). It grows on serpentine outcrops and gravels in the northern Sierra foothills, with a few disjunct populations in the southern Cascade foothills. Bloom time is usually late June into early August. Although not especially common, it often occurs in dense groups, creating spectacular drifts of bright pink at a time when most native vegetation is dormant. Along one back road in northern Yuba County, communities of this plant grow for 2.5 miles (4 kilometers) in openings in the manzanita scrub; the total population may number hundreds of thousands in a good year of high rainfall.

Allium sanbornii var. *congdonii* Jepson (synonym *A. intactum*) resembles variety *sanbornii* closely, but it is more common, a little taller (to 40 centimeters), and more robust; its flowers are white to pale pink, and its stigma head is distinctly three-lobed rather than headlike. It grows in similar habitats but ranges farther south (with some overlap) and generally blooms about four weeks earlier.

Both these onions proved relatively easy to grow from seed in our garden 60 miles (96 kilometers) north of San Francisco Bay. They are kept well watered throughout winter and spring, then allowed to dry at bloom time. Like nearly all California's dry-growing onions, they require complete dryness in summer. They usually bloom the second or third year from seed, and the bulbs increase slowly by vegetative reproduction.

Allium jepsonii (Ownbey & Aase) S. Denison & McNeal

The last member of the *Allium sanbornii* complex is *A. jepsonii*, another late bloomer. It occurs in two disjunct areas in the Sierra Nevada foothills: one on serpentine soils in the north, and the other on volcanic soils in the central foothills. It tends to be the shortest of this group, with a very tight umbel of 20 to 60 white florets on a 20- to 30-centimeter stem; the tepals, though erect, spread at the tips. The plant blooms in late May or early June in the south, and from mid to late June in the north. Although considered rare by the CNPS because of its limited number of known stations, it too blooms in massive numbers in good years and is not formally listed as rare or threatened. Cultivation of *A. jepsonii* is similar to that of the two *A. sanbornii* varieties, with equal success.

Allium fimbriatum Complex

The second group in the *Allium sanbornii* alliance is the *A. fimbriatum* complex, consisting of nine taxa. All of them were once classified as subspecies of *A. fimbriatum*; McNeal (1989) elevated six to full species status, based on careful analysis. The separation of the taxa is quite technical, and so our discussion of them must be as well.

Allium fimbriatum S. Watson

Allium fimbriatum var. *fimbriatum* may be considered the flagship species, since it is the most common member of this complex. It has a loose umbel of 6 to 35 dark rose-purple flowers on a 10- to 20-centimeter stem; the perianth segments are erect but have distinctly flaring tips. The plant's attractive color stands out in its natural habitat of gravelly volcanic or serpentine clays which support little other vegetation. It occurs in the southern foothills of California's Inner North Coast Ranges, a location disjunct from the rest of its range: the Inner South Coast and transverse ranges south to San Diego County, the San Joaquin Valley, and the desert slopes of the southern Sierra Nevada and Tehachapi Mountains. There is one collection from Baja California. The plant generally blooms in May. It is often sought by enthusiasts but has proved very difficult for us to grow from seed, often requiring five to six years to reach blooming size, and never vigorous.

   Allium fimbriatum var. *mohavense* (Tidestrom) Jepson is a little taller (to 25 centimeters), with flowers that range from white to pink to light lavender. It is restricted to the floor and lower mountain slopes of the western Mohave Desert. It blooms from late April through June, depending on elevation. In one area the ranges of varieties *fimbriatum* and *mohavense* are contiguous, and there one can find plants with intermediate characteristics. The intermediates have lavender to purple flowers, but their ovary crests are dentate (toothed) like variety *fimbriatum*, rather than deeply laciniate (slashed, grooved), sometimes with outgrowths, like variety *mohavense*, so they are considered to belong to variety *fimbriatum* despite their hybrid origin.

   Allium fimbriatum var. *purdyi* Eastwood is a narrow endemic of gravelly serpentine clays, mostly along and near the borders between Lake and Colusa counties and contiguous Napa and Yolo counties in the Inner North Coast Ranges. It has 20 to 75 florets on a stout 10- to 37-centimeter stem, blooming from late April through May. The perianth segments are white to pale lavender with darker midveins. The ovary crests have what McNeal (1989) describes as "processes finely dentate to laciniate"; occasionally the ovary crests are entirely absent. The territories of varieties *fimbriatum* and *purdyi* overlap, and where they do, one sees plants that are intermediate in color and size. This is especially the case in a preserve maintained by the federal Bureau of Land Management in a "peninsula" of northernmost Napa County which projects toward Lake County. There we find onions with the robustness of variety *purdyi* but in colors from very pale through medium lavender to near purple, and with variable ovary crests. Because of this variety's narrow range, CNPS has placed *A. sanbornii* var. *purdyi* on its "watch list," but it is difficult to think of it as endangered, given its robust appearance and the huge drifts it forms on soils so toxic they support little other plant material. Interestingly, variety *purdyi* is by far the easiest of the three *A. fimbriatum* varieties to grow from seed. It germinates readily if planted outdoors in late winter and reaches blooming size in two or three years.

Allium sharsmithae (Ownbey & Aase) McNeal

Allium sharsmithae (synonym *A. fimbriatum* var. *sharsmithae*) is another narrow endemic, restricted to serpentine outcrops in the Mount Hamilton Range southeast of San Francisco Bay. Umbels of 5 to 50 dark red-purple flowers appear on a 4- to 17-centimeter stem, usually in mid-May. Its flowers are generally larger than are those of any *A. fimbriatum* varieties, and its ovary crests have distinctive papillate processes. We have seen this allium in one of its better-known locations, the head of Del Puerto Canyon in Alameda County, but since its habitat rarely receives more than 15 inches (375 millimeters) of rain a year, we have not tried to grow it from seed in our wetter coastal climate. This species is not formally listed by either federal or state agencies, but CNPS considers proposal for listing mandatory because of its small range.

Allium parryi S. Watson

This species (synonym *Allium fimbriatum* var. *parryi*) occurs in scattered sites in the southern Sierra Nevada and southern California mountains, as well as one location in northern Baja California, on sandy or (more commonly) clay soils. It blooms from late April to mid-July, depending on location. It has 8 to 50 florets, white with pink midveins, on a 5- to 20-centimeter scape; the flowers fade to red as they age. It can be distinguished from other members of the complex by its color, its ovary crests which tend to be smooth rather than dentate, and its long curving pedicels in fruit, which give the umbel an almost flat-topped appearance.

Allium munzii (Ownbey & Aase) McNeal

Allium munzii (synonym *A. fimbriatum* var. *munzii*) is limited to heavy clay soils in Riverside County, just east of Los Angeles, in grassy openings in a coastal sage scrub habitat. It has 10 to 35 florets, white with pink midveins that turn red as they age, but a taller stem (15 to 35 centimeters) than that of *A. parryi*; it flowers from April to mid-May. Its perianth segments are shorter and broader than in other members of the complex, and its ovary crests are finely and irregularly dentate. McNeal notes that even though its distribution is contiguous with those of both *A. parryi* and *A. fimbriatum*, it does not overlap with either of these taxa. It is listed by the state as a threatened species, with sufficient data on hand to support federal listing.

Allium diabloense (Ownbey & Aase) McNeal

Allium diabloense (elevated from *A. fimbriatum* var. *diabloense*, and some-times misspelled *A. diabolense*) occurs from the area immediately east of San Francisco Bay south to just north of Los Angeles in the Inner South Coast Ranges and is apparently restricted to serpentine soils. Its flowers are white with pink midveins (and sometimes pink tips) and occur in umbels of 10 to 50 on a 7- to 20-centimeter scape. It closely resembles *A. munzii* but differs in having narrower perianth segments and more deeply grooved ovary crests, as well as a longer leaf prior to anthesis. Flowering occurs from early May to mid-June. We have found this spe-cies relatively easy to grow from seed planted in late winter, usually flowering in its third year.

Allium denticulatum (Ownbey & Aase) McNeal

This species (synonym *Allium fimbriatum* var. *denticulatum*) grows in sandy soils on desert slopes north and east of Los Angeles, and flowers from late April to early June. It has 5 to 30 rose-purple flowers on a 5- to 18-centimeter stem. It could be mistaken for an extra-vigorous *A. fim-briatum* var. *fimbriatum*, but its perianth segments are toothed and its ovary crests are smoother. The territories of the two are contiguous but do not overlap. In 1992 we encountered a wonderful blooming of *A. den-ticulatum* east of Lake Isabella, at 4500 feet (1350 meters).

Allium abramsii (Ownbey & Aase) McNeal

This might be considered the oddball member of the *Allium fimbriatum* complex. Its territory is rather disjunct from those of most other mem-bers, being confined to the higher foothills of the central Sierra Nevada, where it can be found growing in disintegrated granitic sands accumu-lated in pockets around the edges of the glaciated granite slabs common here. Its umbels of 6 to 40 rose-purple flowers top 5- to 15-centimeter scapes. The outer three tepals are longer and broader than the inner three, as well as darker in color, and each floret is noticeably more spreading than are those of most members of the complex. The tepals are usually crisped (crinkled at the edges) and occasionally dentate. It is altogether a very attractive onion and, happily for us, it is the easiest of the entire complex to grow from seed, at least in our location. Planted in late winter, it often blooms its second year from seed. It tends to self-seed and naturalize in our mild climate. Bulbs also slowly increase vegetatively.

Other Members of the *Allium sanbornii* Alliance

In addition to the two complexes discussed above, four species belong to the *Allium sanbornii* alliance.

Allium shevockii **McNeal**

A unique member of the *Allium sanbornii* alliance is *A. shevockii*, first published in 1987. A narrow endemic of the southern Sierra Nevada, it grows on volcanic outcrops and talus from 6600 to 8300 feet (1980 to 2490 meters) in an area inaccessible except on foot. It has 12 to 30 florets in a moderately loose umbel on a 10- to 20-centimeter stem, and its single terete leaf may be more than twice as long as the stem. Its perianth segments are distinctly reflexed, white or green below and maroon toward the tips. Another distinguishing feature is long, threadlike rhizomes that terminate in bulblets, in addition to offset bulblets produced around the base of the parent bulb. CNPS considers this species rare, though it is not state listed; data are thought insufficient to support federal listing.

Allium monticola **A. Davidson**

This related species (synonym *Allium parishii* var. *keckii*) from the transverse ranges and northwestern peninsular ranges is found on rocky ridges and talus slopes at elevations of 4,600 to 10,500 feet (1380 to 3150 meters). Its 8 to 25 flowers are pink with rose tips on a 6- to 25-centimeter stem; all the "green" parts of this plant are glaucous.

Allium atrorubens **S. Watson**

In California this species (described above in the section on "Western Alliums with a Single Leaf") is found on the eastern slope of the Sierra Nevada in rocky or sandy soils at 4000 to 7000 feet (1200 to 2100 meters). It is far more common farther east.

Allium nevadense **S. Watson**

Also described earlier (in the section on "Western Alliums with a Single Leaf") is *Allium nevadense*, which occurs in the desert mountains of southeastern California. CNPS regards the pursuit of state listing of *A. nevadense* mandatory because of its limited occurrence within California.

Allium parishii **S. Watson**

This species is found in the Mohave Desert and east into western Arizona. It is more common within California than *Allium nevadense* and is not a likely candidate for listing by CNPS.

Allium howellii **Eastwood**

We turn now to the last group within the *Allium sanbornii* alliance, *A. howellii* and its varieties *howellii*, *clokeyi*, and *sanbenitense*. This onion of the southern half of California is notable for its exserted stamens and prominent ovary crests in all three varieties. All bloom in late spring, with date of anthesis varying according to location. We have grown all three with mixed success.

Allium howellii var. *howellii* is fairly common (Plate 13). It grows on grassy slopes, from east of San Francisco Bay, south through the Inner Coast Ranges and across the transverse ranges and Tehachapi Mountains, and north through the southern Sierra Nevada foothills, as well as in parts of the San Joaquin Valley where it has not been extirpated by agricultural development. It has a moderately open umbel of 15 to 40 flowers, generally pale lavender, on a slender 15- to 30-centimeter stem; it is distinguished from the following varieties by this thin stem.

Allium howellii var. *sanbenitense* (Traub) Ownbey & Aase is less common, confined to eastern San Benito and western Fresno counties, where it grows on thinly grassy slopes in serpentine soils. Its 50 to 90 white to pink florets occur atop a stout scape of 25 to 60 centimeters. This is another species which, though uncommon, may appear in thick clumps or even drifts in a good year.

Allium howellii var. *clokeyi* Ownbey & Aase is the desert version, growing on open slopes amid desert sagebrush scrub in the transverse ranges. McNeal describes it as "locally common," and we would apply that description to all three varieties. Variety *clokeyi* has 50 to 100 white florets, sometimes with pink midveins, on a stout stem of 20 to 40 centimeters. It is striking against the backdrop of scattered high desert plants, many of which have glaucous foliage. It is accustomed to 10 inches (250 millimeters) of rain a year or less, and our efforts to grow it in Sonoma County met with little success. Our experience with the other varieties has been somewhat better; we have got them to bloom their third or fourth year from seed, but the bulbs have not persisted well.

Low-growing Species with Channeled, Prostrate Leaves

We turn next to a group of onions which share the following characteristics: most are low-growing; all have one or two long (compared with scape height), broadly channeled leaves which lie nearly flat on the ground; and all might be called obscure.

Allium cratericola Eastwood

The best-known member of this group is probably *Allium cratericola*, which occurs in several California habitats and varies considerably in form (Plate 14). Alice Eastwood first described it in 1934, based on the form from the southern shoulders of Mount St. Helena, Napa County. Some forms have only a single long, channeled leaf, while others have two; in either case, the leaves are somewhat glaucous. The name implies occurrence on lava-derived soils and volcanic outcrops, but *A. cratericola* also grows in serpentine gravels and granitics. Elevations vary from about 1100 feet (330 meters; Table Mountain north of Oroville, on a lava cap), through 2000 feet (600 meters; Mount St. Helena in Napa County, on lava outcrops), 3500 feet (1050 meters; Walker Ridge, along the Lake

Colusa county line, on a serpentine outcrop), and 4000 feet (1200 meters; Nevada County, on granitic soils), to about 6000 feet (1800 meters; Hell's Half Acre, southeastern Mendocino County, on serpentine-derived soils). Some forms are quite pink, while others are better described as off-white; most have a darker pink midvein. Individual florets have very erect petals, often inward-curving at the tips, and inflorescence diameter varies from 3 to 5 centimeters. All forms have a short stem that is more or less flattened and appears to break easily in late anthesis or early fruiting, so that the seedheads tend to tumble away in the wind. If one is alert to this and collects early, some forms of *A. cratericola* can be grown from seed, but it has taken us many years to achieve blooming-size bulbs.

Allium obtusum J. G. Lemmon

Allium obtusum and its two varieties can also be placed in this group. Variety *obtusum* (synonym *A. ambiguum*) is fairly common, often occurring in gravelly granitic soils and pockets of sand on granitic slabs in the higher foothills and subalpine habitats of the northern and central Sierra Nevada and southern Cascade Range. It has one or two long, channeled leaves, and 6 to 30 white florets with dark purple midveins and erect tepals in an inflorescence of less than 3 centimeters diameter on stems usually less than 2 centimeters. We know it only from the trails that run south from Kings Creek Meadow in Lassen National Park, where it grows in great numbers.

Allium obtusum var. *conspicuum* Mortola & McNeal is less common. It occurs at lower elevations than does variety *obtusum*, confined to granitic central and northern Sierra Nevada foothills and subalpine habitats. Its inflorescence has 10 to 60 flowers, generally pink with purple midveins and erect tepals, and is 3 to 4 centimeters in diameter, on stems of 2 to (reportedly) 17 centimeters. We know it best from a population at about 5500 feet (1650 meters) in El Dorado National Forest in El Dorado County, and from a granite slab at 7000 feet (2100 meters) in eastern Fresno County.

Our efforts to grow these two varieties of *Allium obtusum* have not met with much success. The seeds should be planted in late fall or early winter, and even then germination has been poor for us. The bulbs have required many years to reach blooming size.

Allium tribracteatum Torrey

This is a rare plant confined to volcanic slopes in Tuolumne County, from 4,300 to 10,000 feet (1290 to 3000 meters). Its 10 to 30 florets with erect perianth parts are white to purple and are held in a close umbel on a short, 2- to 7-centimeter scape, above two long, channeled leaves. CNPS regards this California endemic as rare, but it is not state listed, and existing data are thought insufficient to support federal listing.

Allium hoffmannii Ownbey

This species occurs in the southern Klamath Ranges (sometimes called the Siskiyou Mountains) on serpentine outcrops, where it is reported to be locally common. It has 10 to 40 flowers, pink to purple with exserted stamens, and prominent midveins that are often greenish, on a short 5- to 10-centimeter stem, above a single widely channeled leaf. It was considered for federal listing but was judged not to be threatened.

Allium yosemitense Eastwood

Originally collected at the head of Bridal Veil Falls in the Yosemite valley, this species was subsequently found at a second locality not far away, but the type locality was lost for many years. McNeal and Alice Howard rediscovered it in the late 1970s. This plant is very rare and is listed by the state of California, though it has been rejected for federal listing. It grows on open rocky slopes from 2600 to 7300 feet (780 to 2190 meters). Its 10 to 50 white to pink florets are held in a moderately loose umbel atop a 6- to 23-centimeter scape, above two long, widely channeled or flat leaves.

Allium burlewii A. Davidson

The final subject in this group is *Allium burlewii* (synonym *A. johnstonii*), among the oddest California onions. It is a fairly uncommon plant from the southern half of California, occurring in scattered locations in the Inner South Coast Ranges, the Tehachapis, and the southern Sierra Nevada. The *Jepson Manual* describes it as "dull purple, midveins dark" and gives its elevation range as 5900 to 9300 feet (1770 to 2790 meters), but we have seen it as low as 4300 feet (1290 meters) in the Inner South Coast Ranges of San Benito County, where we found it closer to dull light green-brown than dull purple. Its tepals are so erect that they may be described as spreading inward; the whole inflorescence resembles a cluster of BB-sized pale green-brown miniature footballs, encircled by bracts which curl back, creating the effect of an outer ring. Its peculiar appearance has not tempted us to grow it.

Low-growing Plants with Falcate Leaves

Next we consider a group of California onions with low-growing inflorescences and distinctly falcate leaves. These are mostly plants of screes and dry, stony soils.

Allium falcifolium Hooker & Arnold

The most common and best-known of this group is *Allium falcifolium* (synonym *A. breweri*), which occurs on serpentine soils and outcrops from San Francisco Bay north into Oregon (Plate 15). This attractive onion has an inflorescence 2 to 3 centimeters in diameter, with 10 to 30 or more bright rose-purple or maroon florets on a flattened stem usually reaching no more than 5 centimeters, above two or more glaucous, falcate leaves. Individual plants within a single population may be dull, pale pink or off-white, usually with darker midveins. This species is much sought by enthusiasts but has proved difficult in our Sonoma County garden, even though natural populations occur less than 20 miles (32 kilometers) away. It takes four years or more for bulbs to reach blooming size from seed. Once they reach that size, they persist with only very limited vegetative increase.

Allium siskiyouense Ownbey

A related species (once considered a variety of *Allium falcifolium*) is *A. siskiyouense*, which is a little larger and a little taller than *A. falcifolium*, with flowers of bright pink rather than rose purple to maroon. It is considered uncommon in California and grows at higher elevations and farther north than *A. falcifolium*, well into Oregon.

Allium punctum Henderson

Allium punctum is an uncommon plant of rocky flats at 4000 to 5300 feet (1200 to 1590 meters) in far northeastern California (on the Modoc Plateau) and into southern Oregon and western Nevada. Its 6 to 20 flowers with erect perianth parts are held on a short scape (10 centimeters or less); the florets are white to pink with purple midveins.

Allium tolmiei (Hooker) Baker ex S. Watson

Allium tolmiei, described earlier (in the section "Western Alliums with Broad, Falcate Leaves"), reaches northeastern California but is more frequent farther north and east. *Allium tolmiei* is uncommon in California, where it inhabits rocky flats from 5000 to 7300 feet (1500 to 2190 meters).

Allium parvum Kellogg

Like *Allium tolmiei*, the similar *A. parvum* (see above, "Western Dwarf Alliums) is uncommon in far northeastern California. It is confined to northern mountains at higher elevations from 4000 to 9000 feet (1200 to 2700 meters).

Allium anceps Kellogg

The uncommon *Allium anceps* (see above, "Western Alliums with Broad, Falcate Leaves") is found on barren clay and rocky slopes at 4000 to 5200 feet (1200 to 1560 meters) in far northeastern California, southern Oregon, and western Nevada.

Allium lemmonii S. Watson

Allium lemmonii (see above, "Western Alliums with Broad, Falcate Leaves") occurs from northeastern California into Oregon, Idaho, and

Nevada; in California it grows on drying clay soils at 4000 to 6300 feet (1200 to 1890 meters).

Allium platycaule S. Watson

Allium platycaule has been discussed earlier (in the section "Western Alliums with Broad, Falcate Leaves"). We consider it among the most beautiful California species, with its bright pink inflorescence and strongly exserted stamens huddled close above two or more glaucous leaves (Plate 16). In California, *A. platycaule* grows mostly at higher elevations of 5000 feet (1500 meters) and above, on serpentinous or lava-derived soils and screes, near-barren habitats where it provides welcome relief to the eye. We have found it not particularly difficult to grow from seed, though it needs several years to reach blooming size; however, it will not bloom for us in our mild climate near the coast, except in the coldest winters. It seems to require a cold winter to induce bloom.

Allium campanulatum S. Watson

Allium campanulatum (synonyms *A. austinae*, *A. bidwelliae*) heads another group of California alliums that require cold weather to do their best, though we have more consistently flowered this species than any member of this group except *A. platycaule*. *Allium campanulatum* has a fairly loose umbel of 10 to 50 dark rose florets; the erect perianth segments have spreading tips, and the scape, somewhat lax, rises 10 to 30 centimeters above two widely channeled leaves. It is quite common at higher elevations (4500 feet or 1350 meters and above) throughout California (except the South Coast Ranges and south) and east into Nevada. In the West it grows well in ordinary border conditions. We have flowered it after four to five years from seed. Two species in California are closely related to *A. campanulatum*: *A. membranaceum* and *A. bisceptrum*.

Allium membranaceum Ownbey

Allium membranaceum is not common, though it occurs over a wide area of northern California at moderate elevations from 500 to 4500 feet (150 to 1350 meters). It resembles *A. campanulatum*, except that it has white to pale pink flowers on an erect stem that is taller (to 40 centimeters), and flat leaves. *Allium membranaceum* has proved far easier for us to grow from seed than *A. campanulatum* or *A. bisceptrum*. It usually blooms its third year from seed and, unlike the other two—which require a very long cold period to germinate—its seed sprouts with as little as eight weeks of chilling.

Allium bisceptrum S. Watson

Even less common than *Allium membranaceum*, *A. bisceptrum* (synonym *A. palmeri*), known primarily from the eastern slope of the central high Sierra Nevada, has an inflorescence of 10 to 25 florets on sometimes multiple stems 10 to 35 centimeters tall. The individual florets resemble those of both *A. campanulatum* and *A. membranaceum*, except that they are white to pale pink with rose tips but more frequently are entirely rose purple. We have never yet achieved bloom from *A. bisceptrum*.

Medium-sized Alliums with Pink or Purple Flowers

Next we consider some alliums grouped together because of their similar appearance and color: dark red or rose purple to dark or bright cerise, of high value in the garden.

Allium acuminatum Hooker

This species is common and widespread throughout northern California and north into British Columbia, as well as east and northeast into the Rocky Mountains and Arizona. Our favorite location is an extensive population of several thousand plants on the west side of Cedar Pass over the Warner Mountains in Modoc County. This community begins at more than 5000 feet (1500 meters) and culminates in a remarkably dense stand at about 5900 feet (1770 meters). Here *A. acuminatum* might be described as cerise. This species has two or three generally cylindrical leaves and a moderately loose umbel of 10 to 40 rose-purple flowers on a 10- to 35-centimeter stem. (Fernald's variety *cuspidatum* is no longer recognized as distinct.) It requires sunny, dry conditions. Seed from the Warner Mountains took six years to produce its first blooming plants.

Allium bolanderi S. Watson

Allium bolanderi (synonyms *A. mirabile*, *A. stenanthum*) is described in the *Jepson Manual* as having 10 to 20 flowers, rose purple in color, on a 10- to 35-centimeter scape, and as occurring only below 3300 feet (990 meters) in northwestern California from the Mount Hamilton Range north into Oregon. Technical differences are used to distinguish between var. *bolanderi* and var. *mirabile* Henderson. The occurrences we have identified as variety *bolanderi*, based on the description of the bulb and bulb coat, do not quite fit this altitudinal range. We found it at and immediately north of Mendocino Pass, the juncture of Tehama and Glenn counties on the east with Mendocino County on the west, a well-surveyed spot known to be about 5000 feet (1500 meters). We saw the same allium in abundance farther south along Etsel Ridge, a little higher (to almost 5500 feet or 1650 meters). After careful examination, we determined that the plants appeared to be variety *bolanderi*. We later found both these high-elevation locations confirmed by Smith and Wheeler (1992) in their flora of Mendocino County. We have had some success with seed from the Mendocino Pass population; bulbs grown from seeds planted four years previously bloomed in 1998.

Allium peninsulare J. G. Lemmon ex Greene

Allium peninsulare carries a loose umbel of 5 to 35 wine-red to dark rose-purple florets on a 12- to 45-centimeter stem, and thus can be quite tall. *Allium peninsulare* var. *franciscanum* McNeal & Ownbey is uncommon and is confined to the San Francisco Bay area and the Outer Central Coast Ranges. It is characterized by a tight umbel of florets with narrow tepals, technical differences in the shape of the stigma, and occurrence only below 1000 feet (300 meters). *Allium peninsulare* var. *peninsulare* has a looser umbel and wider tepals, and reportedly is found from 1000 to 3500 feet (300 to 1050 meters) and above; we have seen stands at elevations below 1000 feet in Butte County. It is common and widespread in many parts of California, as well as in southern Oregon and in Baja California, but most stands are small; nowhere have we found it in the drifts we see in many other California alliums. Growing variety *peninsulare* from seed has been reasonably successful, with bloom achieved in four years, and the bulbs persisted well.

Allium crispum Greene

Allium crispum is the prettiest in this group, and happily, it has been the easiest to cultivate from seed (Plate 17). It has a moderately loose umbel of 10 to 40 rose-purple flowers on a 15- to 35-centimeter scape, and two or three relatively short terete leaves. Its name derives from the perianth parts, which are crisped, the inner three tepals more strongly so than the outer three. In some forms the inner tepals have edges that are white as well as crisped, a delightful combination. We have also seen occasional albino forms, white to very pale pink, growing among typical plants. *Allium crispum* loves sun and heat and is at least locally common in some parts of its range (the western mountains south of San Francisco Bay, below 2500 feet or 750 meters); in western San Benito and eastern Fresno counties it can produce wonderful drifts of color on hillside after hillside. The seeds are somewhat difficult to germinate; they need to be planted in late fall for spring germination, but if the winter is too mild, they may not germinate until the second year. Given plenty of water during their growing season (late winter to spring) and good light, young plants may bloom their second year.

Plants with Two or More Upright Leaves

The next group of onions consists of those with two or more upright leaves and stems, with the leaves usually flat or somewhat channeled.

Allium lacunosum S. Watson

Allium lacunosum and its varieties *lacunosum*, *davisiae*, *kernensis*, and *micranthum* are rather small, unspectacular plants, with 5 to 45 white to pale pink flowers in relatively close umbels on 10- to 35-centimeter stems. By far the most common is *A. lacunosum* var. *lacunosum*, which can be found on serpentine outcrops below 3500 feet (1050 meters), from the San Francisco Bay area south along the South Coast and through the South Coast Ranges to the Channel Islands off southern California. Its umbel of 5 to 25 florets is quite dense, and it grows on serpentine. We have succeeded in growing it from seed, though only barely, and found it required four to five years to flower—hardly worth the trouble.

The other three varieties are all uncommon. *Allium lacunosum* var. *micranthum* Eastwood is another serpentine grower. It too has an open umbel of 10 to 30 flowers; its three bracts distinguish it, while the other three varieties have only two. It is confined to the Inner South Coast Ranges below 2000 feet (600 meters). *Allium lacunosum* var. *davisiae* (M. E. Jones) McNeal & Ownbey (elevated to species status as *A. davisiae* by some authors) has an open umbel of 10 to 35 florets and is found on open, sandy slopes and ridges from 2000 to 7000 feet (600 to 2100 meters) in the western transverse and San Bernardino ranges of southern California, the eastern side of the Sierra Nevada, and the Mohave Desert. *Allium lacunosum* var. *kernensis* McNeal & Ownbey has a dense umbel of 10 to 45 flowers and occurs on open sandy slopes from 2300 to 4300 feet (690 to 1290 meters) in the southern Sierra Nevada foothills, the Tehachapi Mountains, and the western Mohave Desert. We have seen a single stand of this onion, growing above a deep gully south of Lake Isabella. Its flowers were white, each tepal with a greenish midvein. It grew in clumps from clusters of elongated bulbs. We tried to grow it but found it would not tolerate our wet, humid spring climate.

Allium hickmanii Eastwood

Quite rare, this species grows on wooded, grassy slopes at about 150 feet (45 meters) and is confined to Monterey and San Luis Obispo counties. It has a tight umbel of 4 to 15 florets on a 5- to 17-centimeter stem, with two moderately long, more or less cylindrical leaves. Known from fewer than 20 occurrences, it is a Level 1 candidate for federal listing as a rare species; however, it is already in cultivation and available in the nursery trade.

Allium dichlamydeum Greene

This pretty plant has a moderately close umbel of 5 to 30 or more flowers with erect, hot pink perianth segments, on a stem which varies in height according to habitat. On open coastal bluffs it can be as short as 10 centimeters, while in the shade of coastal woodlands it may achieve 30 centimeters. It grows in dry clay soil on or near sea cliffs along the north coast and the northern central coast of California. Though some authors have classified it as difficult to cultivate, we have not found it so; for us, 8 miles (13 kilometers) from the sea, it consistently blooms in its second year from seed. It is, however, rather tender; during one of our most

severe winters, when the temperatures fell below 24°F (–4°C) four nights
in a row, most bulbs in a large wooden box in an exposed location were
killed. (It has survived 5°F [(15°C], however, in both Oregon and Massachusetts, in frames.)

Allium amplectens Torrey

In contrast to *Allium dichlamydeum*, *A. amplectens* (synonyms *A. attenui-
folium*, *A. monospermum*, *A. occidentale*) is nearly ubiquitous in the California Floristic Province, from the floor of the San Joaquin and Sacramento valleys up to 6000 feet (1800 meters). Its 10 to 50 white to pale
pink flowers are spreading and are held in a moderately close umbel on
a 15- to 50-centimeter stem; it has two to four short leaves which are
more or less cylindrical and which usually disappear by anthesis (Plate
18). It is distinctive in that the flower pedicels wither away after anthesis, so that seed is spread by the wind in dandelion fashion, as the umbel
collapses and the seed capsules scatter.

Allium serra McNeal & Ownbey

Another onion with seed dispersal like that of *Allium amplectens* is *A.
serra* (synonym *A. serratum*). It is very similar to *A. amplectens*, except
that its perianth parts are wider and are rich pink to rose or even cerise;
there are also technical differences in the ovary crests and bulb coats
(Plate 19). It too is common, although its range is more limited: from 100
to 4000 feet (30 to 1200 meters) in the North Coast Ranges, the San Francisco Bay area, and the Inner South Coast Ranges. Both these onions
have been relatively easy for us to grow from seed, usually requiring
three years to flower. The bulbs of both multiply vegetatively, given
good growing conditions (sufficient light and water during their growing season).

Allium praecox Brandegee

This is an uncommon species from shaded, grassy slopes below 2700
feet (810 meters) in southwestern California. It has a loose inflorescence
of 5 to 40 flowers, pale pink with purple midveins, on a tall stem of 20 to
60 centimeters, above two or three widely channeled, keeled leaves.

Allium haematochiton S. Watson

Common to dry slopes and ridges from the Outer South Coast Ranges,
south through the transverse and peninsular ranges into northern Baja
California, this species also grows in seasonally moist, grassy meadows.
The location best known to us is such a meadow on Figueroa Mountain
in Santa Barbara County, at 4000 feet (1200 meters), though this species
is supposedly limited to below 2700 feet (1200 meters). It is quite attractive, with 10 to 30 flowers in a close umbel on a 10- to 40-centimeter
scape, above four to six flat leaves (Plate 20). It is the only rhizomatous

dry-growing onion in California. Its perianth segments are white to rose, with darker midveins. We have found it extremely easy to grow from seed. This is the only onion other than *Allium validum* that we can continue to water all summer long, and have it remain green and continue to grow. It is also the first to start growing in the fall after dormancy. The bulbs multiply readily, forming large clumps, if they receive plenty of water and sun.

Allium hyalinum Curran

Even easier to grow than *Allium haematochiton* is *A. hyalinum*, one of California's few wet-growing onions. It is common in pockets of granitic sands atop depressions in granite slabs (Plate 21), or along streamsides where sand accumulates, at elevations of 100 to 5000 feet (30 to 1500 meters). Its 5 to 25 florets are usually white to pale pink and form a very loose umbel on a 15- to 45-centimeter stem. We have seen one especially beautiful form with cerise flowers, collected many years ago from the floor of the eastern San Joaquin Valley but now extirpated by agricultural development. To call this onion easy to grow borders on understatement: if not carefully controlled, it can become a weed in the garden. It self-sows readily and increases quickly by division. It usually blooms its second year from seed.

Allium unifolium Kellogg

This is a perennial favorite with gardeners because of its pretty colors (pale pink to rose) and tolerance of summer water. It has 15 to 35 flowers in a moderately loose umbel on a tall stem (30 to 80 centimeters). Its two or three leaves are shorter than the stem, and widely channeled or keeled. It is considered uncommon in the wild, though it can grow quite thickly in its preferred habitats of moist clays and grassy streambanks below 3600 feet (1080 meters) in California's Coast Ranges and north into Oregon. It has been easy to grow from seed. Several years ago, we received seed of a richly colored form from Wayne Roderick. This species requires a lot of water up until blooming to do well, and sun for at least half the day. Bulbs multiply rapidly under these conditions. If not given sufficient light, they will still multiply but will not get large enough to bloom. The species may hybridize with *Allium hyalinum* where the two are grown close together.

Allium validum S. Watson

The well-known *Allium validum*, a wet-grower, is responsible for many place names in the state: Leek Mountain, Onion Mountain, Onion Meadow, Onion Creek, and so on (Plate 22). Most of the sites we know are between 4000 and 7000 feet (1200 to 2100 meters), though it can be found above 11,000 feet (3300 meters). The *Jepson Manual* describes the flowers as "white to rose"; we can add light rose purple and the cerise form at Sonora Pass. See the description under "Rhizomatous, Moisture-loving Species" for more details.

Nonnative Alliums

A number of Old World alliums have escaped from cultivation to become naturalized in various parts of North America. A general plant encyclopedia such as the *Royal Horticultural Society Dictionary of Gardening* will help identify any of the following which may be found growing as garden remnants and escapes. Those reported include *Allium ampeloprasum* (wild leek), *A. cepa* (common onion), *A. fistulosum* (Welsh onion), *A. neapolitanum* (flowering onion), *A. oleraceum* (field garlic), *A. porrum* (leek), *A. sativum* (garlic), *A. scorodoprasum* (rocambole, Spanish garlic), *A. triquetrum* (three-cornered leek), and *A. vineale* (field garlic, crow garlic).

Field garlic is a pernicious invader that has become naturalized throughout the United States and many other parts of the world. This weedy plant seems particularly entrenched in the East. In Maryland I've seen a 2-acre (about 1 hectare) lawn in which half the herbage was composed of the leaves of *Allium vineale*! Not only does this species have ugly bulbiliferous heads instead of flowers, it also produces myriad underground bulblets. It can be distinguished from native *A. canadense* by its very slender growth, leaves that clasp the stem for more than half its height, and a single-valved bud spathe with a long appendage.

Bibliography

Abrams, L. 1940. *Illustrated Flora of the Pacific States*. Stanford: Stanford University Press. 1: 380–396.

California Native Plant Society. 1994. *Inventory of Rare and Endangered Vascular Plants of California*. 5th ed. Sacramento: California Native Plant Society. 54–56.

Cronquist, A., A. H. Holmgren, N. H. Holmgren, J. R. Reveal, P. K. Holmgren. 1977. *Intermountain Flora: Vascular Plants of the Intermountain West, U.S.A.* New York: Columbia University Press. 6: 508–522.

Davies, Dilys. 1992. *Alliums: The Ornamental Onions*. London: Batsford; Portland: Timber Press.

Don, George. 1827. "Monograph of the Genus *Allium*." *Memoirs of the Wernerian Natural History Society* 6: 1–102.

Eastwood, Alice. 1934. "New Species in Liliaceae." *Leaflets of Western Botany* 1: 132–133.

Hickman, J. C., ed. 1993. *The Jepson Manual: Higher Plants of California*. Berkeley: University of California Press. 1172–1179.

Hitchcock, C. Leo, et al. 1955–1969. *Vascular Plants of the Pacific Northwest*. 5 vols. Seattle: University of Washington Press.

Hitchcock, C. L., and A. Cronquist. 1973. *Flora of the Pacific Northwest*. 680–684.

Howard, T. M. 1954. "Some Alliums from Texas." *Plant Life* 10: 108–110.

Howard, T. M. 1960. "Alliums of the Southwest Midland." *Plant Life* 16: 135–140.

Jacobson, T. D. 1978. *A Comparative Study of Three Alliances of the Genus* Allium. Dissertation, Washington State University (Pullman).

Jepson, Willis Linn. 1909–1922. *A Flora of California*. Vol. 1. Berkeley: University of California, Jepson Herbarium and Library.

McNeal, D. W. 1970. *Comparative Studies of the* Allium acuminatum *Alliance*. Dissertation, Washington State University (Pullman).

McNeal, D. W. 1989. "A Re-evaluation of the *Allium sanbornii* (Alliaceae) Complex." *Madroño* 36: 122–130.

McNeal, D. W. 1992a. "A Revision of the *Allium fimbriatum* (Alliaceae) Complex." *Aliso* 13: 411–426.

McNeal, D. W. 1992b. "Taxonomy of North American Species of *Allium*." In P. Hanelt, K. Hammer, and H. Knupffer, eds., *The Genus* Allium*: Taxonomic Problems and Genetic Resources*. Proceedings of an International Symposium held in Gatersleben, Germany, 11–13 June 1991. Gatersleben: Institute of Genetics and Crop Plant Research. 195–204.

McNeal, D. W., and M. Ownbey. 1977. "Status of *Allium serratum* (Liliaceae) and Description of a New Species." *Madroño* 24(1): 24–29.

McNeal, D. W., and M. Ownbey. 1982. "Taxonomy of the *Allium lacunosum* Complex." *Madroño* 29(2): 79–86.

Mingrone, L. V. 1968. *A Comparative Study of the* Allium falcifolium *Alliance*. Dissertation, Washington State University (Pullman).

Mortola, W. R., and D. W. McNeal. 1985. "Taxonomy of the *Allium tribracteatum* (Alliaceae) Complex." *Aliso* 11: 27–35.

Munz, Philip A., and David D. Keck. 1973. *A California Flora*. Berkeley: University of California Press.

Ownbey, Marion. 1947. "The Genus *Allium* in Arizona." *Research Studies of the State College of Washington* 15: 211–232.

Ownbey, Marion. 1950a. "The Genus *Allium* in Idaho." *Research Studies of the State College of Washington* 18: 3–39.

Ownbey, Marion. 1950b. "The Genus *Allium* in Texas." *Research Studies of the State College of Washington* 18: 181–222.

Ownbey, Marion. 1972. "*Allium* Species and Varieties." *Plant Life* 28: 63–64.

Ownbey, Marion, and H. C. Aase, 1956. *Cytotaxonomic Studies in* Allium. *I. The* Allium canadense *Alliance*. Pullman: Washington State University.

Peck, M. E. 1941. *A Manual of the Higher Plants of Oregon*. Portland: Binford and Mort.

Smith, G. L., and C. R. Wheeler. 1992. *A Flora of the Vascular Plants of Mendocino County, California*. San Francisco: University of San Francisco. Repr. from *Wasmann Journal of Biology* 48/49: 1–387, especially 96–98.

Traub, H. P. 1967. "Subsect. *Mexicanae* of Sect. *Amerallium*, Genus *Allium* L." *Plant Life* 23: 88–95, 110.

Traub, H. P. 1968a. "The Subgenera, Sections and Subsections of *Allium* L." *Plant Life* 24: 137–163.

Traub, H. P. 1968b. "New Guatemalan and Mexican Alliums." *Plant Life* 24: 127–142.

Traub, H. P. 1968c. "Genus *Allium* L.—Subgenera, Sections, and Subsections." *Plant Life* 28: 132–137.

Traub, H. P. 1982. "Order Alliales." *Plant Life* 38: 119–132.

Watson, Sereno, 1879. "Contributions to Western Botany, I: Revision of the North American Liliaceae." *Proceedings of the American Academy of Arts and Sciences* 14: 213–288.

– 2 –

Amaryllidaceae of North America

ALAN W. MEEROW

The Amaryllidaceae are a cosmopolitan—though chiefly tropical and subtropical—family of herbaceous perennials, mostly bulbous and found in diverse habitats. The family is well marked by its showy, lily-like flowers borne in an umbel at the apex of leafless flowering stems, or scapes, which are initiated terminally inside the bulb (as in the common onion). The flowers are enclosed in bud by two or more bracts. Unlike the ovary of onions (Alliaceae), the ovary of all amaryllids (members of the Amaryllidaceae) is inferior, or below the point in the flower where the tepals (petals) and stamens arise.

The family has three main centers of distribution: South America, South Africa, and Mediterranean Europe and North Africa. Two genera are native to central and eastern Asia, and two to Australasia. Only a single genus, *Crinum*, has native species in both the Old World and the New. In the Western Hemisphere the family occurs from southeastern and southwestern United States and Mexico through Central America and the West Indies, south to Chile and Argentina. Areas of the Americas notable for their diversity include eastern Brazil, northern Chile, and the central Andes of Ecuador and Peru. Only four genera occur natively in North America: *Crinum*, *Habranthus*, *Hymenocallis*, and *Zephyranthes*.

Crinum

There are more than 100 species of *Crinum*, most of them from Africa; perhaps a dozen come from Asia, and even fewer from the American tropics. As might be expected of such a cosmopolitan genus, the habitats of the various species run the gamut from deserts to swamps. Some crinums are deciduous and die back when they are dormant, while others remain evergreen. It is in the genus *Crinum* that we find what may well be the true Goliath of the bulb world: *Crinum asiaticum*, a plant which may exceed 180 centimeters in both height and spread. Numerous hybrids have been produced since 1850. Flowers of two types occur in the genus *Crinum*: nodding trumpet or bell-shaped, bilaterally symmetrical flowers; and erect, radially symmetrical, spidery forms.

Crinum americanum Linneaus

Crinum americanum is the only native North American species. Known as string or swamp lily, it grows in swamps and marshes and along ditches, canals, and streambanks, often as an emergent aquatic, throughout the coastal plain from southeastern North Carolina south into Florida and west to Mississippi. The plants flower from January through November, depending on the locality. The bulb is 6 to 10 centimeters in diameter, with a short neck and brown, papery outer scales. The strap-shaped leaves are bright green, 30 to 90 centimeters long by 2.5 to 5 centimeters wide, and often obscurely toothed along the margins. If the leaves are torn, threads of elastic fiber can be seen joining the torn sections. From the rosette of leeklike foliage rise scapes 45 to 60 centimeters tall, each holding two to six spidery white flowers. Each flower is 10 to 16 centimeters long and consists of six narrow, spreading, white sepals and petals (usually referred to collectively as tepals because they are so similar) which are fused below into a long tube (Plate 23). The free tepals are 6 to 15 centimeters long and are usually reflexed at the tips.

Swamp lily has six stamens; both the staminal filaments and the style are purple-pink in color. The flowers are generally held erect, and are quite fragrant, especially from dusk on into evening. Each flower lasts about two days. As the seed capsules develop, the scape frequently bends over and may even lie on the ground—an adaptation that distributes the seed at a distance from the parent plant. One large, fleshy seed forms in each of the three ovary chambers, and it often ruptures the wall of the fruit in late development. The seeds sometimes begin to germinate while still on the parent plant. Swamp lily, like all other American crinums, is a stoloniferous species; it can escape from the border into a well-watered lawn. It spreads by underground rhizomes and can form a fairly solid ground cover in moist sites.

Crinum americanum as a rule prefers full sun and flowers best in a bright exposure, but it tolerates considerable shade. A steady supply of moisture results in the most vigorous growth. In the southern portions of its range swamp lily remains evergreen if supplied with water throughout the year; to the north, winter dormancy should be expected and even encouraged by withholding water. Swamp lilies raised in containers may have to be repotted every year because their root systems are so extensive.

Two foliar fungal diseases can severely affect the appearance of crinums both in the landscape and in nursery production: leaf spot, caused by *Cercospora pancratii*, and red or leaf scorch, caused by *Stagonospora curtisii*. Fortunately, *Crinum americanum* does not appear to be very prone to infection by either. The symptoms of *Cercospora* infection are irregularly round, necrotic lesions with a golden-brown margin on the leaves. The lesions of *Stagonospora* are elongated red streaks, generally oriented along the longitudinal axis of the leaf. After the center of the lesion becomes necrotic, the margins often remain bright rust-red. A regular program of fungicide application, which alternates between any two broad-spectrum foliar fungicides, controls both diseases. Badly infected leaves should first be removed and destroyed. Interestingly, it has been noted that these fungal diseases are also suppressed when the plants are growing near the coast and receive some salt exposure.

Thrips can sometimes disfigure crinum leaves, and spider mites may infest them during periods of low humidity. Eastern lubber grasshoppers deal the greatest damage to crinums. Insecticide provides adequate control early in the season, as does a biocontrol using a protozoan parasite (*Nosema loctustae*, marketed as Semaspore). When these critters achieve full size, however, the heel of a boot may be the only effective pesticide!

Swamp lily is propagated from seed or by division. Clumps can be lifted in spring and divided with a large, sharp blade. The cuts should be dusted with fungicide, and each offset established in an individual container or replanted immediately.

The large, fleshy seeds of *Crinum americanum* are not long-lived and should be processed soon after collection. If they must be stored, place them in a bag of dry vermiculite or perlite at 45°–50°F (7°–10°C) for one or two months at most. Generally, each capsule contains one to three seeds. The seeds are fully ripe when the capsule wall turns brown, though seeds collected from succulent, fully expanded capsules usually germinate well. Seed can often be collected on the ground near blooming plants because the fruiting stems usually bend to the ground as the weight of the capsules increases. Such seeds often germinate right next to the parent plant. Seed collectors note the large variation in size among seeds even from a single capsule. Those that are less than 1.25 centimeters long or in diameter can usually be discarded because they probably lack embryos. Crinum embryos are large and easily seen if the seed is cut open.

The remains of the fleshy capsule should be at least partially removed from the seed. If the seed is soaked in a mild detergent solution for a few hours, this job is easier. The seeds may be dusted with fungicide or soaked for 10 to 20 minutes in fungicide solution before planting. Crinum seeds should be placed in small pots or cell packs (one seed per unit) of the germinating medium of your choice. No more than half the seed should be covered. It will germinate in full sun or half shade. If a mist propagation system is used, the interval should be sufficiently long to prevent the medium from remaining saturated. The fleshy seeds contain abundant water reserves, and the medium need only be slightly and evenly moist during the first critical weeks of germination. Crinum seeds produce what is sometimes called a dropper: a long cotyledon, from which the primary root and shoot develop, emerges first from the seed and rapidly grows downward. The basal portion of the cotyledon swells and quickly forms a small bulb. Interestingly, light appears to inhibit formation of the bulb.

In containers, growth is best in a peat-based mix at a pH near 6.5. Crinums are gross feeders; incorporate slow-release fertilizer in the soil at the highest rate recommended by the manufacturer. From seed, respectable gallon-container-sized plants can be obtained in a year. Flowering-sized plants will require at least two and possibly three years from seed.

Swamp lily is best suited to waterside gardens throughout its native range; it should not be expected to survive in the open below USDA Zone 6, and it will probably require protection in USDA Zone 7 and below. It prospers best where summer heat and humidity are high. In drier soils growth is not as vigorous, and flowering may be suppressed.

Hymenocallis

Hymenocallis is often mistaken for *Crinum*, but the confusion ends when it blooms. Its appeal as well as its Latin name derives from a curious feature of the flower, a corona or cup formed by outgrowths of the staminal filaments. The petals are linear and often reflexed, justifying the use of spider lily as a common name for this genus too.

There are as many as 60 species of *Hymenocallis*, all native to the American continents and the West Indies. (The genus as treated here is distinguished from its Andean relatives, *Ismene* and *Leptochiton*.) The greatest diversity of the genus is found in Mexico. The North American species of *Hymenocallis* are, unfortunately, in a state of taxonomic confusion. Perhaps 12 species are native to the wetlands and rich forests of the southern United States, with the greatest number of those found in Florida.

Our native *Hymenocallis* species produce globose, ellipsoid, or pear-shaped bulbs and hold two to many persistent or deciduous, linear to widely strap-shaped leaves. One to 12 large, fragrant flowers are borne on the scapes. The ovary generally sits directly on the inflorescence (that is, there is no pedicel or stalk between flower and main stem). The six tepals are narrow and usually spreading, sometimes drooping; the color is in most species white but in a few green or greenish yellow. The tepals are fused below into a long tube that may be flushed green. The six stamens are fused below into a conspicuous, white false corona, or staminal cup, which is often toothed between each free filament. The cup may have a green or yellow central eye. The threadlike free filaments are usually green, at least in their lower parts, and the sticky pollen is orange. (Hawk moths are the main pollinators of the genus.) The inferior, three-chambered ovary contains 2 to 10 ovules per chamber but often only 1 or 2 develop into seed. The mature fruit is a capsule that frequently disintegrates or bursts, exposing the large, fleshy green seeds. These seeds often germinate precociously, close to the parent plant.

A number of our native *Hymenocallis* species (for example, *H. coronaria, H. floridana,* and *H. rotata*) grow as emergent aquatics along clear, spring-fed streams and rivers, in wet glades, or in swamps. These species can be difficult to domesticate unless their native conditions are imitated closely; they often sulk and decline if grown in containers.

Spider lilies produce fleshy green seeds which should be planted immediately in a well-drained but moist germination medium. I've had seeds of several different species commence germination while sitting on my desk awaiting my attention. The cotyledonary petiole is the first structure to emerge from the spongy seed coat (many gardeners mistakenly call this a root). This structure swells at its tip and forms the seedling bulb. *Hymenocallis* can also be propagated by division and by twin-scaling, a technique in which the bulb is cut vertically into a number of segments attached to pieces of the basal plate.

Of all our native species, *Hymenocallis latifolia* is the most accommodating in the garden, adapting to any but the most waterlogged soils, and at least the bulb should be hardy where the ground never freezes. The aquatic species can be garden prima donnas, and the best success in cultivation is achieved by duplicating their habitats as closely as possible. The northern species of the aquatic group are probably the hardiest natives, surviving into USDA Zone 6 with some protection.

Terrestrial Species

Hymenocallis henryae Traub

Closely related to the alligator lily, *Hymenocallis palmeri,* is the green pine lily, *H. henryae,* known from only a few localities in the Florida Panhandle; there it grows in pine flatwoods (low, damp, open forest) or cypress depressions near them. This species bears two or three flowers and has a spreading false corona and tepals that are usually longer than the floral tube. It has a shorter season of bloom (May to June) than the alligator lily, but, like that more broadly distributed species, *H. henryae* has greenish-white tepals.

Hymenocallis latifolia (Miller) Roemer

Hymenocallis latifolia, known as Keys spider lily, is an evergreen species native to Florida and allied to the West Indian members of the genus. It is a littoral plant of coastal dunes, sand ridges, and mangrove swamps of the southern Florida Peninsula and Keys; thus, it is tolerant of salt and alkali and is among the few native species that prefer well-drained sites. It quickly forms a robust clump and is very amenable to cultivation, so it is widely used as a landscape perennial in south Florida. Throughout July, and often into September, it produces many umbels of 7 to 12 fragrant white flowers, 10 to 15 centimeters long. The tepals characteristically hang downward in this species. It forms large clumps of bulbs bearing many somewhat succulent, widely strap-shaped leaves. The ovaries usually contain two (but up to six) ovules per chamber. Some botanists recognize as *H. kimballiae* a form known sparingly in northwest Florida.

Hymenocallis palmeri S. Watson

The alligator lily, *Hymenocallis palmeri*, is a single-flowered species (occasionally two flowers are formed) of cypress swamps, wet prairies, and pine flatwoods, chiefly in south Florida (Plate 24). It flowers from May through August and is notable for three characteristics: very narrow, erect leaves which are channeled down the middle; greenish-white tepals which are usually shorter than the floral tube; and a staminal cup which does not spread at the rim.

Aquatic Species: Hymenocallis coronaria and Its Allies

It is difficult to apply names to the truly aquatic *Hymenocallis* species of the United States. In this group are plants variously known as *H. caroliniana*, *H. coronaria* (Plate 25), *H. crassifolia*, *H. floridana*, *H. occidentalis*, and *H. rotata*. Although differences among the types have been described, including a range of chromosome numbers, as yet no botanist has succeeded in developing a stable taxonomic framework for the group. Variants are found in briskly flowing streams, spring runs, lake margins, wet glades, and river shoals or floodplains from central Florida north through Georgia, Alabama, and the Carolinas, into Tennessee and Kentucky, and west at least to Mississippi. If *H. liriosome* is included as part of this complex, its western limits extend to eastern Texas. Some reports extend the complex even farther north into the southern Ohio River Valley. Southern representatives of this group tend to bear two or three flowers per inflorescence, while more northern aquatic spider lilies carry up to seven or eight.

All these species are rhizomatously spreading perennials, and all have particularly showy, expansive staminal coronas with a prominent green or yellow eye. They are best cultivated in heavy, wet clay or muck soils and seem to resent stagnant conditions, preferring a steady flow of water for best growth. Members of this group flower either in late spring or in summer. They have leaves which are eventually deciduous, but all flower with their leaves. The leaves, while variable in length and width, are consistently dark green and usually channeled down the middle.

Hymenocallis duvalensis Traub

Hymenocallis duvalensis is a small spider lily found in moist woods or streamsides from Jacksonville, Florida, west to the eastern fringes of the Florida Panhandle, north to southeastern Georgia, and south to about Gainesville, Florida (Plate 26). It bears narrow leaves and two flowers with a much narrower staminal cup than any of the preceding species do. It flowers from April to June, and it is sometimes abundant in shadier locations than are typical for most other spider lilies.

Hymenocallis galvestonensis (Herbert) Baker

Hymenocallis galvestonensis (synonyms *H. eulae, H. choctawensis*) is a very distinctive spider lily which has unfortunately long been confused taxonomically with *H. liriosome*. Any acquaintance with the former quickly dispels the confusion. *Hymenocallis galvestonensis* is an upland plant, typically found in the understory of rich woods. Nowhere common across its known range from eastern Texas to western Florida, it is sometimes locally abundant, as it is on the Appalachicola River bluffs of Torreya State Park in northwestern Florida. Unlike any other native spider lily, *H. galvestonensis* has grayish or almost blue-green leaves. The leaves appear in spring but die back during the summer. The flower scapes emerge as the leaves begin to deteriorate or after they disappear completely. The scape of this species is rounded rather than compressed or even decidedly two-edged, as is the case for the other species in the United States.

Hymenocallis liriosome (Rafinesque) Shinners

The clan of aquatic spider lilies is extended from Mobile, Alabama, to eastern Texas by *Hymenocallis liriosome*, which flowers in the spring. It is most common in the vicinity of the Gulf of Mexico, usually in shallow water, but it reportedly occurs inland to southern Arkansas. Very dark, almost black bulb coats and an intense lilylike fragrance distinguish it. The 30- to 60-centimeter scape is sharply two-edged and bears up to six large flowers (up to 20 centimeters wide) contemporaneously with the leaves. Like the other aquatic spider lilies, *H. liriosome* has a very wide-spreading staminal cup which sports a prominent yellow eye.

Zephyranthes

The rain lilies, as the two genera *Zephyranthes* and *Habranthus* are popularly called, get their common name from their delightful habit of bursting into flower one or two days after a rainstorm, any time from spring to fall (depending on the species). In certain respects, rain lilies are tropical stand-ins for crocuses, announcing the conclusion of the dry season much as spring crocuses herald winter's demise in temperate regions. Alternating periods of wetness and drought often stimulate successive flowerings. The ephemeral flowers, funnel-shaped and usually upfacing, appear singly on hollow, leafless stems a few days after a rain. The bracts surrounding the single flowers are fused partially or completely into a tube. *Zephyranthes* is widespread throughout the warm temperate and tropical Americas, extending as far north as the southeastern United States. Many species and hybrids are found in Mexico, with another cluster of diversity from southern Brazil into Argentina.

Zephyranthes atamasca (Linnaeus) Herbert

Two spring-flowering species of the southern United States, *Zephyranthes atamasca* and *Z. simpsonii*, have large flowers as rain lilies go. They are quite similar, 20 to 30 centimeters in height with very narrow leaves. *Zephyranthes atamasca* var. *treatiae* (S. Watson) Meerow (sometimes treated as a distinct species) can be seen flowering by the hundreds along wet roadside ditches at the margins of pinelands throughout the northern half of Florida. *Zephyranthes atamasca* var. *atamasca* is found from northern Florida to Virginia in the shade of moist, even swampy woods. It produces clumps of offset bulbs, and its 7- to 10-centimeter-long flowers spread open widely; in contrast, variety *treatiae* rarely offsets, and the flowers are not as wide. Variety *treatiae* is less hardy but still capable of surviving temperatures below 20°F (−7°C). The pure white or pink-tinged flowers of this species are 5 to 7 centimeters wide.

Zephyranthes simpsonii Chapman

Zephyranthes simpsonii, which has twice the number of chromosomes as *Z. atamasca*, is found in peninsular Florida (Plate 27). The flowers are more cup-shaped than those of *Z. atamasca*. In both species, each bulb, in some cases no more than 1.25 centimeters in diameter, is capable of producing several scapes over a period of several weeks from late March through mid-May. Leaves emerge in late winter to early spring. After flowering and seeding, the foliage of the native rain lilies dies back for the summer and fall months.

Zephyranthes pulchella J. G. Smith

Zephyranthes pulchella is lovely autumn-flowering yellow rain lily from the western Gulf Coast, related to *Z. citrina*, an exotic that is widely available in the bulb marketplace. Its leaves are linear and sedgelike, growing from black-coated bulbs up to 5 centimeters in diameter which characteristically form a long neck. The golden-yellow flowers are about 2.5 centimeters long. In the wild, *Z. pulchella* is found in the coastal prairies and wet roadsides of eastern Texas, and it demands moist conditions in cultivation. The leaves grow through the winter and spring, dying off with the advent of summer. It is hardy at least through USDA Zone 8, and possibly in Zone 7 with protection. *Zephyranthes jonesii*, *Z. refugiensis*, and *Z. smallii* are three narrowly distributed sulfur-yellow rain lilies of Texas that are thought by most botanists to be hybrids of *Z. pulchella* with the night-blooming *Z. chlorosolen*.

Zephyranthes chlorosolen

A group of night-flowering, long-tubed *Zephyranthes* (sometimes treated as a separate genus, *Cooperia*) extends up from Mexico into the Gulf Coast and southwestern United States. Most have very narrow, grayish, succulent leaves, and white or yellow flowers. *Zephyranthes chlorosolen* (synonym *Cooperia drummondii*) is the most widely distributed of this group; it is very common in Texas and occurs in Louisiana, New Mexico, southern Kansas, and Oklahoma. It also ranges into northern Mexico. Plants seemingly identical to this species have been collected in Brazil—one of several biogeographic mysteries with which the rain lilies plague botanists. *Zephyranthes chlorosolen* flowers from summer to fall, bearing rather drab white flowers, cuplike in aspect, with tubes 7 to 12 centimeters long. They are sweetly fragrant at night and last no more than one or two days. *Zephyranthes chlorosolen* is remarkably forgiving as a garden plant and can be observed growing profusely in abandoned fields. The bulbs offset generously and the plants self-sow readily.

Zephyranthes traubii (Hayward) Moldenke

Zephyranthes traubii, similar to *Z. chlorosolen* but smaller in all its parts, is found in moist, coastal prairies and wet roadsides across a more restricted range in eastern Texas, flowering in the summer and fall.

Zephyranthes drummondii D. Don

The giant prairie lily, *Zephyranthes drummondii* (synonym *Cooperia pedunculata*), is probably the white cooperia of choice for gardening purposes. Found across a fairly broad area of Texas and in northern Mexico, and reportedly observed in Louisiana as well, the giant prairie lily sports flowers that are handsomer than those of *Z. chlorosolen*, from March through midsummer and sometimes continuing through autumn if conditions are optimal. While the tube of this species is shorter than that of *Z. chlorosolen*, the limb of the flower spreads widely to more than 5 centimeters. Unlike the other cooperias, *Z. drummondii* has a noticeable flower stalk (or pedicel) between the ovary of the flower and the top of the scape. The gray leaves are wider than those of most cooperias, up to 2 centimeters broad, and may remain evergreen through much of the year. The dark-coated bulbs can swell to 7 centimeters in diameter. Giant prairie lily exhibits the same garden tolerance as *Z. chlorosolen* and is hardy throughout most of the southeastern United States on the Gulf Coast and coastal plain.

Habranthus

The genus *Habranthus* is often confused with *Zephyranthes*, and for good reason. Like the latter genus, *Habranthus* consists of diminutive plants that produce single-flowered, hollow scapes and have a tubular bract. Unlike the radially symmetrical flowers of *Zephyranthes*, those of *Habranthus* are bilaterally symmetrical (or zygomorphic) and have stamens of four different lengths. The seeds of *Habranthus* possess a noticeable oblique wing; seeds of *Zephyranthes* do not. The two genera have similar chromosome numbers and produce fertile hybrids when crossed.

The majority of *Habranthus* species are found from southern Brazil to Argentina. Another cluster of species occurs in Mexico. No species have been described from the large, intervening distance between these two centers of distribution. Only a single species is known from the United States, and, oddly enough, it is considered a variety of a species otherwise found in Argentina and Uruguay.

Both *Habranthus* and *Zephyranthes* are fast-growing from seed and flower in a year or two after germination. Seed is often produced freely on the plants, but the flowers of stock material can easily be cross-pollinated to increase the amount of fruit set. Some species readily naturalize from self-sown seed as long as the seeds contact soil (rather than mulch). The seeds mature rapidly and dehisce abruptly; if they are not harvested or prevented from maturing, the resulting plants can become pests in a collection under glass. The mature fruit is a three-celled capsule containing as many as 100 black, D-shaped (*Zephyranthes*) or flat, obliquely winged (*Habranthus*) seeds less than 1 centimeter long. The seed should be sown as soon as it is collected, or it may be air-dried for 24 hours and then stored at room temperature in a sealed plastic bag for no more than a few weeks at most without loss of viability. Rain lilies have very few pests and diseases, but southern blight (*Sclerotium rolfsii*) and fusarium can damage the bulbs if they are consistently overwatered.

Habranthus tubispathus var. *texensis* Herbert

Habranthus tubispathus var. *texensis*, known as Texas copper lily, flowers in summer and fall on the roadsides, seasonally dry fields, and prairies of central Texas and southwestern Louisiana. The inconspicuous leaves emerge in winter. The 2.5-centimeter flowers are yellow-orange in color, permeated with streaks of rusty bronze. This plant is best managed at the margins of cultivation, preferring neglect and dry soil to excessive irrigation and high fertility. One theory about the Texas copper lily's entry into the United States posits that it accompanied early Spanish missionaries from South America, but no one has been able to prove this or any other hypothesis of origin.

Bibliography

Flagg, R. O. 1961. *Investigations in the Tribe Zephyrantheae of the Amaryllidaceae.* Dissertation, University of Virginia.

Flagg, R. O., and W. S. Flory. 1976. "Origins of Three Texas Species of *Zephyranthes.*" *Plant Life* 32: 67–80.

Herndon, A. 1987. "A Morphometric Comparison of *Hymenocallis palmeri* and *Hymenocallis floridana* (Amaryllidaceae) in Southern Florida." *Sida* 12: 295–305.

Meerow, A. W. 1985. "Notes on Florida *Zephyranthes.*" *Herbertia* 41: 86–94.

Ogden, S. 1994. *Garden Bulbs for the South.* Dallas: Taylor.

Shinners, L. H. 1951. "The North Texas Species of *Hymenocallis* (Amaryllidaceae)." *Field and Laboratory* 19: 102–104.

Smith, G. L., and W. S. Flory. 1990. Studies on *Hymenocallis henryae* (Amaryllidaceae). *Brittonia* 42: 212–230.

– 3 –

The *Brodiaea* Alliance: *Bloomeria,*
Brodiaea, Dichelostemma, and *Triteleia*

PARKER SANDERSON AND JANE McGARY

The bulbous genera we are here calling the brodiaea group are ubiquitous in the Far West, but except for a few species, they are little known to gardeners, even within their native region. This is surprising, because within this group are some of the showiest and most widely adaptable western bulbs. They include plants of dry and moist habitats and warm to fairly cold climates; all, however, have evolved in a climatic regime of wet winters and dry summers. They have a strikingly varied color range: purple-blue, violet, pink, yellow, red, and white. They are easy to propagate from seed, and many also increase by copious offsets.

This group is usually perceived as comprising five morphologically similar genera: *Brodiaea, Bloomeria, Dichelostemma, Triteleia,* and *Muilla.* The first four, which are native to the West Coast, are discussed in this chapter; *Muilla* is covered in chapter 10 ("Bulbs of the Southwest"). Over the century and a half during which the botany of the West has developed, many species have wandered among these genera, with the result that any list of them contains a plethora of rejected synonyms. All the species now distributed among *Dichelostemma* and *Triteleia* were once in *Brodiaea* (*Bloomeria* was once regarded as an *Allium*), and wildflower enthusiasts still refer to all of them casually as brodiaeas (pronounced "bró-dee-uhs").

All these genera are restricted to western North America. The Chilean genus *Leucocoryne* was formerly included in *Brodiaea*. Another South American genus, *Ipheion*, has passed through *Triteleia* on its remarkably complex taxonomic journey. Other genus names that have been associated with some of these species include *Brevoortia, Calliprora, Hesperoscordum, Milla, Seubertia,* and even *Ornithogalum.*

Botanists were even perplexed regarding the family affiliation of brodiaeas. Before the huge family Liliaceae was split into many smaller ones, there was some controversy about whether these genera belonged to the Liliaceae or the Amaryllidaceae. There is now consensus that they should be assigned to the new family Alliaceae (the onion family), within the greater group of the Liliaceae.

These plants have the following common characteristics. They grow from corms with fibrous tunics, each of which produces a few long, rather narrow leaves and, when mature enough, a scape (flowering stem). In nature the corms are likely to grow quite deep in heavy clay soil, where they spend their dormant period in a cool environment with some residual moisture. The flowers are borne at the end of the scape in an umbel, on pedicels (individual flower stalks) that range from quite short—resulting in a congested inflorescence—to very long. Flower shapes include wide open and starry, bowl, cup, trumpet, and tube. Although they inhabit many situations, most of them grow among grasses, herbs, and shrubs which support their slender stems. Most species flower rather late in the growing season, often after their foliage has withered. The seed capsules have a "beak" at the tip, formed by the withered style, which splits open along with the longitudinal seams to release the dark, angular seeds.

Cultivation

The tendency to flower after the foliage dies makes brodiaeas a little difficult to place in the traditional garden. Take a cue from nature, and plant them among small perennials or low-growing ornamental grasses such as *Festuca ovina* and *Deschampsia caespitosa*; for example, the commonly grown *Triteleia laxa* is lovely emerging from plantings of *Dianthus* (pinks). They can also add interest to a planting of dwarf bearded irises, since they flower later than the irises. Short-stemmed species like *Brodiaea terrestris* are appropriate in the rock garden. All these plants look best spaced closely in groups of at least a dozen, then left to form clumps. The individual species descriptions that follow include guides to moisture requirements and cold hardiness. In the wild some species grow among shrubs, but in most temperate climates, all revel in full sun.

Seed of the more common species often appears in exchange lists and the catalogs of commercial collectors. The seed of most species disperses quickly once the capsules split, so it should be harvested after the scape has withered but while the capsule is still slightly green. It germinates best when obtained as early as possible in the season of its collection and planted in fall, exposed to cool conditions, and kept moist. After germination the seedlings should be protected from frost. Keep them watered until they turn yellow and wither; then reduce watering but keep the pots in a cool place. The first-year bulbs are small and can be hard to identify, so many growers prefer to leave them in the seed pots for two seasons. They should be fed two or three times during the growing season with a weak solution of liquid fertilizer. Once they are large enough to move on, they can be planted directly into the garden or—our preference—in larger pots in a plunge bed to gain strength for another year or two. Most species flower the third or fourth year from germination, given a sufficiently warm climate and good nutrition. Propagation is also easy by means of offset corms, dug and separated during the dormant season.

Brodiaeas are quite amenable to pot culture, but the growth habit of most does not lend itself to the production of "show" pots in the British style. A representative collection, however, can be maintained in deep clay or plastic mesh pots, plunged in sand in a bulb frame or cool greenhouse, and kept rather dry in summer. Plants should be repotted every second or third year to maintain their vigor.

Bulbs of a few species are grown commercially in large quantities. Gardeners are most likely to find *Triteleia laxa* 'Queen Fabiola' ('Koningin Fabiola'), a large-flowered, adaptable clone. A Dutch selection is *T. ixioides* 'Starlight', with very numerous pale yellow flowers. There are two garden hybrids in wide circulation: 'Corrina', a tall, violet-flowered plant of uncertain parentage, and *T. ×tubergenii*, a hybrid of *T. pedunculares* and *T. laxa* with large umbels of lavender flowers. U.S. growers are beginning to take an interest in these plants, and Jim and Georgie Robinett have introduced large-flowered clones of *T. laxa* under the names 'Humboldt Star' and 'Sierra Giant'. There is great potential for further exploration and nursery introductions.

Conservation

The greatest threat to lowland brodiaeas is agriculture and urban development. Cattle grazing, which is widespread at most elevations in the West, may also harm these palatable plants. There are a few very restricted endemic species, especially on offshore islands. Nonetheless, most species are so widely distributed and so enthusiastic about maintaining their populations by seed that they still form a prominent element in the flora of the West.

The only federally listed endangered species in this group are *Brodiaea filifolia* and *B. pallida*. The California Native Plant Society has categorized the status of some other species in that state as follows: rare—*Bloomeria humilis, Brodiaea kinkiensis, B. orcuttii, Triteleia grandiflora* var. *howellii*; extremely rare—*T. clementina*; uncommon—*Brodiaea appendiculata, B. californica* var. *leptandra, T. ixioides* subsp. *cookii, T. lugens*; and endangered—*Brodiaea coronaria* subsp. *rosea, B. insignis*. In Oregon, *T. crocea* and *T. hendersonii* var. *leachiae* are classified as rare (*T. laxa* is considered endangered in Oregon at the margin of its range, but it is very common in California).

The Plant

The first task in identifying these plants is to determine which genus is before us. The drawings on pages 84–85 explain the terms *stamen* and *staminode*—essential to understanding this group—in graphic terms. A staminode is a modified stamen that lacks a pollen-bearing anther at the tip. Another important feature is the structure of the leaves, with or without a keel (a raised, longitudinal central structure on the underside); this can be difficult to see at the time of flowering, when the leaves of most species are withered, especially in those with very narrow leaves.

The following informal key can be used with plants in flower. Note these exceptions, however: the rare *Brodiaea orcuttii* does not have staminodes, and the common *Dichelostemma capitatum* has six fertile (pollen-bearing) stamens, but it is distinguished from *Triteleia* by its three-lobed stigma.

A   Three fertile stamens and three flattened, infertile
    staminodes . . . . B
    Six fertile stamens and no staminodes C
B   Leaves with a keel; flowers in tight umbels . . . .
    . . . . *Dichelostemma*
    Leaves without a keel; flowers in loose umbels . . *Brodiaea*
C   Leaves flattened and keeled . . . . D
    Leaves round in cross section . . . . *Muilla*
D   Filaments of anthers flattened or threadlike . . . . . *Triteleia*
    Filaments cup-shaped at base . . . . *Bloomeria*

Bloomeria

This genus of entirely coastal distribution has one common species, popularly called goldenstars, and one rare one. Both are plants of grassland and the thin evergreen brushland called chaparral in the West.

Bloomeria crocea (Torrey) Coville

The more common of the two species was first identified as an *Allium* (by Torrey) and has also been called *Bloomeria aurea*. It is found in the South Coast Ranges south to northern Baja California. Not often seen in cultivation, it is hardy to about 20°F (–7°C) if protected from excessive freezing and thawing and given a very dry summer dormancy. Where it can be accommodated, it is a pleasing garden subject, producing an airy spray of deep golden flowers in June or July. It flourishes in the bulb frame. Propagate it by seed; it makes few offset corms.

    Bloomeria crocea usually has a single basal leaf, withered by flowering time; it does not roll inward when withering, and the keel is obvious.

The narrow, wide-spreading tepals (perianth segments) are separated almost to the base. The flowers are borne in an umbel of 10 to 35 or more, atop a stem 15 to 60 centimeters tall (typically about 25 to 30 centimeters). They are rather small and bright golden yellow, with green central stripes on the exterior (underside). The diagnostic cup-shaped base of the filaments looks like a little yellow crown surrounding the bright green ovary. The three-lobed stigma extends well beyond the stamens. The only native plant with which it might be confused is the yellow-flowered *Triteleia ixioides*, but their ranges do not overlap, and the *Triteleia* has brown central exterior markings and a stigma shorter than its stamens.

Bloomeria humilis Hoover

This species is distinguished by its much shorter scape, usually less than 8 centimeters tall. Its perianth segments are tighter at the base rather than opening out almost flat. It is a rare endemic, restricted to Monterey County and northern San Luis Obispo County, where *Bloomeria crocea* also occurs. It has been successfully cultivated in troughs by California gardeners.

Brodiaea

This widespread genus is characterized, as we have seen, by the combination of three stamens plus three staminodes and by unkeeled leaves. Plants have rather open, umbel-like flower heads in various shades of purple, violet, and lavender (white-flowered individuals may appear rarely), usually with darker purple midveins on the tepals. The gardener will wish to verify plants grown from seed, since the species can be difficult to distinguish out of flower, and this means opening up an individual floret and looking at it, perhaps with a hand lens. The diagnostic features that must be examined to identify species are as follows:

- Shape of the flower: Are the perianth segments widely spreading from near the base, so that the flower is flat and starry in appearance, or are they ascending from a noticeable tube, so that it has a flaring funnel shape? Is there a constriction above the ovary, or not?
- Details of the staminodes: Are the margins flat or inrolled, like a scroll? How wide are they relative to the tepal? Are they the same width for their whole length (linear), or wider at the base? Do they lean toward or away from the stamens?
- Details of the anthers and filaments: Are the anthers narrow (linear) or broad (obcordate)? Are there any appendages on the filaments?

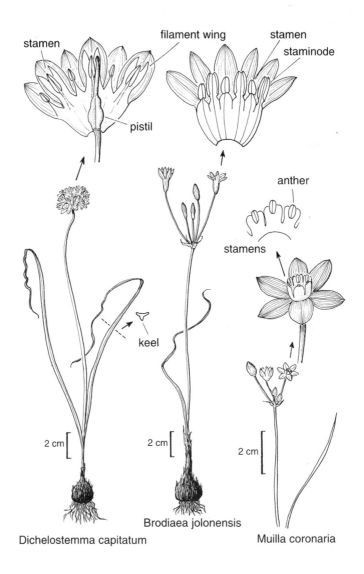

stamen

filament wing

stamen

staminode

pistil

anther

stamens

keel

2 cm

2 cm

2 cm

Brodiaea jolonensis

Dichelostemma capitatum

Muilla coronaria

Representative species in the *Brodiaea* complex, showing plant form and details of stamens and staminodes. Drawing by Linda Vorobik.

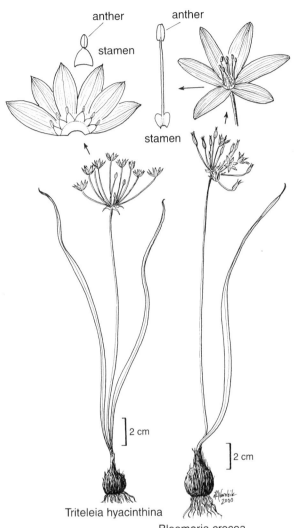

anther

stamen

anther

stamen

]2 cm

]2 cm

Triteleia hyacinthina

Bloomeria crocea

As noted in the introduction to this chapter, many entities formerly included in *Brodiaea* have now been moved to *Triteleia* or *Dichelostemma*. Several species still in *Brodiaea* were once called *Hookera* (not *Hookeria*, as the name appears in the Biota of North America Program index), a genus no longer recognized. All *Brodiaea* species occur in California, but a few extend up into the Pacific Northwest, and one reaches southern British Columbia. Unless otherwise stated, places mentioned in this section are all in California.

Brodiaea appendiculata Hoover

This is an uncommon species of low-elevation foothill grasslands, with a distribution centered on San Francisco Bay and extending to the inland North Coast Ranges and the western base of the central Sierra Nevada. It is very similar to *Brodiaea californica* but is separated from it on the basis of two characters: the filaments of *B. appendiculata* have two thread-like appendages not present in *B. californica*, and the free outer portions of the perianth segments of the former are less than twice the length of the fused portion (the tube), while the reverse is true of the latter species. The perianth segments are violet, with recurved tips; the staminodes are erect and white, with inrolled margins. Although it is not documented in cultivation, the plant should be hardy to about 20°F (–7°C) and would require a dry summer dormancy.

Brodiaea californica Lindley

This robust-appearing plant is common in grassland and chaparral of the northern Coast Ranges and the western foothills of the northern Sierra Nevada, to 2670 feet (800 meters) elevation. On a stout stem from 20 to 70 centimeters tall, it bears funnel-shaped flowers varying from light to dark purple, or sometimes pinkish, with dark midveins. The flower is not constricted above the ovary, and the staminodes are narrow, linear, and wavy. Differences between this and the similar *Brodiaea appendiculata* are noted under that species.

There are two varieties: *Brodiaea californica* var. *californica*, the typical form, and *B. californica* var. *leptandra* (Green) Hoover, a smaller plant with narrower, dark violet perianth lobes and more deeply inrolled staminode margins. The latter is uncommon in Napa, Lake, and Sonoma counties, where it often grows on serpentine. This species is a good candidate for gardens because it is the largest of its genus and flowers late. In warm climates it often self-sows. Variety *leptandra* is also said to produce offsets freely. Seed is often available. In the early 1990s selections from a Tehama County population in shades of white to pink were offered by the Robinetts; it is hoped that these remain in cultivation.

Brodiaea coronaria (Salisbury) Engler

The most northerly species in the genus ranges from northwestern California to southern British Columbia. In Oregon and Washington it is found primarily west of the Cascades, but it extends east through the Columbia River Gorge into Yakima County, Washington, and Wasco County, Oregon. Known to wildflower enthusiasts as blue dicks or harvest brodiaea, it is a common plant of thin grassland, often flowering in great numbers in early summer. The northern populations were formerly called *Brodiaea grandiflora*.

The flower, in varying shades of violet, has ascending perianth lobes, unconstricted above the ovary. The staminodes are wider at the base and lean inward toward the stamens; their margins are strongly inrolled. It is among the less showy brodiaeas with its short stems and few-flowered umbels, but it should appeal to gardeners in colder climates.

Brodiaea coronaria subsp. *rosea* (Greene) Niehaus, known as the Indian Valley brodiaea, is endemic to serpentine formations in Tehama, Lake, and Glenn counties of California. It is distinguished from subspecies *coronaria* by its corm tunic, which is thin rather than thick; its shorter stems (not exceeding 7 centimeters); and its rose to pinkish purple perianth, along with several microscopic details. It is listed as endangered by the state of California.

Brodiaea elegans Hoover

This pretty plant is found in a wide variety of habitats, mostly open and sunny, from northern California up through western Oregon to the Columbia River (Plate 28). It is easy to grow in dry parts of the garden, where it flowers in early July. The blossom is violet-purple, sometimes with a rosy tint. It is distinguished from *Brodiaea californica* by its staminodes, which are wide at the base rather than linear; and from *B. coronaria* by its staminodes, which do not lean in toward the anthers. In addition, its perianth tube is a smoothly tapered funnel shape, rather than the bell shape of *B. coronaria*. *Brodiaea elegans* subsp. *hooveri* Niehaus has been separated on the basis of its slightly inrolled staminodes; it is recorded at low elevations in southwestern Oregon.

Brodiaea filifolia S. Watson

This species was documented long ago, but it had the misfortune to be native to sagebrush (*Artemisia*) scrub areas on the coast of southern California that are now heavily developed. As a result, it is a federally listed endangered species. It has become extinct in parts of its former range but is reported to survive in Riverside and San Diego counties and on San Clemente Island; however, it is being maintained in cultivation. Its range suggests that it is quite tender to frost. It is a small, slender plant, 20 to 30 centimeters tall, with one to four reddish violet flowers per stem.

The tube is narrowly cylindrical, and above it the lobes spread widely. It has insignificant, flat staminodes which reflex against the perianth lobes.

Brodiaea insignis (Jepson) T. Niehaus

The Kaweah brodiaea draws its common name from its limited range in the drainages of the Kaweah and Tule rivers of Tulare County, where it grows in open oak woodland in the foothills. It is listed as endangered by the state of California because its habitat is threatened by development and grazing. Stems 7 to 25 centimeters tall bear flowers in the rose-lavender range of colors. The unconstricted perianth spreads widely; the stamens are strongly inrolled. The latter feature, together with its geographic distribution, separates it from the otherwise similar *Brodiaea filifolia* and *B. kinkiensis*. Plants are in cultivation; they are likely to benefit from hot, dry summers and winter temperatures no lower than 20°F (−7°C).

Brodiaea jolonensis Eastwood

This strictly coastal species occurs in clay soils in grassland and light woodland from Monterey south to northern Baja California, and on Santa Cruz Island offshore. It is of low stature (5 to 15 centimeters), with fairly short pedicels (1 to 4 centimeters). It has an ascending, unconstricted perianth and wide-based staminodes that lean in toward the anthers. It can be told from the similar *Brodiaea coronaria* by its small size and by the only slightly inrolled staminode margins. Another similar species is *B. terrestris*, also short; however, *B. jolonensis* has a purple ovary, while that of *B. terrestris* is green. *Brodiaea jolonensis* is reported to be amenable to cultivation and would be suitable for the rock garden, but most bulbs of its native region come into growth in late winter, so it might need some frost protection.

Brodiaea kinkiensis T. Niehaus

Endemic to San Clemente Island, one of the Channel Islands off the southern California coast, this species is state listed as rare. It grows in clay soil in grassland and experiences no freezing temperatures in nature. It is very similar to *Brodiaea filifolia*, a rare species of the nearby mainland, but is separated on the basis of its abruptly pointed staminode which does not reflex against the perianth. The small, rather pale blue-violet flowers are borne on pedicels that are longer than the dwarfish (2 to 3 centimeters) stems. The species is maintained in cultivation, and if material were obtained, it would be most suitable for a pot in the frost-free greenhouse.

Brodiaea minor (Bentham) S. Watson

Another short species, officially known as the dwarf brodiaea, this one is native to grassland and gravelly clay soils on the dry, open flats of the

Sacramento and northern San Joaquin valleys and adjacent foothills in California. Here it experiences winters with frequent frost (to 20°F or −7°C), wet spring runoff conditions, and blazing hot, dry summers. From a stem 2 to 10 centimeters tall, small flowers 1.5 centimeters in diameter are borne on short 1- to 3-centimeter pedicels. The light blue-violet flower is tightly constricted above the ovary, then the tepals spread widely, producing an urnlike shape (Plate 29). *Brodiaea pallida* and *B. purdyi* have similar flowers, but both are taller (to 25 centimeters). Brian Mathew (1987) writes that it is a good species for the bulb frame.

Brodiaea orcuttii (E. Greene) Baker

The odd man out in the genus has no staminodes but only three fertile stamens; it is also unusual for its widely channeled, more or less cylindrical leaves. Neither the gardener nor the casual plant-hunter is likely to encounter this botanical curiosity, which is endemic to Riverside and San Diego counties of southern California, from sea level to 5330 feet (1600 meters), growing in moist grassland near streams and vernal (summer-dry) pools. It is state listed as rare. It attains 8 to 25 centimeters in flower. The perianth is violet, with a tubular base and widely spreading lobes. Material from populations at higher elevations should be able to withstand a few degrees of frost.

Brodiaea pallida Hoover

This federally listed endangered species is restricted in the wild to a single population near Chinese Camp, Tuolumne County, in the western foothills of the central Sierra Nevada. It grows on a serpentine formation in a vernally moist streambed site that has been threatened by development—no doubt for vacation homes. Specimens are maintained in cultivation. The plant has an ascending perianth constricted above the ovary. The staminodes are erect, inrolled, and deeply bilobed at the tip. *Brodiaea pallida* is reported to hybridize in nature with *B. elegans*.

Brodiaea purdyi Eastwood

Named for Carl Purdy, an early twentieth century nurseryman who identified many populations of California bulbs and then destroyed them by collecting them for sale, this species is very similar to *Brodiaea minor*, from which it is separated by its taller stature (10 to 25 centimeters) and narrower perianth segments (4 to 5 millimeters). It is native to the foothills of the northwestern Sierra Nevada, particularly Butte and Tehama counties, at elevations from 330 to 2000 feet (100 to 600 meters), growing in open coniferous woodland, often on serpentine. It is fairly cold hardy and has survived temperatures to 0°F (−18°C) in western Oregon, growing in gravelly soil kept dry in summer. It is not, however, a very attractive plant owing to its narrow tepals.

Brodiaea stellaris S. Watson

In the coastal forests of northern California, where the dry summers are tempered by ocean mists, *Brodiaea stellaris* can be found in openings on serpentine soils below 3330 feet (1000 meters), from Sonoma County north to Humboldt County. It is distinguished by its combination of widely spreading perianth lobes and staminodes that are equal in width to the perianth lobes. It is a short-stemmed plant (2 to 6 centimeters tall), bearing a few blue-violet flowers of ascending shape with recurved tips. The erect, flat staminodes are held close to the stamens and are notched at the tips. According to the *Jepson Manual* (Hickman 1993) it is difficult in cultivation, but nurseries in northern California have offered it, and it is hard to see why it should present any unusual problems to the specialist grower.

Brodiaea terrestris Kellogg

A rock gardener's delight, *Brodiaea terrestris* grows in grassland and oak woodland along the coast of California from San Diego in the south to Humboldt County in the north, preferring sandy soils (Plate 30). It is quite variable in size: the scape ranges from 2 to 20 centimeters in height, and the pedicels from 1 to 15 centimeters long. Despite its usual shortness, it has a substantial appearance and produces numerous, showy blue-violet flowers. These are ascending and unconstricted in shape. The staminodes are widened at the base and narrower than the perianth lobes, with margins only slightly inrolled. The most similar species is *B. jolonensis*, which has a different range and a purple ovary, whereas *B. terrestris* has a green ovary. Two subspecies are distinguished: *B. terrestris* subsp. *terrestris*, with stems 7 centimeters or shorter, flowers 25 millimeters in diameter or smaller, and leaves crescent-shaped in cross section; and *B. terrestris* subsp. *kernensis* (Hoover) Niehaus (synonyms *B. coronaria* var. *kernensis*, *B. elegans* var. *australis*), with taller stems, larger flowers, and leaves more flattened in cross section. The latter has a less extensive range and is especially common in the Tehachapi Mountains. Both subspecies of this handsome species are easy to grow from seed or offsets. They should not be baked in summer, so a site in light or afternoon shade is appropriate for the garden in a hot climate; however, they do not require summer water.

Dichelostemma

The small genus *Dichelostemma* includes some of the most easily grown species in this group and certainly the showiest—*D. ida-maia*. The genus name is from the Greek for "toothed crown" and refers to the appendages at the base of the stamens which fuse to form a serrated ring, or crown. The pronunciation of the name is not very stable, but "Dick-uhlo-stem'-ma" is often heard, and enthusiasts shorten it to "dicks" in common names. Karl S. Kunth set up the genus in the first half of the nineteenth century, but as late as the 1960s many of its present members were placed in *Brodiaea* by most U.S. botanists. The treatment in this section follows that of Glenn Keator (in Hickman 1993).

The distinctive characteristics of *Dichelostemma* are as follows. The corms are spherical and usually sessile; that is, the offset corms develop close to the parent corm, rather than at the end of stolons. As in *Brodiaea,* the flowers have three fertile stamens (except for *D. capitatum,* which has six stamens of unequal size). The leaves have a keel. The flowers are held in close umbels, giving these plants a different visual effect than the airy inflorescences of most *Brodiaea* species.

Dichelostemma capitatum A. Wood

The smallest member of the genus is also the most wide-ranging, found in open woodland, grassland, scrub, and desert from northern Mexico north to Douglas County, Oregon, and east to Utah and New Mexico. It is most common west of the Sierra–Cascade barrier, throughout California and in southern Oregon, often in vast populations. It has gone under many names over the years, including *Brodiaea capitata, B. pulchella, Dichelostemma lacuna-vernalis,* and *D. pulchellum.* An earlier edition of the influential *Jepson Manual* confused it with *D. congestum.* Wildflower enthusiasts call it blue dicks, but a name more grounded in folk practice is grass nuts, a reference to Native Americans' use of the corms as food; in fact, it was even cultivated by indigenous people. It is easily grown in almost any soil, but it should be kept fairly dry in summer.

The scape, 10 to 40 centimeters tall, bears a tight head of blue-purple flowers; pink shades and albinos are sometimes seen. This is the only *Dichelostemma* species that has six stamens, but the inner three are larger than the outer three. This trait distinguishes it from the superficially similar *D. congestum,* which also flowers later in spring. *Dichelostemma capitatum* subsp. *pauciflorum* (Torrey) G. Keator is a desert-dwelling plant of the Great Basin region which extends into Mexico; it has a few whitish flowers and is of little horticultural interest.

Dichelostemma congestum (Smith) Kunth

The ookow—from one of the Native American names for this food plant —is the common species of the Pacific Northwest (Plate 31). It ranges from California's Sacramento Valley to British Columbia, growing in open woodland and grassland from sea level to 6700 feet (2000 meters), often on north-facing slopes. It is easily grown and tolerates summer water in a cool situation, but it cannot survive the combination of heat and wet soil. It should be planted in masses because of its small size. Obtaining plants is no problem, since they flower in two to three years from seed. Nonflowering plants typically have leaves much larger than flowering ones. The plant is better in the ground than in a pot, where it presents an awkward appearance. The very dense inflorescence that gives this species its name is a raceme borne on a stem 20 to 80 centimeters tall. The flowers are blue-purple, sometimes quite dark. The three inner stamens are fertile, while the three outer ones are reduced to tiny stubs. This character and its later flowering season (April to June) separate the species from *Dichelostemma capitatum*, which may co-occur with it.

Dichelostemma ida-maia (A. Wood) E. Greene

The undoubted star of the entire brodiaea group is the firecracker flower, the only species with bright red flowers (Plate 32). Distributed in the North Coast Ranges of California as far north as Curry County, Oregon, it is not found in large populations, perhaps as a result of the activities of bulb collectors; however, it is not considered threatened. Its unusual name is said to commemorate Ida May, the daughter of a stagecoach driver who directed an early botanist to the plant.

This is probably the most popular "brodiaea" in horticulture and is grown commercially. It is easily raised from seed, flowering in three years. If given deep planting in well-drained soil and a dry summer dormancy, it can take winter temperatures as low as 15°F (–9°C), though A. M. D. Hoog characterizes it as "not hardy" in Holland. Its tall stems are stout and do not usually need support, but they may be knocked over by wind. In nature, however, it is often seen growing up through shrubs at forest margins. The stems may twist and bend, though it is not a climber like the related *Dichelostemma volubile*.

The relatively broad, stiff leaves are withered by flowering time in early summer. A stem to 100 centimeters bears a dense umbel of pendent flowers. These have long (25 millimeters), narrow, bright red tubes tipped with very reduced, reflexing, green to creamy yellow lobes. (Carl Purdy reported finding an all-yellow form of *Dichelostemma ida-maia*, but it has not been found again.) The unusual form is an adaptation to pollination by hummingbirds, which find ample reward in the inflated nectaries near the base of the tube. The flowers remain attractive for a long period. The corms have very fibrous tunics and multiply by producing new corms on short stolons.

This species hybridizes with *Dichelostemma congestum* to produce forms that have been called *D. venustum* (synonym *Brodiaea venusta*). The flowers resemble *D. ida-maia* in shape but are held more horizontally and are intermediate in color, usually bright rose purple; the plants vary in size and robustness. Wild forms have been found in Del Norte and Trinity counties of California, and a named cultivar, 'Pink Diamond', is now offered by Dutch bulb growers. These hybrids are usually sterile and must be multiplied by "scoring" the corm. They also produce new corms on stolons, like *D. ida-maia*.

Dichelostemma multiflorum (Bentham) A. A. Heller

The handsome species known as wild hyacinth is a plant of foothills and mountains from near sea level to 6700 feet (2000 meters) from the San Francisco Bay area to southern Oregon. It prefers clay soils in grassland and scrub and flowers in June. It is a garden-worthy species, likely to be hardy to 15°F (–9°C) or slightly colder. The leaves are very long (30 to 85 centimeters) and glaucous. The very dense, spherical inflorescence contains 10 to 35 flowers, which are held erect in an umbel—a feature that distinguishes it from the similar *Dichelostemma congestum*, which has a raceme. The color varies from rosy to bluish purple, with a darker midvein. The rather long perianth tube is strongly constricted, and above the narrow point the lobes open out widely.

Dichelostemma volubile (Kellogg) A. A. Heller

The snake lily is as striking for its oddity as *Dichelostemma ida-maia* is for its beauty. Its flowering stem coils and twines up through shrubs and other plants (often, poison oak) for as much as 2 meters to carry the inflorescence into the sunlight. Failing the presence of stouter neighbors, it may twine together with others of its kind, producing a ropelike effect. By the time the flower opens in June, the scape may actually have withered at the base and become free of the corm; the energy and moisture in the long stem are sufficient to sustain the flowers and the ripening seeds.

The species is widespread in the central and northern foothills of the Sierra Nevada and in California's North Coast Ranges. In cultivation it is hardy to about 15°F (–9°C) and should be given a dry summer dormancy. Plants grown from seed can flower in three years, but it takes a few more years for them to build up to producing a good display. They can be cultivated in a deep pot with the addition of a stake or, perhaps, an ornamental wire support for added weirdness value.

The twining stem is an infallible identifying trait. The strongly keeled leaves are withered by flowering time. The dense, numerous flowers are rosy lavender and urn-shaped. The corms grow deep in the soil and offset sparingly.

Triteleia

The many species and varieties of this genus include a number that are showy, hardy, and easy to grow. The individual flowers of the inflorescence tend to open simultaneously, whereas in *Brodiaea* and *Dichelostemma* they open in succession; thus, the visual effect is more pleasing. In addition to the purple-blue range common in the brodiaea group, *Triteleia* includes white- and yellow-flowered species. The genus is widely distributed in the Far West, with 12 species occurring in California and 7 in the Pacific Northwest states. The genus name comes from

Greek roots meaning "three" and "complete," referring to the fact that all the flower parts are in threes; it is pronounced variously as "try-tuh-lée-uh" and "try-tée-lee-uh," probably reflecting the American versus British approaches to botanical names, respectively.

Triteleia species have sessile (nonstoloniferous), spherical corms with fibrous tunics. The inflorescence is umbel-like and open. The flowers have a funnel-shaped perianth tube, sometimes relatively long, and six flaring lobes. There are six fertile stamens without appendages on the flattened, threadlike filaments; the anthers are attached at their middle to the filaments, which usually lean away from the stigma. The leaves have a keel. Species are distinguished primarily on the basis of the color of various parts of the flower, the level at which the stamens are attached to the perianth tube, and details of the stamens.

Triteleia bridgesii (S. Watson) E. Greene

This species inhabits forest edges in lower foothills from the central Sierra Nevada north to southern Oregon, often growing in rocky situations. It has not stimulated much horticultural interest and is said not to be very cold hardy. It varies from 10 to 50 centimeters in height and has flowers in various shades of purple. It differs from *Triteleia grandiflora* subsp. *howellii* in that its perianth tube is tapered at the base, while that of *T. grandiflora* is rounded. Other distinguishing characteristics are that all six stamens are attached to the tube at the same level and that the tissue at the throat of the flower is translucent and shiny.

Triteleia clementina Hoover

This very rare species is endemic to San Clemente Island off southern California, where it grows on damp cliffs and rock walls. It is maintained in cultivation, where it probably requires frost-free conditions and some moisture year-round. The light blue flowers, which are not showy, are borne on rather long pedicels atop a 30- to 40-centimeter stem. The filaments are attached at two different levels, and the anthers are purple.

Triteleia crocea (A. Wood) E. Greene

Native to the dry Siskiyou Mountains on both sides of the border between California and Oregon, *Triteleia crocea* is unusual in having two subspecies, one with blue flowers, one with yellow. It grows on sunny slopes and in sparse conifer woodland and is reported to be difficult in cultivation; outside its native region, a bulb frame, kept dry all summer, would probably suit it best. This is a rather short plant of 10 to 30 centimeters. The flowers of both color forms are small (less than 20 millimeters) and have greenish median stripes and widely spreading lobes. The filaments are attached at two levels, distinguishing this species from *T. bridgesii*. The blue subspecies differs from the more widespread *T. laxa* primarily in size and in its more linear filaments. *Triteleia crocea* subsp.

crocea has bright yellow flowers and is found throughout the range of the species. *Triteleia crocea* subsp. *modesta* (Hall) Munz has pale blue flowers with slightly fringed perianth tips and is said to be restricted to the Trinity Mountains of California.

Triteleia dudleyi Hoover

A true alpine plant, *Triteleia dudleyi* occurs at elevations from 10,000 to 11,700 feet (3000 to 3500 meters) in the southern Sierra Nevada in open pine (*Pinus*) forest. This region is cold and snowy in winter, hot and dry in summer; its bulbous plants (for example, *Calochortus kennedyi*) are notoriously recalcitrant in cultivation, but *T. dudleyi* has done well in a bulb frame, flowering in its third year. A short (10 to 30 centimeters) scape bears relatively large pale yellow flowers which darken to purplish as they dry. The stamens are attached at one level. The diagnostic feature is the presence of short, blunt appendages outside the lavender anthers; the only other yellow-flowered species with these appendages is *T. ixioides*, in which the appendages are conspicuous and pointed.

Triteleia grandiflora Lindley

This species has a northerly distribution from northernmost California up to British Columbia and east into Idaho, western Montana and Wyoming, and northern Utah. It was formerly regarded as two species, *Brodiaea douglasii* and *B. howellii*; the latter is now called *Triteleia grandiflora* subsp. *howellii*. It occurs in hills from the coast inland and in sagebrush steppe, sometimes near conifers. As the name implies, it is showy in bloom. Its wide range should offer clones suitable to many different garden situations. The eastern populations have adapted to winter temperatures of −20°F (−29°C) or even lower. This is definitely a plant that needs attention from horticulturists.

This tall-growing (to 70 centimeters) species is distinguished from all others by the rounded or cuplike form of the base of the perianth tube and by the fact that the ovary stalk is not as long as the ovary itself. The flowers of both subspecies vary from very pale blue to deep blue. *Triteleia grandiflora* subsp. *grandiflora* has showier flowers because the outer perianth lobes are strongly ruffled and flared. In *T. grandiflora* subsp. *howellii* (S. Watson) Hoover the two series of perianth lobes are rather similar (Plate 33). The filaments are flattened and inserted at the same level in subspecies *howellii*, whereas they are not very flattened and are unequally attached in subspecies *grandiflora*. The latter subspecies is more common in the eastern part of the species' range.

Triteleia guadalupensis

The southernmost triteleia is a rare plant found only on Guadalupe Island of Mexico. It is similar and undoubtedly closely related to *Triteleia lugens* but differs in its more widely reflexed perianth lobes and larger size over all. Lee Lenz (personal communication) has described it as bright yellow with dark veins. We have not heard of its being in cultivation.

Triteleia hendersonii Greene

The only yellow-flowered species found north of California occurs in dry hills from Lane County south to Josephine and Jackson counties of southwestern Oregon, growing in dry hills on or near serpentine. Little known in cultivation, it is of moderate stature (20 to 60 centimeters). The flowers, borne on relatively short pedicels, are pale yellow to white with a strong purple median stripe on each lobe. The filaments are attached at the same level and are of equal length; the anthers are blue. *Triteleia hendersonii* var. *leachiae* (Peck) Hoover is a rare plant of the Siskiyou Mountains in Josephine, Curry, and Douglas counties. It is of short stature (to 25 centimeters) and has white rather than yellow flowers, also striped with purple.

Triteleia hyacinthina (Lindley) E. Greene

Thin grasslands from central California north to British Columbia and east to Idaho are dotted in late spring with great numbers of this plant, commonly known as white brodiaea (Plate 34). It may be seen from sea level to 6700 feet (2000 meters). The regions where it grows are dry in summer, but this species prefers swales that are quite damp in spring; it is often seen in association with *Camassia*. It is so easily grown that some western gardeners refuse it space, fearing its propensity to self-sow; however, it should not be regarded as a threat, since it is not stoloniferous and is easy to remove where not wanted. The medium-height (10 to 40 centimeters, usually around 25) scape bears a dense but not crowded head of white flowers, more or less flushed purple on the outside. They are bowl-shaped, with a short perianth tube and widely flared ascending lobes. *Triteleia hyacinthina* can be distinguished from other white-flowered species by its short pedicels (those of *T. ixioides* subsp. *cookii* and *T. peduncularis* are quite long) and by its yellow anthers (those of *T. lilacina* are lavender).

Triteleia ixioides (S. Watson) E. Greene

This is a variable species found mostly in coastal California; it extends barely into southern Oregon. It inhabits forest margins and scrub and is said to prefer gravelly or sandy soils. The good yellow color and substance of many forms attract gardeners, though not all the subspecies are reputed easy to grow. The shorter forms are suitable for the rock garden. The easiest to grow is *Triteleia ixioides* subsp. *scabra* (Greene) Lenz, which appears to be the source of most material in cultivation. In the 1990s the Dutch grower Wim de Goede selected a strain of it which he named 'Starlight' and propagated it in great numbers, so it is now offered in many major bulb catalogs. It features a very large inflorescence with as many as 60 blossoms opening in succession over a long period. Its cold hardiness has not yet been well reported, but it should survive winter lows in the range of 15° to 20°F (–9° to –7°C). Repeated freezing and thawing are not well tolerated.

Triteleia ixioides has a funnel-shaped perianth tube much shorter than the lobes, which flare out flat or even reflex a little. The anthers are surrounded by a tall, crownlike ring of sharply pointed appendages, the distinctive feature of this species. The flowers, mostly yellow, have purple or brownish median stripes on the exterior. Four subspecies are recognized: *T. ixioides* subsp. *anilina* (Greene) Lenz (sometimes misspelled *analina*), with dull yellow flowers drying bluish, a perianth tube shorter than 7 millimeters, anthers usually blue, and shorter appendages that curve toward the anthers; *T. ixioides* subsp. *cookii* (Hoover) Lenz, a rare serpentine-dweller of the Santa Lucia Range, with a white to very pale yellow perianth, strongly reflexed lobes, and appendages that curl away from the anthers; *T. ixioides* subsp. *ixioides*, with bright golden-yellow flowers and perianth tube 7 to 10 millimeters long; and *T. ixioides* subsp. *scabra* (Greene) Lenz, with pale yellow flowers, cream to yellow anthers, and long appendages that curve outward (Plate 35). The height of the scape varies both among and within subspecies, from 20 to 80 centimeters, but subsp. *scabra* is usually the tallest.

The *Jepson Manual* states that this species hybridizes in the wild with *Triteleia hyacinthina*, producing a sterile plant known as *T. ×versicolor*. It was known from Point Lobos on the central California coast but may now be extinct.

Triteleia laxa Bentham

This species, widespread in California and reaching barely into southern Oregon, is the best-known triteleia in gardens. Wildflower books claim that its common name is Ithuriel's spear, but we think this is merely the poetical fancy of some early writer; it is difficult to imagine it in the everyday lexicon of rural Californians. More likely to be authentic is the peculiar name "wally basket," perhaps derived from a Native American word. It grows in a variety of habitats, including grassland, open woodland, and brushy areas, slopes, and flats which are sometimes quite moist in spring. It is so variable that it is difficult for the nonbotanist to imagine how some of the more extreme manifestations can belong to the same species, and Keator in the *Jepson Manual* notes that "more study [is] needed."

The essentials of *Triteleia laxa*, as now defined, are flowers in some shade of blue to purple (white forms are not uncommon); stamens attached at two different levels; large flowers (greater than 20 millimeters); and linear filaments. Beyond that, it may be anything from 20 to 60 centimeters tall in giant forms. The most spectacular is a form—possibly tetraploid—found in various sites in the Sierra Nevada foothills in Tulare and Mariposa counties; on long, lax stems, it bears huge heads of pale lavender flowers. It is bewildering that this form is not in general cultivation, even by the authors of this chapter!

Several named strains or clones exist. The usual one in gardens is *Triteleia laxa* 'Queen Fabiola' (or 'Koningin Fabiola'), selected in Holland; it is a strong-growing plant, perhaps a hybrid, with rich violet flowers on stems about 40 centimeters tall. The Robinetts selected and named two other tall forms: 'Humboldt Star', with numerous blue-purple flowers, and 'Sierra Giant', with more red-violet flowers on longer pedicels. Crossed in Holland with *T. peduncularis*, this species gave rise to the hybrid *T. ×tubergenii*, which resembles it and is quite vigorous.

Triteleia lemmonae (Watson) Greene

This is the only *Triteleia* species endemic to Arizona, where it is found in Apache, Coconino, and Gila counties. It grows in sparse pine woodland at elevations between 5000 and 7000 feet. The flowers are bright yellow fading purplish. The perianth lobes are more than twice as long as the tube. The anthers are sagittate (arrowhead-shaped), and the stigma obscurely lobed. We know of no record of it in cultivation, but its elevational range suggests that it would not be too difficult to grow. It is likely, however, to prefer a dry winter and more moisture in late summer than the California species enjoy.

Triteleia lilacina E. Greene

The specific name *lilacina* refers not to the color of this flower, which is pure white without any purple stripe, but rather to the color of the anthers. The species is restricted to volcanic substrates in the foothills of north central California, especially at the northern end of the Sacramento Valley, and is said to be difficult in cultivation. It grows 30 to 60 centimeters tall. The rather small flowers have a short, shallow tube which is described as "glassy-beaded" when fresh and translucent when dry. It was once known as *Brodiaea hyacinthina* subsp. *greenei* and is very similar to *T. hyacinthina*, differing only in its linear filaments and in the color of its anthers (those of the latter species are yellow).

Triteleia montana Hoover
Triteleia lugens E. Greene

These two species are combined here because they are extremely similar, according to their descriptions. They differ only in the distributions cited for them—*Triteleia montana* in the northern to central Sierra Nevada, and *T. lugens* in the North Coast Ranges—and in the length of the filaments ("of two lengths" for *T. lugens*, and "more or less equal" for *T. montana*). Keator (in Hickman 1993) states that *T. lugens* is "related to *T. ixioides*" and that its "scattered occurrences need further study." Both species differ from *T. ixioides,* however, in lacking the prominent ring of append-ages outside the anthers. They are found in open montane forests, and both are fairly small, slender plants. They have yellow flowers with dark brown median stripes, and their anthers may be either yellow or blue. *Triteleia montana* is in cultivation but has been found rather difficult. It is likely to require fairly cool conditions in summer, since it grows among trees at high elevations to 6700 feet (2000 meters).

Triteleia peduncularis Lindley

This plant is easily identified by the very long pedicels that give it its name. From a stem of variable height (10 to 80 centimeters), numerous flower stalks extend straight up and outward for as much as 16 centi-meters. The bowl-shaped white flowers are often flushed with purple on the outside. The ovary is also distinctive, being bright yellow. *Triteleia peduncularis* grows in vernally wet habitats such as streamsides, pool margins, and low grasslands, often on serpentine, at elevations to 2670 feet (800 meters) along the coast of central and northern California. Easy in cultivation, it tolerates moisture until about midsummer, after which it should have a dry period. It hybridizes readily in gardens with *T. laxa,* a cross that produced the popular hybrid *T. ×tubergenii.*

Bibliography

Hickman, James C., ed. 1993. *The Jepson Manual: Higher Plants of California.* Berke-ley: University of California Press.

Hitchcock, C. Leo, and Arthur Cronquist. 1973. *Flora of the Pacific Northwest: An Illustrated Manual.* Seattle: University of Washington Press.

Jepson, Willis Linn. 1912. *A Flora of California, Parts 1 to 7.* Berkeley: University of California.

Mathew, Brian. 1987. *The Smaller Bulbs.* London: Batsford.

– 4 –

The Genus *Calochortus*

FRANK CALLAHAN

The genus *Calochortus* of the family Liliaceae is restricted to western North America and Mesoamerica. Its northernmost extension is in southern British Columbia (*C. macrocarpus*), and its eastern limit is in the Dakotas (*C. gunnisonii* and *C. nuttallii*). The most southerly species is *C. ghiesbreghtii*, which occurs in Guatemala at 90° north latitude. *Calochortus kennedyi* is the species with the greatest west-to-east distribution— from Mount Pinos in California (118°40′ west longitude) through Arizona and the Mexican states of Sonora, Chihuahua, and Coahuila, to Big Bend National Park in Texas (102° west longitude). The westernmost point of the genus is near Cape Blanco, Oregon (124°33′ west longitude), where there is a population of *C. tolmiei*.

The greatest concentration of species is in California, where almost half the known species (52 taxa) occur. Oregon ranks second, with 19 taxa. Six species are endemics of ultramafic substrates—soils with a very high concentration of iron and magnesium, sometimes called serpentine. Most inhabit acidic soils; *Calochortus striatus* is the lone species that is endemic to alkaline soils.

Calochortus has no close relatives in the Old World, but the genus *Tulipa* bears a remote resemblance to *Calochortus*. No other genus in North or South America is closely related to it. I believe that the genus *Calochortus* exhibits enough distinctive characteristics to warrant consideration as a monotypic family, now that botanists have subdivided the Liliaceae.

History

The botanical history of the genus *Calochortus* is tied to the exploration of the West. Lewis and Clark collected the type specimen of *C. elegans* "on the headwaters of the Kooskoosky" in present-day Idaho. Frederick

Pursh (1814) proposed the genus *Calochortus* and described *C. elegans* in *Flora Americana* (1 September, p. 240). Pursh chose the Greek compound *calo-chortus*, meaning "beautiful grass." *Elegans*, like many other specific epithets applied to the genus, is a redundant adjective: I have never met a calochortus that was not elegant, superb, or splendid!

Lewis and Clark missed many calochortus during their expedition because the other species native to the lands they passed through were not in bloom at the time. Around the same period, Mexico was being explored botanically, and in 1816 Alexander Humboldt, A. J. A. Bonpland, and Carl S. Kunth described two calochortus under the names *Fritillaria purpurea* and *F. barbata*. Although these species mimic *Fritillaria* in some respects, their morphology links them to *Calochortus*.

The ambitious plant explorer David Douglas, visiting the American West in the 1820s, discovered two additional species, *Calochortus macrocarpus* and *C. nitidus*. Douglas's second expedition, in the 1830s, led to the first collections of *C. albus, C. luteus, C. pulchellus, C. splendens,* and *C. venustus.*

In the early years of collecting and categorizing, *Calochortus* was somewhat confused with *Fritillaria*. George Bentham (1834) grouped the species with nodding flowers into his genus *Cyclobothra*. John G. Baker (1874) divided the genus *Calochortus* into four subgenera with 21 species and several varieties. Sereno Watson (1879) revised Baker's work and unified the genus into three sections with 32 species. Carl Purdy (1901) presented an additional revision of the genus, bringing the U.S. species to 40. W. L. Jepson's flora of California (1921) lists 24 species within that state. Abrams (1923) identified 41 species in the three Pacific Coast states.

Marion Ownbey (1940) delineated 57 species and 13 varieties. He accepted Watson's concept of three sections within the genus *Calochortus* and expanded the concept of 12 subsections. This chapter follows Ownbey's treatment, with a few alterations. My revision of Ownbey's outline of the genus is as follows:

Section I. *Calochortus* (formerly *Eucalochortus*)
    Subsections: 1. *Pulchelli*
                    2. *Eleganti*
                    3. *Nudi*
                    4. *Nitidi*
Section II. *Mariposa*
    Subsections: 5. *Venusti*
                    6. *Macrocarpi*
                    7. *Nuttalliani*
                    8. *Gunnisoniani*

Section III. *Cyclobothra*
　　Subsections:　9. *Weediani*
　　　　　　　　10. *Ghiesbreghtiani*
　　　　　　　　11. *Barbati*
　　　　　　　　12. *Purpurei*

My treatment recognizes 71 species and 15 varieties. It includes the following revisions to Ownbey's treatment:

OWNBEY	CALLAHAN
C. douglasianus	*C. nitidus*
C. nitidus	*C. eurycarpus*
C. coeruleus var. *nanus*	*C. coeruleus* var. *fimbriatus*
C. coeruleus var. *westonii*	*C. westonii*
C. elegans var. *oreophilus*	*C. elegans* var. *nanus*
C. lobbii	*C. subalpinus*
C. nuttallii var. *bruneaunis*	*C. bruneaunis*
C. nuttallii var. *panamintensis*	*C. panamintensis*
C. nuttallii var. *aureus*	*C. aureus*
C. hintoni	*C. fuscus*

Ownbey did not botanize in Mexico but described Mexican species from old, faded, often incomplete herbarium specimens. In addition, other botanists later described several species he did not identify. Ownbey did, however, correctly describe *C. ambiguus* (from Jones), *C. foliosus, C. minimus, C. monanthus, C. nigrescens*, and *C. persistens*.

Conservation

All *Calochortus* species have been severely affected by human activities. The leading problem is livestock grazing, since these plants are very palatable. *Calochortus monanthus* is possibly extinct; its former habitat has been entirely converted to pasture. Other species presently threatened by grazing are *C. coxii, C. excavatus, C. greenei, C. longebarbatus, C. macrocarpus, C. obispoensis, C. palmeri* var. *palmeri, C. pulchellus* (extirpated in pastureland), *C. simulans* (extirpated in pastureland but surviving between fencelines and roads), *C. striatus, C. superbus*, and *C. uniflorus*. *Calochortus tiburonensis* is listed as threatened because of its small population and restriction to ultramafic soils. In Mexico, livestock grazing and cutflower production threaten *C. balsensis*.

　　Urbanization has resulted in direct habitat loss to many species. Most of the former habitat of *Calochortus umbellatus* lies within the present city of Berkeley, California. Finally, the destruction of livestock predators, such as bear, cougar, bobcat, and coyote, has caused explosive growth in populations of deer, rabbit, and mice. These herbivores, along with overgrazing by domestic cattle, sheep, and goats, have wreaked terrible damage on western American rangelands. Plants not grazed are trampled, and the soils are severely compacted.

The best public collection of calochortus can be viewed in season at Tilden Park, situated in the hills west of the University of California, Berkeley, campus. Another must-see nearby is the University of California Botanic Garden, a gem among California gardens.

Economic Value

All parts of calochortus plants are edible; there are no known toxins in the genus. Native Americans have long utilized the bulbs as food. The sego lily (*Calochortus nuttallii*) is the state flower of Utah in recognition of its use as a food by traveling Mormon settlers.

There is a growing cutflower industry utilizing this genus in both Europe and Mexico. Calochortus are also the object of renewed interest among gardeners and the nurseries that serve them. Several species, such as *Calochortus albus, C. luteus,* and *C. venustus,* are grown commercially in large quantities by Dutch bulb nurseries and are appearing in widely distributed bulb catalogs.

The Plant

Calochortus plants grow from true bulbs, which are mostly elongated and ovoid. The bulbs have coats or tunics—membranous in sections *Calochortus* and *Mariposa,* and fibrous-reticulate in section *Cyclobothra.* Offsets, or offset bulbs, grow on the sides of mature bulbs; they are not numerous. Some species produce bulbils in the axils of the lower leaves. From each bulb rises a single scape, or stem, which may or may not branch above ground. The linear to ensiform (swordlike) leaves include a basal leaf, often quite large, and smaller leaves arranged up the stem. Stems and leaves are generally glabrous (without hairs). The lower leaf may be withered by the time of flowering. The typical calochortus is a slender, erect plant, adapted to growing where it has the support of surrounding grasses and herbs.

The showy flowers are borne several to a stem in most species, held on pedicels accompanied by bracts opposite them on the stem. The perianth segments are three narrow sepals, which are long and conspicuous in some species, and three broad petals. The flowers may be upfacing or, less commonly, pendent; their shapes include nearly flat to rounded bowl and cup forms, and nearly globose (spherical) ones in species whose petals are incurved, such as *Calochortus albus.*

Identifying the species often relies on details of the petal, which are depicted on page 106. The most fascinating features of these plants are the colorful marking patterns and the structures of the gland, or nectary, on the lower part of the petal. The gland, which produces the bait for pollinating insects, is usually dark in color and entirely or partially covered with trichomes (multicellular hairlike structures). The region around it typically has trichomes as well; in some species—called cat's-ears—the entire upper surface of the petal is quite hairy. These trichomes are crucial to species identification and must be examined with a strong hand lens or microscope. The figure on page 107 shows categories of trichomes.

Each flower has six stamens, inserted on the base of the perianth segments and larger at the base; the anthers are linear to oblong. The ovary has three cells, each with two locules. There are three stigmas, which persist after the flower withers. The seed capsules, which may be orbicular, oblong, or linear, are borne upright in most species but pendent in a few. Some species have winged capsules, while others have a simple triangular cross section. The seeds of some species are flat disks (usually whitish), while those of others are irregularly shaped and thicker.

Species

The following discussion is divided according to the three sections of the genus. A botanical key to these follows. This key, however, is useful primarily for plants in seed.

> Section I. *Calochortus*. Capsules orbicular to oblong, three-winged; inflorescence subumbellate; seeds irregular, not flattened or waferlike; bulb coats membranous.
> Section II. *Mariposa*. Capsules oblong to linear, three-angled, upright; seeds mostly waferlike and thin, rarely thickened; bulb coats membranous.
> Section III. *Cyclobothra*. All characters of section II, except bulb coats thick, coarsely hairy, fibrous-reticulate.

Section I. *Calochortus*

Subsection 1. *Pulchelli*: Flowers and capsules globose to subglobose, pendent; bulbs with membranous tunics.

Calochortus albus Douglas ex Bentham

The white globe lily comprises two races in California. One is a plant of the foothills of the western Sierra Nevada to 4000 feet (1200 meters), and

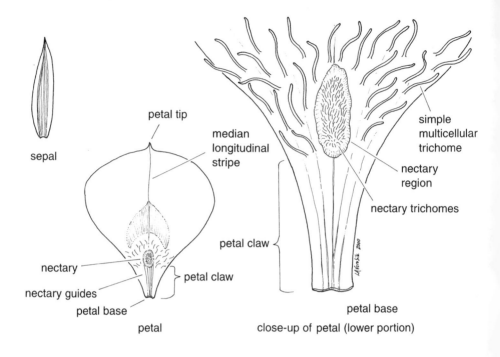

sepal

petal tip

median
longitudinal
stripe

simple
multicellular
trichome

nectary
region

nectary trichomes

nectary

nectary guides

petal base

petal claw

petal claw

petal base

petal

close-up of petal (lower portion)

Parts of a *Calochortus* tepal. Drawing by Linda Vorobik.

the other has a coastal distribution from San Francisco Bay south just into Mexico in northern Baja California. Near sea level in San Luis Obispo County, it tastes the salt winds off the Pacific, which often dwarf the plants. Farther inland, in protected habitats near York Mountain, the flowers have a rich burgundy color reminiscent of the fine wines grown in this region; this is known as forma *rubellus*. The species grows in a multitude of soil types, avoiding only wet sites, and is often seen on brushy north-facing slopes. It is known to hybridize with *Calochortus monophyllus*. The plant is relatively easy to cultivate, though it cannot survive cold continental climates without protection. This May-bloomer may reach a height of 50 centimeters or even more. Its large, globose, pendent flowers, as many as eight on the scape, range from off-white with a light yellow or beige flush through many shades of pink. The sepals are shorter than the petals, so the flower has a compact, spherical appearance. The only similar species are *C. amoenus*, with a deep pink flower which is much smaller and has prominent sepals, and *C. pulchellus*, with conspicuously fringed petal margins.

106

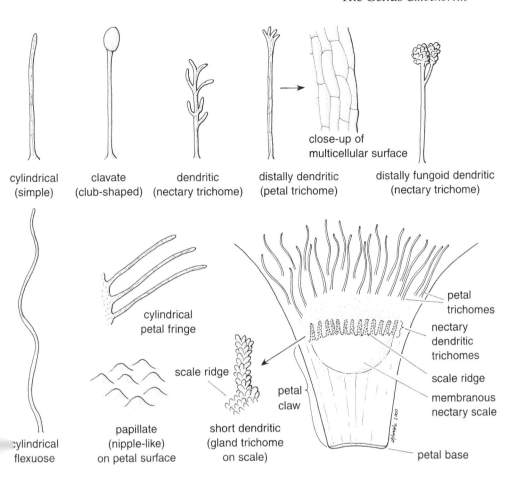

cylindrical (simple)

clavate (club-shaped)

dendritic (nectary trichome)

distally dendritic (petal trichome)

close-up of multicellular surface

distally fungoid dendritic (nectary trichome)

cylindrical petal fringe

cylindrical flexuose

papillate (nipple-like) on petal surface

scale ridge

short dendritic (gland trichome on scale)

petal claw

petal trichomes

nectary dendritic trichomes

scale ridge

membranous nectary scale

petal base

Types of trichomes found in different species of *Calochortus*. Microscopic examination of these structures is an aid to identifying species. Drawing by Linda Vorobik.

Calochortus amabilis **Purdy**

Known as Diogenes' lantern for its sunny yellow blooms, this species ranges along the Coast Ranges of California from Mendocino County south almost to San Francisco Bay; there is one very disjunct population in the Vulcan Peak region of San Diego County (Plate 36). The exquisite, globelike pendent flowers with large, elegant yellow sepals are charming on open hillsides and in woodland. The species inhabits a wide range of soils at elevations from 230 to 3000 feet (70 to 900 meters). It performs well in cultivation in mild climates, surviving temperatures in the low twenties Fahrenheit (around –4° to –7°C). *Calochortus amabilis* may reach 50 centimeters in height but is usually somewhat shorter. The petals are entirely yellow. The nectary has long, unbranched hairs surrounded by a few more or less clavate (club-shaped) petal hairs. The petals are mostly hairless above the gland except at the margin, which has a fringe of short hairs; the rather similar *C. pulchellus* has sparse hairs over most of the petal surface.

Calochortus amoenus Greene

The southern Sierra globe lily is native to the western slopes of the southern Sierra Nevada at elevations from 1670 to 5000 feet (500 to 1500 meters), growing on well-drained, decomposed granitic soils. Up to 50 centimeters tall, it has rose-lavender flowers in which the petals are darker than the sepals. The nectary is only slightly depressed and bears dendritic (branching) hairs; the petals have long hairs. This is an easy garden plant, hardy to about 20°F (–7°C) and tolerant of a wide range of soils, provided it receives no summer water.

Calochortus pulchellus Bentham

Endemic to low elevations from 670 to 2670 feet (200 to 800 meters) in the area of Mount Diablo in Contra Costa County, California, this species is known as the Mount Diablo fairy lantern. It grows to 30 centimeters tall and bears lime-yellow, globe-shaped flowers. The unbranched hairs of the nectary form a hemispherical cone. Tolerant of a wide variety of soils but frost-tender, it is a good candidate for gardens in very mild climates.

Calochortus raichei Farwig & Giard

This species is endemic to ultramafic residual soils in a small area of rugged topography in Sonoma County, California, known as The Cedars—hence the proposed common name, Cedars fairy lantern. It is closely related to *Calochortus amabilis* and *C. pulchellus*, but the plants are taller (to 35 centimeters) and the foliage is quite glaucous. The yellow flowers have long, tapering hairs in the nectary zone, with scant, red-based hairs on the inner surface and margin of the petals. The Cedars is named for the presence of *Cupressus sargentii* (Sargent cypress), a common associate of this calochortus. As a plant of low elevations from 670 to 1000 feet (200 to 300 meters) in a mild climate, *Calochortus raichei* is probably not suitable for gardens in cold-winter areas.

Subsection 2. *Eleganti*: Flowers broadly campanulate (bell-shaped), held upright; petals densely bearded; capsules elliptic-oblong, three-winged, pendent; bulbs with membranous tunics.

Calochortus apiculatus Baker

This species is named for its apiculate (sharply pointed) anthers, but its most important diagnostic feature is the dark subcircular gland. It is one of three species that extend north into British Columbia; the others are *Calochortus lyallii* and *C. macrocarpus*. It is a common feature of mountain meadows in Glacier National Park. Its range also encompasses northeastern Washington, adjacent Montana, and southwestern Alberta, at elevations from 4000 to 7330 feet (1200 to 2200 meters). It is obviously adapted to cold winters and is a good choice for northern gardeners to grow in scree settings. The creamy flowers are densely fringed and hairy, carried on stems to 30 centimeters tall.

Calochortus coeruleus (Kellogg) Watson

Beavertail grass ranges from Susanville, California, south through the mountains to Amador County, California, usually growing on west-facing slopes above 4000 feet (1200 meters) elevation. *Calochortus coeruleus* may be distinguished from the similar *C. elegans* and *C. tolmiei* by its large, oblong anthers and its petals, which are not papillose on the inner surface. The flowers are pale bluish lavender, borne on stems usually not exceeding 10 centimeters. This plant is best suited to cooler climates on the West Coast.

Calochortus coeruleus var. *fimbriatus* Ownbey ranges to the north of the typical species, growing mainly in the vicinity of Mount Shasta, California, and in southeastern Jackson County, Oregon. This variety, which was badly confused in Ownbey's monograph, is much smaller than the typical *C. coeruleus* and is distinguished by a strongly fimbriate (fringed) petal margin. The flowers are pale lavender. Coming from elevations of 3330 to 6700 feet (1000 to 2000 meters), this variety is also suited to cooler climes.

Calochortus elegans Pursh

The elegant cat's ear is the basis for the genus *Calochortus* because it was the first to be described. Lewis and Clark collected it where it is most heavily concentrated, in northeastern Oregon, southeastern Washington, and adjacent western Idaho. In Oregon its southernmost point is in the mountains between Lime and the Snake River Canyon. There is an isolated population north of Boise, Idaho. It is found at elevations from 3330 to 5330 feet (1000 to 1600 meters). The climate in this area is continental, with long, cold winters and hot, dry summers. *Calochortus ele-*

gans is a diminutive species, rarely growing over 8 centimeters in height, and small-flowered. It is distinguished from the closely related *C. coeruleus* by its anthers, which are long apiculate, and by the petals, which are papillose and sparsely fringed and bearded. *Calochortus elegans* grows with *C. eurycarpus*, *C. macrocarpus* var. *maculosus*, and *C. nitidus* on Jim Creek Ridge, overlooking the Snake River, in extreme northeastern Oregon.

Calochortus elegans var. *nanus* Wood was first collected in June 1866 west of Yreka in far northern California (Plate 37). It is common in the Klamath Ranges north to Diamond Lake, Oregon, and south to Glenn County, California. It tends to occur in the *Abies* (fir) zone at relatively high elevations from 3330 to 6700 feet (1000 to 2000 meters). It is separated from typical *C. elegans* by its distribution, a shallowly fringed gland scale, sparser and thicker petal hairs, and fringed petals. Nevertheless, the two entities are quite closely related.

Calochortus elegans var. *selwayensis* (St. John) Ownbey is easily distinguished from the former varieties by its small, short, transverse, linear, undepressed gland, and its petals, which are heavily bearded only halfway to the tip. It is found at elevations of 3330 to 6700 feet (1000 to 2000 meters) in the Bitterroot Mountains of Idaho and Montana, where it can best be viewed in the pass above Lolo Hot Springs, southwest of Missoula, Montana.

Calochortus monophyllus (Lindley) Lemaire

Calochortus of the subsection *Eleganti* are commonly called pussy ears or cat's ears from the dense "fur" on their petals, and this species is known as yellow pussy ears. It occurs from the southern Cascades in Jackson County, Oregon, to the western foothills of the Sierra Nevada in Tuolumne County, California, at 3330 to 5700 feet (1000 to 1700 meters) elevation. It is unique in its subsection in the strong yellow color of its flowers and the shape of gland and overall flower. The Oregon populations have a reddish blotch on the petal claw, a feature missing in many Sierra Nevada populations. These are little plants, seldom more than 10 centimeters tall. The petals are densely covered with subclavate hairs. This hardy mountain species accepts many soil types.

Calochortus subalpinus Piper

The Pacific Northwest, from Mount Adams in southwestern Washington south to Douglas County, Oregon, is the home of this plant of high-elevation open screes, alpine meadows, and scablands. Growing at elevations from 3330 to 8330 feet (1000 to 2500 meters), it flowers late—from early July to mid-August. Most plants are less than 20 centimeters tall. The creamy white sepals are usually marked with a purple glandular spot. The trichomes of the petal glands are strongly branched, and the hairs surrounding the gland usually yellow. This species tolerates severe cold and many soil types, so it is a good choice for northern rock gardens.

Calochortus tolmiei Hooker & Arnott

This widespread, variable species has had several synonyms, including *Calochortus coeruleus* var. *mawei, C. elegans* var. *lobbii, C. glaucus, C. mawei,* and *C. purdyi.* It is found from sea level to 4330 feet (1300 meters) elevation, from the Columbia River south to Santa Cruz County, California. The Oregon plants tend to be larger and more robust, often attaining 30 centimeters in height; those around San Francisco Bay are diminutive in comparison. The species accepts most soils and is fairly cold hardy. In cultivation it flowers earlier than any other calochortus. It produces offsets readily. *Calochortus tolmiei* is distinguished from the similar *C. coeruleus* and *C. elegans* by its usually branching stem and the fact that the petals are less conspicuously fringed and have dense hairs all the way to the tip. The flowers are typically white, flushed to deep lavender toward the base. Some coastal populations have flowers that are entirely lavender.

Calochortus westonii Eastwood

This plant is restricted to the southern Sierra Nevada in the Greenhorn Mountains. The best colonies are at Shirley Meadows, a popular ski area; Shirley Meadows star tulip has been offered as an English name (Plate 38). *Calochortus westonii* is close to *C. coeruleus*, from which it is best distinguished by its short flowering stems—mostly 6 centimeters tall—amid broad, near-vertical leaves up to 20 centimeters tall. The flowers are white with pink centers, with sparse hairs toward the petal tips. This species grows with *Abies* (fir) and spends the winter under a heavy blanket of snow at elevations around 6700 feet (2000 meters).

Subsection 3. *Nudi*: Flowers campanulate, more or less erect; petals obovate to cuneate, not fringed, with scant hairs; capsules elliptical, three-winged, pendent (except *Calochortus nudus*); bulbs with membranous tunics, often producing basal offsets.

Calochortus nudus Ownbey

Shasta star lily, as that common name implies, occurs in its best forms around Mount Shasta in northern California (Plate 39). The finest population I know is near Bartle, in open meadows surrounded by lodgepole pines (*Pinus contorta*). The species ranges from Jackson County, Oregon, south in both the Klamath and Cascade ranges and into the Sierra Nevada as far as El Dorado County, California. In the southern Cascades, south of the Pit River, hybrids between *Calochortus nudus* and *C. minimus* occur; these plants are quite fertile, suggesting close genetic relationship of these species. *Calochortus nudus* thrives in soils that are vernally wet and later dry out. It prefers higher elevations from 3330 to 8000 feet (1000 to 2400 meters) and cooler climates than *C. uniflorus*. This species can reach 20 centimeters in height and bears pale to deep lavender flowers. The nectary is a scale fringed along the top edge, but hairs on the rest of the petal are very scant.

Calochortus uniflorus Hooker & Arnott

This widely distributed species ranges from San Luis Obispo County in central coastal California to Lane County in the southern Willamette Valley of Oregon, at elevations from near sea level to 5000 feet (1500 meters). It often grows in lowland, vernally wet meadows, and in cultivation it often thrives in sites that receive summer water. For the most part, it is too plain-looking to warrant the gardener's attention, but some populations are superb, such as one near the University of California, Santa Cruz. It is sad to note that the southernmost known population, about 2 miles (3 km) north of Arroyo de la Cruz in San Luis Obispo County, was destroyed by a range improvement program, as John Erwin and I found when we reviewed the site.

Calochortus uniflorus is a short plant, not more than 10 centimeters tall. The petals of the cup-shaped flowers are usually light lavender, unmarked or crossed by a darker purple band. There is a fine, translucent nectary scale with scant yellow hairs just above it; the remainder of the petal is hairless. Despite its name, this species is often multiflowered. There exist two races, one diploid ($2n = 20$) and one tetraploid ($2n = 40$). In southern Oregon, hybrids between the diploid race and *C. tolmiei* are common. Wherever the two meet, a series of very fertile hybrids is found. This situation may have given rise to the dubious taxon *C. indecorus* Peck. Only two herbarium specimens of that species exist, and their exact collection sites are unknown. It is interesting that neither Ownbey nor Peck noted hybrids between *C. tolmiei* and *C. uniflorus*. The only valid difference between Peck's *C. indecorus* and *C. uniflorus* is the lack of basal bulbil production in the former. (If I were using the same criterion for a new species, any population of *C. albus* with bulbils in the leaf axils would constitute one.)

Calochortus umbellatus Wood

Oakland star tulip is a plant of hill slopes, not of vernally wet flats. Its range is strictly maritime, from northern Mendocino County to Santa Clara County, at elevations from 330 to 2330 feet (100 to 700 meters). The best form of this species occurs on Ring Mountain in Marin County, California, in downslope grasslands. This area is more famous for another species, *Calochortus tiburonensis*. Its locales suggest that it is not very cold hardy. *Calochortus umbellatus* is typically about 15 centimeters tall and is often multiflowered; I have seen as many as 15 blossoms on a single plant. The nectary is scalelike, with stubby hairs cresting its edge. The petals are mottled rose pink near the scale, with substriations (faint penciled lines) on the petal claw.

Subsection 4. *Nitidi*: Flowers campanulate, suberect to erect; petals obovate, cuneate (triangular-lanceolate and clawed in *Calochortus lyallii*); bulbs with membranous tunics.

I divide this subsection into two subgroups or alliances. Species of the first subgroup (*C. greenei*, *C. longebarbatus*, *C. nitidus*) have strictly erect petals with long hairs. Those of the second (*C. coxii*, *C. umpquaensis*, *C. howellii*, *C. lyallii*, *C. eurycarpus*, *C. persistens*) have campanulate flowers, which are densely bearded in the first four; *C. eurycarpus* has only a few long hairs above the gland, while *C. persistens* is densely hairy above the gland but lacks long petal hairs. The capsules are three-winged and erect, except pendent in *C. coxii*, *C. persistens*, and *C. umpquaensis*. All members of this subsection are relatively northern in distribution, mostly in Oregon.

Calochortus coxii R. Godfrey & F. T. Callahan

Cox's mariposa is a rare ultramafic endemic, restricted to a ridge complex south of Roseburg and north of Myrtle Creek in Oregon (Plate 40). Its preference for serpentine soils should be kept in mind when cultivating it: add a little Epsom salts to the planting mix. *Calochortus coxii* grows 20 to 30 centimeters tall. The flowers have dense white hairs on the inner petal surface, with transverse rows of dendritic hairs in the nectary zone. A narrow band of yellow hairs is situated just above the nectary zone. The outer petal surface often shows a yellow flush with pink striations. This species, along with *C. howellii*, *C. umpquaensis*, and a yet undescribed variety of *C. elegans*, exhibits linear rows of trichomes over the entire inner surface of the basal leaf; no other calochortus has this trait. All four of these plants are Oregon endemics.

Calochortus eurycarpus Watson

This northerly species ranges from southeastern Washington south through the Wallowa and Blue mountains of Oregon, where it is especially abundant along the upper ridges on the Oregon side of the Snake River Canyon. It extends east through central Idaho to Wyoming and Montana. There are two disjunct populations, one near Elko, Nevada, and another in northwestern Utah. It is a plant of high plateaus and vernally moist basins from 3670 to 7330 feet (1100 to 2200 meters) elevation,

FRANK CALLAHAN

growing with *Abies lasiocarpa* (alpine fir) at the upper end of its range and with *Juniperus occidentalis* (western juniper) at the lower end (Plate 41). Each plant bears one to five flowers, which may be white, lavender, or reddish, usually with a red blotch centered on the petal, which is broadly obovate. Scant, long hairs are situated near the nectary, which is composed of clustered yellow dendritic hairs. The three-winged capsule is erect and elliptic-oblong. I have had only moderate success in cultivating it in an area with milder winters than it experiences at home.

Calochortus greenei Watson

Greene's mariposa occurs from 3330 to 7330 feet (1000 to 2200 meters) elevation on residual volcanic clay soils which shrink and swell markedly with moisture fluctuations. Its range extends from Keene Creek Ridge in Jackson County, Oregon, south of the Siskiyou summit to Table Rock in Siskiyou County, California, the type locality. Most of its habitat has been severely degraded by cattle grazing and by an invasive weed, the Eurasian star thistle. This is another classically tulip-shaped flower. Growing to 30 centimeters tall, it is stouter in appearance than *Calochortus longebarbatus* and has more tangled, long hairs on the petal surface; the hairs just above the nectary are bright yellow. The scale ridge is adorned with rows of dendritic trichomes with distinct pink nectary guides on the petal claw. Each scape may bear two to four flowers. The stout, upright capsule has a short style.

Calochortus howellii Watson

Howell's mariposa is known primarily from the Illinois Valley of Josephine County, Oregon, at elevations from 1330 to 3670 feet (400 to 1100 meters). It is another ultramafic endemic with a rather large population base, indicating that it is propagating itself satisfactorily by seed (a "high recruitment rate," in technical terms). The plant is erect and 30 to 40 centimeters tall. The cream-white flowers have purple hairs surrounding the nectary; the petal claw is yellow-green (Plate 42). The nectary bears a series of transverse dendritic trichomes. Growers have met with limited success in cultivating this species.

Calochortus longebarbatus Watson

This is a plant of high mountain meadows from 5000 to 8330 feet (1500 to 2500 meters) which seeks out a perfect hydrological regime. Grazing and erosion have severely reduced its populations on many sites; it is a kind of ecological barometer or miner's canary for alpine meadows. The extensive range of the species has many gaps, indicating loss of habitat. It occurs in eastern and south central Washington down to Oregon's Hood River Valley; after a large gap, in Klamath and Jackson counties of southern Oregon; and after another hiatus, in Shasta County, California. Like many plants of cold, semiarid steppes, it is difficult to cultivate in most gardens; the bulbs appear to need a clay soil with some moisture over most of the year. The long-haired mariposa has a flower of classic tulip form. It grows up to 60 or 70 centimeters tall and bears lavender-pink blooms with a reddish blotch just above the gland. The inner surface has long hairs, hence its name. The nectary region has rows of dendritic white hairs. Bulblets are produced in the cauline bract (the axil of the basal leaf).

Calochortus longebarbatus var. *peckii* Ownbey, known as Peck's mariposa, is an endemic of south central Oregon, a semiarid region with cold winters and hot summers; in fact, Oregon's coldest temperature ever, –59°F (–50°C), was recorded in its habitat. The largest populations are centered on Big Summit Prairie in the Ochoco Mountains. This variety's elevation range is 5000 to 6700 feet (1500 to 2000 meters). It differs from typical *C. longebarbatus* in that it is a sterile triploid: it does not set seed and instead is ultrabulbiferous—a single 12-inch-square (30-centimeter-square) plot yielded nearly a thousand offset bulbs! The petal angles sharply from petal claw to assume a vertical orientation, rather than being rounded like the typical species. The transverse color band on the petal is darker. This variety reaches 20 to 30 centimeters in height.

Calochortus lyallii Baker

This species is strikingly different from other members of subsection *Nitidi*; with its triangular-lanceolate, long-clawed petals and small flowers, it almost resembles *Calochortus westonii* or members of subsection *Elegantes*. It ranges from extreme southern British Columbia down along the eastern slopes of the Cascade Range to Yakima County, Washington, at elevations from 3330 to 8330 feet (1000 to 2500 meters). It is a rain-shadow species, found in several sagebrush (*Artemisia*) localities together with *C. macrocarpus*. I have had limited success in cultivating it. Each 20-centimeter scape bears one to nine flowers, which are white to lavender, usually with a lavender crescent above the nectary and a similarly colored spot on the sepal. The petals are ovate to lanceolate-acute, with scattered hairs and a fringed margin. The nectary is composed of transverse, compact dendritic trichomes. The capsule is erect.

Calochortus nitidus Douglas

The giant mariposa was badly confused by Ownbey, an error carried over by Peck in *A Manual of the Higher Plants of Oregon* (1961). Ownbey's *Calochortus douglasianus* is a synonym of *Calochortus nitidus*. This "tulip" once ranged in the lowlands of southeastern Washington, but its habitat there has been entirely destroyed by grain farming and grazing, and we have been unable to locate any surviving populations in Washington. We did, however, find plants east of Moscow, Idaho, south into the Snake River and Salmon River canyons, and on Jim Creek Ridge in Oregon, as well as a very disjunct population in Jackson County, Oregon.

Elevations range from 5000 to 7000 feet (1500 to 2100 meters). *Calochortus nitidus* bears some resemblance to *C. longebarbatus*, but the nectary hairs are much longer, some with a yellow cast; the gland differs in being small, shallow, and centralized; dark bands of color extend almost halfway up the petal; and it lacks a bulbil in the basal leaf axil. *Calochortus nitidus* is a real garden charmer, showy because of its size at 20 to 30 centimeters. It is a tetraploid species native to dry habitats. It is interesting to speculate about this: as the wet, cool climate at the end of the Pleistocene gave way to today's drier regime, the changes may have favored tetraploid individuals, which are more robust and better able to handle extreme conditions. Most plants that grow above the Arctic Circle are tetraploids, while the lowest proportion of this type resides in stable tropical zones.

Calochortus persistens Ownbey

This species is known from a limited area around the Oregon-California border: one small population on Bald Mountain west of Talent, Oregon, and some in the mountains west of Yreka, California. It grows at around 6000 feet (1800 meters) elevation in scree zones, in mineral soils on summit slopes. I have found it quite amenable to cultivation in its native region. The large leaf (resembling that of a tulip) is conspicuous in late spring, but the plant does not flower until late June. The flowers may be white or strong pink. The nectary is composed of transverse bands of dendritic trichomes, with a row of dense yellow trichomes at the upper edge. Following seed set, the capsule becomes pendent, retaining the dried perianth—hence the species name. This trait, called marcescence, is unique in the genus.

Calochortus umpquaensis Fredricks

Probably no other calochortus is surrounded by as much confusion and controversy as is the Umpqua mariposa. A collection by Thomas Howell (no. 727, Douglas County near Roseburg, 8 June 1887) of *Calochortus howellii* set the stage for an unusual chain of events. Ownbey, Peck, and Chambers all cited the Umpqua Valley of Douglas County as the northernmost station of *C. howellii*. Reggie Miller, founder of the Glide Wildflower Show, was probably the first person to recognize the distinctness of the local plant. In the early 1950s Miller collected herbarium specimens of the Umpqua mariposa on soapstone upriver from the Talcott Ranch, sent them to a university (probably Oregon State at Corvallis), and made comparisons with *C. howellii*. When I talked with her in the early 1970s, she commented, "That's the one the botanists have been calling *Calochortus howellii*, but it's not." She noted the dark purple spot at the base of the petals and the drooping seed capsule, two to three times longer than that of *C. howellii*. Miller remarked, "The plant has a very different stature than that of *C. howellii*." If the botanists had paid

attention to her find, the plant's identity probably would have been set-
tled much sooner.

Calochortus umpquaensis is known from two population centers at
elevations from 2000 to 3670 feet (600 to 1100 meters) in southwestern
Oregon: one near Peel, and another which I discovered near Tiller.
(Howell's collection turned out to have been mislabeled as to location.)
It is restricted to ultramafic soils. The plant is 20 to 30 centimeters tall.
The flower is white with a blackish purple center (Peel population) or a
deep burgundy center (Tiller). The nectary consists of rows of transverse
dendritic trichomes, and the petal claw is marked with nectary guides.
This plant performs well in cultivation in its native region and should be
suitable for cold-winter areas.

Section II. *Mariposa*

Subsection 5. *Venusti*: Flowers campanulate and erect;
sepals lanceolate obtuse-attenuate; petals obovate to
cuneate; nectaries of varying shapes; capsules always
erect, three-angled; seeds flattened and set horizontally in
the capsule; bulbs with membranous tunics.

Calochortus argillosus (Hoover) Zebell & Fiedler

The clay mariposa is common in San Benito County and is also found in
the Santa Clara Valley and near Somersville in Contra Costa County,
California, usually growing in heavy, compacted clays. The plant
reaches 50 centimeters in height and bears one to four flowers. The erect
perianth is bell-shaped; the white to purple petals have a central red spot
and are sparsely hairy. The sublunate nectary is densely covered with
short hairs, and there is a longitudinal bar on the petal claw. This species
has done well in cultivation.

Calochortus catalinae Watson

Catalina mariposa, named for its occurrence on one of the Santa Barbara
Islands, also ranges from southern San Luis Obispo County south to San
Diego County in California. It is the common mariposa of the Hollywood
Hills and frequents open grassland on slopes. It responds well to cultivation, but it is somewhat tender, as one would expect from its altitudinal range (near sea level to 670 feet or 200 meters). The plants grow 40
centimeters or more tall. The flowers are white to lilac, upright, and not
fully reflexed. A large, diamond-shaped purple blotch surrounds the
green nectary. Scant long hairs are in the nectary region. The capsule is
three-winged, a trait unique in this section. Plants are bulbiliferous.

Calochortus dunnii Purdy

Dunn's mariposa ranges from the Vulcan Mountains of San Diego County, California, to mountains south of Tecate in northern Baja California, at elevations from 5000 to 5700 feet (1500 to 1700 meters). It flourishes on mafic gabbro soils, where it has little competition. It has performed poorly in cultivation, despite the fact that it shares much of its habitat with the easily grown *Calochortus albus*; *C. splendens* also grows here. The flowers are broadly campanulate and erect, white, with a reddish blotch above the yellow hairs attending the nectary. The nectary is U-shaped and densely matted with fine hairs.

Calochortus flexuosus Watson

The twining mariposa occurs from the southern California deserts to the southern tip of Nevada, in southwestern Utah, and in central Arizona, with a disjunct population in southwestern Colorado (Plate 43). It is primarily a species of desert and foothills at elevations from 3330 to 8330 feet (1000 to 2500 meters), but it can be cultivated elsewhere. It is unusual in the genus in its preference for alkaline soils. The 10- to 30-centimeter flower stems are usually twining in habit, supporting the plant on shrubs and grasses; otherwise, they are decumbent. The one to four flowers are campanulate and erect, white to lavender with lavender blotches above and below the rather square nectary. A transverse yellow band crosses the nectary, and short, scant, sinuous hairs appear to both sides of the nectary.

Calochortus leichtlinii Hooker

This species occurs at elevations from 4,000 to 13,300 feet (1200 to 4000 meters) in Jackson, Klamath, and Lake counties of southern Oregon and in the Sierra Nevada of California from Modoc County south to Tulare County. It is up to 40 centimeters tall, bearing one to five flowers. The petals are white to light lavender with a pink blush and a red blotch above the nectary. The nectary is ovate to triangular, with hairs that flow toward a central point and toward the petal claw. This species is separated from its close allies *C. luteus*, *C. superbus*, and *C. vestae* by its sagittate (arrowhead-shaped) anthers and inflated seed coat. It is reported to be difficult in cultivation.

Calochortus luteus Lindley

The yellow mariposa is native to California from Shasta County south to Tulare County in the Sierra Nevada foothills, and along the Coast Ranges from Mendocino County to Santa Barbara County; it also grows on Santa Cruz Island. It is a species of low to moderate elevations from sea level to 2330 feet (700 meters). It is not only widespread but also extremely numerous, turning the grassy hillsides yellow in early June. It is easy in cultivation in warmer climates and is grown commercially in

Holland, where the bulbs are held in storage until being planted in early winter to prevent their emerging too soon and succumbing to frost. A floriferous named variety, 'Golden Orb', has been introduced by Wim de Goede. The populations vary quite a bit in appearance. The plants can reach 50 centimeters but are usually shorter. The one to seven flowers range in color from white to the more usual bright butter yellow, with a central blotch of red. The nectary is more or less lunate (crescent-shaped) and has scant long hairs above.

Calochortus monanthus Ownbey

This species is probably extinct. Its entire habitat has been severely over-grazed, leaving only about 3 percent of the original native plant community intact. We have surveyed the area during the blooming period and have found no trace of this mariposa in more than two decades. E. L. Greene collected only about six plants in 1876, along the Shasta River near Yreka, California. They were described as being up to 30 centimeters tall and bulbiferous. The single flower had a pink perianth, narrowly bell-shaped; the 4.5-centimeter petals had a dark red chevron filled with dense hairlike processes. The form of the capsule is not known. The plant was probably restricted to the ultramafic section of the Shasta River, suggesting a narrow adaptation.

Calochortus palmeri Watson

Palmer's mariposa has a very narrow range in central to southern California, from San Luis Obispo County to the Tehachapi, San Bernardino, and San Jacinto mountains. It is a species of vernally moist meadows, often in association with *Pinus coulteri* (big-cone pine) and *P. jeffreyi* (Jeffrey's pine). It usually grows in granitic residual soils with some clay content at elevations from 4000 to 7330 feet (1200 to 2200 meters). It is rare in cultivation. This species reaches 30 to 50 centimeters tall and bears one to six flowers on the scape. The flower is broadly campanulate, white to rose lavender; the nectary is yellow and hairy. *Calochortus palmeri* is distinguished by its clavate hairs and white anthers from *C. splendens*, which has fungoid hairs and bluish anthers.

    Calochortus palmeri var. *munzii* Ownbey differs from the typical species in that it lacks basal bulblets and has paired rather than unequal pedicels and a nectary that is glabrous or purple haired. This variety is known from the San Jacinto Mountains at 4000 to 7330 feet (1200 to 2200 meters).

Calochortus simulans (Hoover) Munz

The San Luis Obispo mariposa is endemic to central San Luis Obispo County, California, in the Coast Ranges at elevations from 670 to 3670 feet (200 to 1100 meters). Grazing has degraded much of its range. It reaches 50 centimeters, bearing one to three large flowers. The petals are white, often with a lavender-pink flush externally, especially toward the tips. The nectary is situated in a red spot with a darker red-brown spot at the apex; the nectary hairs are folded at a 90° angle toward the apex. The species is adapted to ultramafic and numerous other soil types but is reported to be difficult to grow; success has been achieved in a bulb frame, kept dry in summer.

Calochortus splendens Bentham

This southerly species ranges from Colusa County, California, to lower Baja California, Mexico, from near sea level to 9330 feet (2800 meters) elevation. It is also found offshore on Santa Catalina Island and the Coronados Islands of Mexico. The northern and southern habitats are strikingly different. In its southern outpost, up to 30° north latitude, its associates are cardón cactus (*Pachycereus pringlei*), the boojum or cerio tree (*Fouquieria columnaris*), and several species of agaves. The northern outpost features open grassland to broken chaparral; here the plants are more robust. *Calochortus splendens* grows 30 to 60 centimeters tall. The pale to rich lavender petals have a purple spot near the nectary, which uniquely features fungoid (cauliflower-like) trichomes. In southern populations the nectary is absent in some plants. The species is rarely bulbiliferous, and the capsule is three-angled and linear. Difficult in cultivation, *C. splendens* has been hybridized with *C. superbus*, resulting in sterile offspring.

Calochortus striatus Parish

The alkali mariposa is found from southern Nevada to the Mohave Desert of southern California, at 2670 to 6330 feet (800 to 1900 meters) elevation. The finest populations for photography are at Ash Meadows, Nevada, where the alkaline salts cover the ground like heavy frost. This plant indeed tolerates extreme alkalinity and survives today in vernal salt meadows. The plant is 5 to 25 centimeters tall and lacks basal bulblets. The one to five erect, campanulate flowers are pale lavender with pronounced striations, hence the name. It has been grown, but it is very difficult.

Calochortus superbus J. Howell

This species has a disjunct northern outpost in Siskiyou County, California, northwest of Mud Lake, where it grows in a juniper-sagebrush woodland along with *Calochortus macrocarpus*. More generally, it is found from Shasta County south to Kern County and through the North Coast Ranges to Lake and Sonoma counties, at 670 to 5700 feet (200 to 1700 meters) elevation. It does remarkably well in cultivation. The plants reach 50 centimeters and have basal bulblets. Flower color is quite variable: white or bright yellow. The nectary hairs bend toward the petal apex. The shape of the gland varies as well, from a sharp chevron to a gentle crescent like that of *C. luteus*. These two species hybridize readily, and it can be difficult to distinguish the yellow forms of *C. superbus* from *C. luteus* where their ranges overlap; *C. superbus* tends to be taller and fewer-flowered and has narrower capsules.

Calochortus syntrophus Callahan

Callahan's mariposa is a very narrow endemic, known from The Cove in Shasta County, California, at 1747 feet (524 meters) elevation (Plate 44). I published its description in *Herbertia* in 1993. It is up to 40 centimeters tall, with one to four flowers. The white petals have a triangular reddish blotch above the nectary, which has dense orange hairs in a horseshoe shape, surrounded by scant longer hairs. The plants exhibit division of the main bulb and often grow in clumps, hence the name, which means "thriving together." This calochortus has proven difficult to grow, even near its native area.

Calochortus venustus Bentham

This well-known and amazingly variable Californian species ranges from El Dorado County to Kern County in the Sierra Nevada, and in the Coast Ranges from south of San Francisco Bay to Los Angeles County. Habitats include open grassland and mountain meadows from 1000 to 9000 feet (300 to 2700 meters) elevation. This plant tolerates a wide range of soils, including serpentine. It is reported to be difficult in cultivation outside its native range, but it is so attractive that efforts are made to please it throughout the gardening world. Depending on elevation and soil, it varies in height from 10 to 60 centimeters. The sepals are recurved, and the petals campanulate. Petal color varies from strong red without blotches (as found near Mount Pinos) to white, yellow, and purple. Gardeners have selected strains in brilliant sunset shades of orange overlaid with wine red. The petals are usually blotched midway and have a paler blotch near the apex. The nectary, the best diagnostic feature, is more or less square and densely covered with angled hairs that point toward the petal apex.

Calochortus vestae Purdy

This is a plant of northern coastal California, from Humboldt County to Napa and Sonoma counties, at 1000 to 9000 feet (300 to 2700 meters) elevation. It is a tetraploid species with large flowers and tall stature. The plants rise to 60 centimeters in height, bearing one to three flowers. These may be white to red or purplish; the petals are usually well penciled below the nectary guides and have a median blotch (usually red) above. The nectary is not depressed and is transverse and doubly lunate in shape. This species is closely related to *Calochortus superbus*, if not indeed a direct descendant of it, differentiated by its chromosome doubling. It is somewhat tolerant of cultivation.

Subsection 6. *Macrocarpi*: Flowers with sepals greatly exceeding the petals; nectary triangular with branched processes; bulbs with membranous tunics.

Calochortus macrocarpus Douglas

The Great Basin mariposa is widespread in the interior Northwest, from British Columbia to Montana, with scattered populations in Idaho, south through most of eastern Washington and Oregon to northeastern California. It occurs west of the Cascades in Jackson County, Oregon, and there is a small disjunct population in northern Nevada. It is adapted to loose volcanic soils, though it is found on ultramafic soils in the Blue Mountains of Oregon. It is often seen growing on hillsides among scattered conifers, or in the open on raised formations where drainage is especially good. Its elevation range is 4330 to 7000 feet (1300 to 2100 meters)—the latter on Steens Mountain, Oregon.

This is a big, showy calochortus, growing 50 centimeters or more tall. The one to five large flowers, held erect, are purple, often with a green median stripe and a dark, transverse purple band above the gland. The nectary is depressed, triangular to heart-shaped, with a fringed membrane enclosing the simply forked trichomes. The very long, narrow, pointed sepals are a prominent distinguishing trait. The capsule is linear-lanceolate, acuminate, and three-angled; the seeds are set horizontally in the capsule and are quite flat. The seeds do not germinate as readily as those of many other species, and the plant has proven difficult in cultivation.

Calochortus macrocarpus var. *maculosus* Nelson & McBride is found in northeastern Oregon at elevations from 2330 to 7330 feet (700 to 2200 meters) along the Snake, Grand Ronde, and Imnaha canyons, extending to Lewiston, Idaho. It is distinguished by the flower color, which is white to very pale lavender with a conspicuous reddish-purple crescent above the gland. The capsule is narrower than that of the typical species; the seeds lie at an angle of about 30° in the capsule and are thicker. This plant of hot canyons, rarely found on the flats, is also difficult to grow.

Subsection 7. *Nuttalliani*: Glands circular-depressed, mostly surrounded by a broad membrane; bulbs with membranous tunics; seeds flat; chromosome base number eight.

Calochortus aureus Watson

This exquisite calochortus is generally confined to alkaline soils at 2500 to 8330 feet (750 to 2500 meters) elevation within its range in central to southern Utah, northern Arizona, and northwestern New Mexico. The plants are usually small (to only 10 centimeters tall, rarely 20 centimeters). The one to three yellow flowers are broadly campanulate, with a strongly marked reddish-brown band crossing above the nectary (Plate 45). The hemispherical nectary has long clavate hairs above it.

Calochortus bruneaunis Nelson & McBride

Closely related to *Calochortus nuttallii*, this species ranges from southwestern Montana through eastern Idaho into extreme northwestern Utah, northern Nevada, and southeastern Oregon. Its habitat is juniper-pine-sagebrush woodland at 2,330 to 10,670 feet (700 to 3,200 meters) elevation. Though also widespread, it is no easier than its cousin in gardens outside its homeland, but it has performed well in a Pacific Northwest bulb frame, dry in summer. *Calochortus bruneaunis* is distinguished from *C. nuttallii* by the fact that the former has only a few (or no) short hairs near the nectary and a longitudinal reddish bar on the petal claw. The nectary is subcircular and slightly depressed, surrounded by a yellowish zone on the lower petal.

Calochortus clavatus Watson

The club-haired mariposa, among the more taxonomically complex species, is restricted to California. The typical species is distributed in the South Coast Ranges from Stanislaus County south to Los Angeles County, growing in grassland, chaparral, and forest (especially *Pinus attenuata* [knobcone pine]), often on ultramafic to alkaline soils. It is a lowland and foothill plant, from near sea level to 6000 feet (1800 meters). *Calochortus clavatus* is perhaps the tallest mariposa, to 60 centimeters or more. The one to four cup-shaped flowers are usually red-brown at the base and yellow with some banding above the gland; the petal hairs are distally clavate. The nectary is circular and surrounded by a fused membrane; its trichomes are dendritic.

Calochortus clavatus var. *avius* (Watson) Jepson is limited to El Dorado and Amador counties, a locality quite disjunct from other known populations. The largest populations are in the El Dorado National Forest. The plants are tall and robust (to 90 centimeters) and bear one to eight flowers. This has proven vigorous in cultivation.

Calochortus clavatus var. *gracilis* Ownbey, the slender mariposa, comes from the San Gabriel Mountains in Los Angeles County, at elevations from sea level to 3330 feet (1000 meters); this is another good candidate for the garden. It is of smaller stature (to 30 centimeters) and bears only three or four flowers on slender stems. The petal hairs are scant, and there is a reddish-brown line above the small, shallow nectary.

Calochortus clavatus subsp. *pallidus* (Hoover) Munz, by contrast, is a very tall mariposa (to 90 centimeters). Its epithet comes from the light yellow color of the petals. The petal hairs are subclavate and the nectary hairs not strongly branching. Its homeland is in San Luis Obispo County from the La Panza Range to the Tembler and Caliente ranges.

Calochortus clavatus subsp. *recurvifolius* (Hoover) Munz is a coastal plant, found mostly on the ocean bluffs of the Hearst Ranch in San Luis Obispo County. Its epithet refers to the strongly recurved leaves. (Some populations of *C. kennedyi* also exhibit strongly recurved leaves, especially in windy, exposed sites.) It is relatively short, to 20 centimeters, and does well in cultivation.

Calochortus concolor (Baker) Purdy

This species occurs from the San Bernardino Mountains of southern California south to Baja California, at elevations from 2000 to 8700 feet (600 to 2600 meters). It is commonly found in grassland and chaparral, where the tall (to 60 centimeters) plants grow up through the shrubs, and in pine forests. In the southern part of its range it is associated with cacti and boojum trees and co-occurs with *Calochortus splendens* in decomposed granitics and volcanic residuals. Like all these desert species, it is problematic to grow. *Calochortus concolor* bears one to seven erect flowers. The petals are flushed reddish on the exterior and are yellow within, with long, dense hairs above the nectary. The nectary is small and subconical, with unbranched trichomes. The petal claws usually bear a reddish-brown blotch.

Calochortus excavatus Greene

The Inyo mariposa is restricted to Inyo and Mono counties in northeastern California, where its survival is threatened by habitat degradation caused by grazing and groundwater extraction. It is especially abundant during heavy rainfall years in the Alabama Hills near Lone Pine, and also in vernally moist meadows. It favors decomposed granitic and residual volcanic soils. It has been very difficult to cultivate here in the open, but Jane McGary (personal communication) has flowered it in the moisture-controlled conditions of the bulb frame. The plants, to 30 centimeters tall, have one to eight flowers which are often arranged some distance apart along the scape. This species is distinguished from the similar *C. nuttallii* by the fact that its basal leaf does not wither before anthesis (opening of flowers). The flowers vary from white to lavender, with a smoky blue to reddish-brown median stripe on the outside of the petals. The nectary is transversely oval to subcircular with strongly branching yellow trichomes. Scant, long reddish-brown hairs surround it.

Calochortus invenustus Greene

This species has an unusually disjunct distribution: Santa Clara County just south of San Francisco Bay, San Diego County in far southern California, the southern Sierra Nevada, and the Bodie Hills of Nevada. It grows at 5,000 to 10,000 feet (1500 to 3000 meters) elevation in sagebrush-juniper woodland, chaparral, and pine-fir (*Pinus-Abies*) forest. The plants may attain 40 centimeters and bear as many as eight flowers. These are white tinged with lilac to strong lavender, usually purple below the nectary and with scant yellow hairs above it. The nectary is circular, with a fringed membrane. It is distinguished from *Calochortus nuttallii* by its narrower, more wedge-shaped petals. It is difficult to cultivate outside its native range.

Calochortus kennedyi Porter

Kennedy's mariposa is among the great desiderata of keen gardeners, who are enchanted by its brilliant floral hues but frustrated by the challenge of growing it (Plate 46). It grows in the border area of the United States and Mexico, from Mount Pinos, California, through the southern California desert and Arizona to Sonora, Chihuahua, and Coahuila states of Mexico, as far east as Big Bend National Park in Texas. It is typically a plant of boulder-strewn outwash plains and ridgetops of shattered rock. The bulbs are very drought-tolerant and can remain dormant for as much as eight years in the desert. The plants often refrain from sprouting until the soil has become saturated. This is among the most adaptable species in regard to soil type and elevation (2000 to 8330 feet or 600 to 2500 meters). Even though it occurs in areas with both winter and summer rainfall, it is difficult to manage in cultivation outside its native range.

The plants vary in height according to elevation, from less than 10 centimeters on mountain summits to 40 centimeters in more protected areas. The one to seven erectly poised flowers may be dark red, scarlet, orange, or yellow; the yellow form has been invalidly called variety *munzii*. Populations in Arizona often exhibit all three color phases, while the red to orange forms seem to predominate in Mexico. I have been unable to locate the species in New Mexico. The petals bear a dark blotch around the gland and scant hairs above the nectary. The nectary is depressed and round to transversely oval with a membrane (fused trichomes); the trichomes are simple to forked.

Calochortus nuttallii Torrey

The eastern range of the sego lily, state flower of Utah, reaches 102° west longitude and thus parallels that of *Calochortus kennedyi* for the easternmost extension of the genus in the United States. This species is found in the western parts of North and South Dakota, in eastern Montana, most of Nebraska, western Colorado, extreme northwestern New Mexico, most of Utah, and northwestern Arizona, with several disjunct populations in Nevada. It is a plant of prairie and rolling grassland at 2330 to 7330 feet (700 to 2200 meters) elevation, well adapted to colder climates, but I have found it a challenge to grow in mild southern Oregon. The plant varies from 10 to 40 centimeters in height and bears one to four erect, campanulate flowers of white, lilac, or magenta. The petals are yellow toward the base, with a reddish, irregular band above the nectary. Scattered subclavate (round-tipped) hairs surround the nectary, which is circular with a membranous sheath enclosing dense, short, branched trichomes.

Calochortus panamintensis (Ownbey) Reveal

The Panamint mariposa is found in the high desert mountains around Death Valley, California, growing on metamorphic complexes and decomposed granitics. Unlike its relatives Calochortus bruneaunis and C. aureus, this species enjoys high elevations—up to 10,670 feet (3200 meters). At lower elevations in protected valleys, plants may reach 50 centimeters tall, but on the summit colonies often flower at only 5 centimeters. The flowers are white and, unlike other members of the section, have no markings above the nectary; the petal claw is reddish-brown. This rare plant can be assumed to be a great challenge for the gardener.

Subsection 8. Gunnisoniani: Flowers with transverse, oblong nectary, narrow gland membrane, and distally branched gland-tipped hairs on the petal; seeds thin with hexagonally reticulate coats; bulbs with membranous coats.

Calochortus ambiguus (Jones) Ownbey

Found mostly in Arizona, this species has a few populations in extreme southwestern New Mexico; it may also extend into Mexico, since its known range is on the international border. A plant of higher elevations from 3330 to 9000 feet (1000 to 2700 meters), it is adapted to interior climates with cold, dry winters. It does well in cultivation where continental climates prevail, but it has been difficult in milder areas. Growing to 50 centimeters in height, it blooms in April and May, producing two to five flowers per stem. The petals may be white, pink, or lavender, with a dark lavender band above the nectary. A green zone surrounds the subcircular to transversely lunate nectary, which is covered with yellow, distally enlarged, branching, gland-tipped hairs.

Calochortus gunnisonii Watson

This species, closely related to Calochortus ambiguus, occupies the more northern part of the Rocky Mountain region, from extreme southwestern South Dakota to central Montana and south through Wyoming, Colorado, eastern Utah, far eastern Arizona, and central New Mexico. It flowers from June to August, depending on elevation—it occurs from 3,330 to 10,000 feet (1000 to 3000 meters) in elevation. It is adapted to long, cold, dry winters and hot summers with some rainfall, and does not do well without a sharp winter dormancy. This tall (to 60 centimeters) plant bears three to five flowers of various colors: white to purple, or yellow. It is distinguished from *C. ambiguus* by its acute anthers and its nectary, which is wider in the transverse direction, with small, simple trichomes below the nectary.

Section III. *Cyclobothra*

Subsection 9. *Weediani*: Scape slender, tall, branched; not bulbiliferous; flowers erect; petals densely bearded; nectaries slightly depressed with membranously united trichomes.

Calochortus plummerae Green

Plummer's mariposa is found in mountains and outwash plains of Los Angeles, San Bernardino, and Riverside counties in southern California, from 1670 to 6330 feet (500 to 1900 meters) elevation. It cannot tolerate extreme cold, but it has done well west of the Cascade Range in Oregon. The plants are tall, especially as they age, with the branching scape reaching 50 centimeters or more. The two to six flowers vary from white through pale pinks to dark rose. The broadly ovate petals are rarely fimbriate (fringed), densely bearded with yellow hairs, and glabrous (smooth) toward the distal end. The gland is subconical, with hairs that are more or less united at the base.

Calochortus obispoensis Lemmon

The San Luis mariposa is endemic in San Luis Obispo County, California, usually on ultramafic soils at 330 to 1670 feet (100 to 500 meters) elevation; however, near Arroyo Grande it grows on decomposed sandstone. The plant, to 40 centimeters tall, can produce from 2 to 70 flowers; I once observed a plant with almost 100 blossoms in a year after a severe fire—a record for the genus. The greatly reduced (10 to 20 millimeters), heavily bearded petals make this species unique (Plate 47). The petals are orange with reddish-brown tips, densely bearded with yellow hairs over the lower half and with reddish-brown hairs to the petal apex. The nectary is subconical and is hollow inside, with active nectar-producing glands. This rare plant has not succeeded in gardens.

Calochortus tiburonensis A. J. Hill

This species is known only from Ring Mountain in Marin County, California, on ultramafic soils. Its remaining habitat has been set aside as a preserve. Plants range from 10 to 50 centimeters in height, depending on age. The one to eight flowers are erect and bell-shaped. The hairy petals are light yellow-green, dotted with purple-brown, oblanceolate in shape, with margins ciliate to the apex. The nectary is transverse, sharply crescent-shaped, with papillose membranes; the plant is unlike any other in this section and exhibits similarities with section *Calochortus*.

Calochortus weedii Wood

This species ranges from western Riverside and San Diego counties in southern California into Baja California, at 1670 to 6330 feet (500 to 1900 meters) elevation. It is another tall one (to 60 centimeters) and quite variable. The two to six erect flowers are bell-shaped. The yellow-orange petals are flecked with reddish brown and are densely hairy, often to the apex. This apical hair and the fringed petal margin differentiate it from *Calochortus plummerae*. The nectary is circular, slightly depressed, and nearly hairless. In cultivation it has proven short-lived; it may bloom for two or three years and then perish.

Calochortus weedii var. *vestus* Purdy, from the Santa Lucia Range in Monterey County and near Santa Barbara, differs from the typical *C. weedii* in having rather square petals, densely bearded, with conspicuous reddish-brown hairs at the petal apex. The nectary is longitudinally oblong-conical.

Calochortus weedii var. *peninsularis* Ownbey is found on granitic and metamorphic soil complexes in the western foothills (1670 to 2000 feet or 500 to 600 meters) of the Sierra San Pedro Martir of Baja California, south to 30° north latitude. It is distinguished by its pale yellow petals which lack fringe and are scantily bearded below the midpoint; the color marks it as distinct from *C. plummerae*.

Calochortus weedii var. *intermedius* Ownbey is restricted to Orange County, California, from near sea level to 2330 feet (700 meters). Its petals are rounded with a conspicuous fringe at the apex and are often reddish at the tips on the reverse. The petal claw is deep red.

Subsection 10. *Ghiesbreghtiani*: Mesoamerican species ranging from northern Chihuahua (Mexico) to Guatemala; rarely bulbiliferous in the leaf axils; flowers small, campanulate, erect; nectaries present or lacking, or found on both petals and sepals.

Calochortus exilis Painter

Limited to Hidalgo state, Mexico, this is a plant of high elevations from 8,330 to 10,000 feet (2500 to 3000 meters), at home with firs (*Abies*). Winter frosts are common where it grows, but they are of short duration;

there is some snow. This is definitely a species for the rock garden. A short (to 10 centimeters) stem bears two to four flowers. The petals are white to light yellow, glabrous except near the base, where they are densely bearded with short hairs. The nectary is inconspicuous, but nectariferous tissue is present. This species differs from *Calochortus venustulus* in its short stature, longer and narrower basal leaf, smaller flowers, and short, wide capsule.

Calochortus fuscus Schultes

Known only from the district of Temascaltepec in México state, Mexico, at 3000 to 7670 feet (900 to 2300 meters) elevation, *Calochortus fuscus* Schultes (synonym *C. hintoni*) is common in oak and pine forest on volcanic residual soils. This too would be suitable for rock gardens. The plant is flexuous, or twining, with a branching scape to 30 centimeters. The two to four flowers are erect, dark red, and glabrous except for a dense beard near the base. The nectary, though present, is inconspicuous.

Calochortus ghiesbreghtii Watson

Spottily distributed, this plant occurs in the mountains of Hidalgo, Querétaro, and Chiapas states in Mexico, and after a large gap in the genus's southernmost station in Guatemala. It is an unusual calochortus in that it grows well on limestones. It has adapted to a subtropical climate with little winter frost, even within its altitudinal range from 4000 to 8700 feet (1200 to 2600 meters); it does well in mild-climate gardens. The two to four flowers on a 40-centimeter stem are white (rarely yellow), broadly campanulate, and held erect on elongate pedicels (Plate 48). The nectary is an inverted V with a deeply laciniate membrane edged with short hairs. The anthers are linear-lanceolate and apiculate.

Calochortus ownbeyi (ined.) McDonald v. Patterson, Ness

This species (see Ness, 1989) is another subtropical calochortus, found in Mexico from Chihuahua to Jalisco states, growing on granitic substrates near Puerto Vallarta and on volcanics elsewhere. It associates with pines and oaks in open forest at 1670 to 8330 feet (500 to 2500 meters) elevation. Stems to 35 centimeters bear two to five flowers. The cauline leaves are small and short, and bulbils are produced in the leaf axils. The flowers are white, with long white hairs to the midpoint of the petals (Plate 49).

Calochortus pringlei Robinson

Restricted to the Mexican states of Morelos and Puebla at elevations from 7000 to 8000 feet (2100 to 2400 meters), this plant does well in cultivation in milder climates but must be protected from frost. Because its flowers are erect (despite Ownbey's description of them as "nodding") and on the basis of characteristics of the gland, I am placing it in subsection *Ghiesbreghtiani* in contrast to other authors' assignment of it to the *Barbati*. On a scape to 40 centimeters, it flowers in August and September; the flowers, usually two, are dark red with yellow or red hairs (Plate 50). The gland is lunate, and the petal apex serrate.

Calochortus venustulus Greene

The range of this species is entirely in Mexico, from northern Chihuahua to the Federal District, at 1,670 to 11,700 feet (500 to 3500 meters) elevation. In the northern part of its range it experiences winter temperatures down to –10°F (–23°C), and it is adapted to a wide range of soils; not surprisingly, it does rather well in cultivation. A plant of moderate height (20 to 35 centimeters), it bears two to five white to bright yellow flowers, erect and 2 to 4 centimeters in diameter (Plate 51). The petals are densely hairy to the midpoint or beyond. The gland is longitudinally oblong. Rare individuals produce bulbils in the leaf axils. *Calochortus venustulus* var. *imbricus* Reveal & Hess differs in having scalelike trichomes covering the petal surface.

Subsection 11. *Barbati*: Flowers nodding; petals bearded; often bulbiliferous in upper leaf axils; bulb coats fibrous-reticulate.

Calochortus balsensis G. Mendoza

This plant is restricted to the coastal mountains of Guerrero state, where it is reported from Chilpancingo, in a tropical climate. It is best seen on steep outcrops or among cacti and agaves, situations which protect it from herbivores. Most of its habitat is overgrazed, so it is rare on the meadows where it once grew. It is also collected and sold as a cutflower. It performs well in cultivation, blooming in August and September, but it must be protected from any frost. *Calochortus balsensis* has very glaucous foliage. The stems, to 60 centimeters tall, bear two to four globose yellow flowers, 3 to 4 centimeters long (Plate 52). The petals have yellow hairs with reddish spotted bases; the gland is depressed and triangular.

Calochortus barbatus (Humboldt, Bonpland, & Kunth) Painter

The type species for this section ranges from southern Chihuahua in the Sierra Madre Occidental to the transverse volcanic belt of central Mexico and Oaxaca. It occurs at elevations from 5000 to 9700 feet (1500 to 2900 meters), usually on volcanic soils in pine, fir, and oak forest. It does well in cultivation and is adapted to cooler climates. The plants, to 40 centimeters tall, bear two or more campanulate, pendent flowers. The sparsely bearded petals are yellow to orange. The nectary is slightly depressed, subcircular, and hairless. The petal tips are undulate and serrate; the three-angled capsule is erect. *Calochortus barbatus* subsp. *chihua-*

huanus Painter, confined mostly to Chihuahua state, differs in that the petals are purplish, the sepals yellow, and the petal margins hairy.

Calochortus marcellae Nelson

This limestone endemic occurs at elevations from 3,330 to 10,000 feet (1000 to 3000 meters), from Nuevo León state to San Luis Potosí state in Mexico. Ownbey (1940) annotated early collections of it under the name *Calochortus spatulatus*. The erect plants, to 50 centimeters tall, bear one to three flowers. The petals are dark carmine, sparsely to densely bearded above the nectary, which is round and bordered by basally fused hairs. Bulbils are produced prolifically in the leaf axils.

Calochortus nigrescens Ownbey

This species is reported from "Los Tepates, Puebla." John Erwin and I were unable to identify this town or site, but we finally found *Calochortus nigrescens* in the Sierra de Tamazulapan in northern Oaxaca (Plate 53). It is a small plant (to 10 centimeters) of open, rocky, dry meadows, growing with cacti and oaks at around 6700 feet (2000 meters) elevation. The one or two nodding flowers are deep reddish black and densely hairy. The nectary is circular, and the plant is quite bulbiliferous. It has done well in mild-climate gardens.

Subsection 12. *Purpurei*: Plants erect; most bear bulbils in the leaf axils; stems leafy; flowers nodding; petals sparsely bearded; bulb tunics fibrous-reticulate.

Calochortus cernuus Painter

This uncommon species, known only from the Mexican state of Morelos in the Sierra de Tepoxtlan (6700 to 9330 feet or 2000 to 2800 meters), near Cuernavaca, is clearly related to *Calochortus spatulatus*. The only major difference is its lack of the nectary hairs usually seen in the latter species. It grows to 40 centimeters in height, bearing two pendent purplish flowers which are yellow within. The petals are fringed. The nectary appears as a blotch, a small, central region of nectary tissue, and is without hairs. I have not heard of it being cultivated.

Calochortus foliosus Ownbey

This is apparently a rare species, reported only from Campanario near Morelia in México state. I was unable to find it at the type locality, though *Calochortus purpureus* was abundant there. From Ownbey's description, it is very similar to *C. purpureus*, if not indeed identical with it. The plant is said to be very leafy, hence the specific epithet, and to grow to 40 centimeters tall, with two bluish flowers.

Calochortus hartwegii Bentham

This species is distinguished from all others in this subsection by its robust stature and large flowers. Its range is from Zacatecas to Aguascalientes, Nayarit, and Jalisco states in Mexico, at 6700 to 8330 feet (2000 to 2500 meters) elevation. It grows on volcanic residual soils and is often common in scabland habitats, pine and oak woodland, and open fields. (It grows with the rare Martinez pinyon [*Pinus maximartinezii*] in the mountains of Jalisco.) Its climate is subtropical, with only mild nighttime frosts, and it is a choice candidate for warmer gardens. Plants range in height from 20 to 40 centimeters and are stout, bearing two or three large (to 5 centimeters long), pendent flowers, which may be purple, reddish purple, yellow, or greenish purple (Plate 54). The petals are usually glabrous or may have scant hairs below the midpoint and a longitudinal line of short hairs. The subtriangular gland is naked and not depressed. Bulbils are not produced.

Calochortus purpureus (Humboldt, Bonpland, & Kunth) Painter

This woodland calochortus grows among pines and oaks in the Mexican states of Chihuahua, Guanajuato, Jalisco, and Oaxaca, where it is especially abundant in the western transvolcanic belt on old lava flows at 6,700 to 10,000 feet (2000 to 3000 meters) elevation. It is intermediate in size (50 centimeters) between *Calochortus spatulatus* and *C. hartwegii*. The two to four pendent, purplish to purplish-brown flowers are usually yellow within. The petals are more or less ciliate and sparsely bearded toward the apex. The nectary is subcircular and naked. It produces many bulbils in the leaf axils.

Calochortus spatulatus Watson

This species has an enormous range in Mexico, occurring in the Sierra Madre Occidental from Chihuahua to Guerrero, at 6,700 to 10,000 feet (2000 to 3000 meters) elevation. It may be so widespread because it reproduces freely by both bulbils and seed. It is very similar to *Calochortus cernuus* in size and general appearance. Stems to 50 centimeters bear one to four pendent flowers of purple to reddish purple. The inner petal surfaces have scant hairs; the nectary is round and surrounded by trichomes. It is a good candidate for cultivation, and propagation material is easily obtained.

Cultivation

Calochortus can be propagated from seeds, bulbils, bulblets, or tissue culture. The seeds usually require some moist stratification (chilling, not freezing) for optimal uniform germination. The chilling period varies according to the origin of the species: those from mild coastal climates require four to six weeks, while inland species may need several months. The best results are obtained from seed of the current year, planted in fall. Newly germinated seedlings are grasslike; the seed coat usually hangs onto the tip of the emerging cotyledon. When germination occurs outdoors and frost can be expected, the pots of seedlings should be moved into a frost-free place to grow on. Germination is epigeal in sections *Cyclobothra* and *Mariposa*: the cotyledons rise above the surface with the seed coats at their tips. It is hypogeal in section *Calochortus*, where the seed remains below ground as a food reserve and a single grasslike leaf protrudes from it. Continue to water seedlings as long as they appear green and growing, and do not "bake" them afterward but keep them cool and rather dry; use clean water free from pathogens.

Some species produce sizable bulbs the first year from seed, but in others the bulbs may be so small that they are hard to pick out. In the latter case it is best to grow them on in the seed pot for a second year, providing adequate nutrients in the form of a little bone meal or a low-nitrogen soluble fertilizer. The young bulbs are typically brown, narrow, and elongated; the smallest ones are hard to distinguish from peat fibers in the compost.

Some species increase well by division or offsets from the bulb and can be separated when they are dug or repotted. The bulbils that form in the leaf axils of some species can be collected and planted just like seeds, but the resulting plants will flower sooner than seedlings. Bulbil cultivation is also useful to maintain select strains, since the bulbils are asexually produced.

Depending on species, available moisture, and nutrition, calochortus grown from seed can reach the blooming stage in two to six years. The grower can reduce this time by several years by extending the time during which water and nutrients are supplied. Water quality is important: chlorinated water is not well tolerated, and water containing a high concentration of microorganisms may induce damping off or other fungal damage to roots or bulbs.

Only a few species are currently available from bulb suppliers, but rising interest in bulbs and in unusual plants generally should stimulate more commercial production. The extended period necessary to produce flowering-size bulbs, coupled with the fact that many calochortus species are not very cold hardy, has limited growers' motivation to work with the genus. *Calochortus luteus* and *C. albus* are presently on the market at moderate cost.

Conservation should always be the highest priority when one contemplates collecting seeds, bulbils, or bulbs in the wild. Bulbs may be collected where their habitat is about to be destroyed by road building, development, or water impoundment projects. No more than 10 percent of the seed should be collected from a population, and the collector should carefully plant a few seeds while working.

Once bulbs of some size have developed, they may be planted out in the open where the climate is suitable, or in a bulb frame where it is not. Shade should be provided for most coastal species being grown in hot interior climates. Conversely, interior species need full sun when grown in coastal regions. Most calochortus are pioneer plants which need open soil conditions for optimal growth. Slightly acidic, sandy loam soils are best, and drainage is of the utmost importance. Avoid strong fertilizers, organic or otherwise; a half-strength solution of low-nitrogen fertilizer, applied while the plants are in growth, is adequate.

The bulbs are eaten by rodents such as gophers, mice, voles, and rats and must be protected from these tunneling pests. Deer and rabbits are fond of the plants, especially the flowers and seed capsules.

Gardeners outside western North America usually want to know about the adaptability of these plants, but it is difficult to predict how a given species will respond to conditions outside its native range. The species descriptions above note which species are known to be frost-tender, but beyond this, management of water availability may be more crucial than temperature to the survival of the plants. Virtually all calochortus experience a long annual period of dry dormancy: those from warm regions and low elevations get it in summer, and those from high elevations and monsoon (summer-rainfall) climates get it in winter. In Holland, growers prevent frost damage to calochortus by keeping the bulbs in temperature-controlled rooms until very late fall and then planting them out in their sandy fields; the late planting and consequent late emergence protect the plants from Holland's cold winter conditions. Few gardeners, however, can provide this kind of care. Finally, subtropical species flower in August and September and must be protected from any frost during the winter.

Soil media for optimal growth are usually half organic material such as leafmold or sphagnum peat (or a combination of these) and half coarse, clean sand. This formula has been used by the noted grower, Boyd Kline, with great success in southern Oregon. The only caveat is that this mixture offers little protection for the bulbs in subzero temperatures; sand is a poor insulator, and the bulb beds should be covered with a deep mulch in cold areas. If the bulbs are being grown in pots, these can be moved into a frost-free building for the winter.

Ultramafic species do well on their favored substrate because of its fungicidal properties, and growing them may require a sterile soil medium. Very low levels of mycorrhizal activity are recorded on these soils. A number of serpentine dwellers are also accumulators of heavy metals, especially nickel complexes. In short, ultramafic and, to some degree, mafic soils restrict plant prosperity. These soils tend to be sterile, lacking the calcium and many trace minerals needed for optimal growth. The characteristics of the soils limit the intrusion of competitive plants that cannot survive there, so calochortus and other plants (often bulbous) with low nutritional requirements tend to dominate there.

Soil depth is also important: the medium should be 25 to 30 centimeters deep. This allows the bulbs to "draw down" to the optimal perennating depth. Individual plants of some species can live as much as 60 years, so consider this when planting them in the garden.

The placement of calochortus in gardens is largely determined by the available drainage. Very few species can tolerate constantly moist sites, especially during their dormant season in summer. The rock garden is obviously suitable in terms of soil, but many calochortus are so tall that they may not be pleasing among the mats and cushions of this setting; they are better planted near shrubs of similar height. In nature most species grow among grasses and other plants that lend their stems some support.

Especially in Britain, many gardeners grow calochortus as specimens in pots, where their water regime can be carefully managed. The growing area should be very well ventilated but protected from strong winds, since these plants will not have the support of grasses and shrubs that they enjoy in the wild. The pots should be as deep as possible, since calochortus bulbs can pull themselves down to depths of 20 centimeters or more. Plunging the pots in sand to the rim helps to maintain a proper level of residual moisture and coolness during the dormant period and prevents the bulbs from becoming desiccated; remember that even though their native habitats may experience no summer rainfall, the bulbs are far below the soil surface, well insulated from the blazing summer sun.

Bibliography

Albee, B. J., et al. 1988. *Atlas of the Vascular Plants of Utah*. Salt Lake City: Utah Museum of Natural History and University of Utah.

Anderson, E. 1968. "Calochortus." *Lily Yearbook* 31: 54–56. Kew: Royal Horticultural Society.

Balls, E. K. 1963. "Californian Liliaceae." *Lily Yearbook* 26: 38–48. Kew: Royal Horticultural Society.

Beauchamp, R. M. 1986. *A Flora of San Diego County, California*. National City, California: Sweetwater Press.

Brock, R. 1988. *Research Report:* Calochortus greenei, *Habitat and Threat Analysis*. Woodland Hills, California: Hardman Foundation.

Brooks, R. R. 1987. *Serpentine and Its Vegetation*. Portland: Dioscorides.

Caicco, S. L. 1992. Calochortus nitidus: *Species Management Guide*. Boise: Idaho Department of Fish and Game.

Callahan, F. T. 1993. "A New Species of *Calochortus* (Liliaceae-Tulipeae) from Shasta County, California." *Herbertia* 49: 20–27.

Chickering, Allen. 1938. *Growing Calochortus.* Rancho Santa Ana Botanic Gardens, Horticultural Monographs, 7. Rancho Santa Ana, California.

Coleman, R. G. 1977. "North American Ophidites." *DOGAMI Bulletin* 95: 95–183.

Cronquist, A., et al. 1977. *Intermountain Flora: Vascular Plants of the Intermountain West.* Vol. 6, *Monocotyledons.* New York: Columbia University Press.

Fahn, A. 1956. "On the Structure of Floral Nectaries." *Botanical Gazette* 1956: 464–470.

Farwig, S., and V. Girand. 1987a. "A New Species of *Calochortus.*" *Fremontia* 15(2): 18.

Farwig, S., and V. Girand. 1987b. "*Calochortus raichei,* a New Species from California." *Herbertia* 43: 2–9.

Fredricks, N. A. 1989. "Morphological Comparison of *Calochortus howellii* and a New Species from Southwestern Oregon." *Systematic Botany* 14: 7–15.

Godfrey, R., and F. T. Callahan. 1988. "A New *Calochortus* from Douglas County, Oregon." *Phytologia* 65(5): 216–219.

Henderson, D. M., et al. 1977. *Endangered and Threatened Plants of Idaho.* University of Idaho Forest, Wildland, and Range Experiment Station, Contribution 73. Moscow, Idaho.

Hill, A. J. 1973. "A Distinctive New *Calochortus* (Liliaceae) from Marin County, California." *Madroño* 22: 101–103.

Hitchcock, C. L., and A. Cronquist. 1973. *Flora of the Pacific Northwest.* Seattle: University of Washington Press.

Hoover, R. F. 1944. "*Mariposa,* a Neglected Genus." *Leaflets of Western Botany* 4: 1–4.

Howell, J. T. 1985. *Marin Flora.* Berkeley: University of California Press.

Kearney, T. H., and R. H. Peebles. 1951. *Arizona Flora.* Berkeley: University of California Press. See also *Supplement,* 1960.

Kruckeberg, A. R. 1984a. "California Serpentine." *Fremontia* 11(4): 11–17.

Kruckeberg, A. R. 1984b. "The Flora of California's Serpentine." *Fremontia* 11(5): 3–10.

Lloyd, R. M., and R. S. Mitchell. 1973. *A Flora of the White Mountains, California and Nevada.* Berkeley: University of California Press.

McClaran, M. 1979. "Chromosome Numbers for *Calochortus tiburonensis* (Liliaceae)." *Madroño* 26: 191.

McDonald, H. P. 1996. "The Genus *Calochortus* in California, Part I." *Fremontia* 24(3): 25–28.

McDonald, H. P. 1997. "The Genus *Calochortus* in California, Part II." *Fremontia* 25(1): 20–25.

McGregor, R. L., et al. 1977. *Atlas of the Flora of the Great Plains.* Ames: Iowa State University Press.

McGregor, R. L., et al. 1986. *Flora of the Great Plains.* Topeka: University Press of Kansas.

Mozingo, H. N., and M. Williams. 1980. *Threatened and Endangered Plants of Nevada.* Reno: U.S. Forest Service and Bureau of Land Management.

Munz, P. A., and D. D. Keck. 1968. *A California Flora.* Berkeley: University of California Press.

Nesom, L. L. 1983. "New Species of *Calochortus* (Liliaceae) and *Linum* (Linaceae) from Northern Mexico." *Madroño* 50: 250–254.

Ness, B. D. 1989. "Seed Morphology and Taxonomic Relationships in *Calochortus* (Liliaceae)." *Systematic Botany* 14: 495–505.

Ownbey, M. 1940. "A Monograph of the Genus *Calochortus*." *Annals of the Missouri Botanic Garden* 27: 371–561.

Peck, M. E. 1954. "A New *Calochortus* from Oregon." *Leaflets of Western Botany* 7/8: 190–192.

Purdy, C. 1901. "A Revision of the Genus *Calochortus*." *Proceedings of the California Academy of Sciences*, 3rd ser., *Botany* 11: 107–158.

Rzedowski, J. 1978. *Vegetación de México*. Mexico City: Editorial Limusa.

Schmidt, M. G. 1976. "Calochortus." *Pacific Horticulture* 37(4).

Siddall, J. L., K. L. Chambers, and D. H. Wagner. 1979. *Rare, Threatened, and Endangered Vascular Plants in Oregon: An Interim Report*. Salem: Oregon Natural Area Preserves Advisory Committee to the State Land Board.

Smith, G. L., and C. R. Wheeler. 1992. *A Flora of the Vascular Plants of Mendocino County, California*. San Francisco: University of San Francisco.

Watson, S. 1879. "Contributions to American Botany, IX: Revision of the North American Liliaceae." *Proceedings of the American Academy of Arts and Sciences* 14.

Weber, W. A. 1967. *Rocky Mountain Flora*. Boulder: University of Colorado Press.

Yanovsky, E. 1936. *Food Plants of the American Indians*. USDA Miscellaneous Publications 237. Washington, D.C.: Government Printing Office.

Zebell, R. K., and P. L. Fiedler. 1992. "A New Combination in *Calochortus* (Liliaceae)." *Madroño* 39(4): 306.

– 5 –

The Genus *Erythronium*

MOLLY M. GROTHAUS

Erythroniums, spring-blooming members of the lily family, are beautiful additions to the partially shaded areas of the garden. They thrive in humus-rich soil. The reflexed flowers are carried on bare stems that rise above a pair of leaves. The leaves themselves are plain green in some species but spotted or mottled with red and silver in others.

Therein lies a tale. All across Europe and on into China and Japan, and in North America east of the Rocky Mountains, erythronium foliage is spotted or plain green. West of the Rocky Mountains, it is either mottled (marbled) or plain green. Asa Gray, when he was Harvard Professor of Natural History in 1842, was the first to recognize the relationship between the flora of eastern North America and those of China and Japan. He hypothesized a uniform Arcto-Tertiary forest which stretched across much of the northern part of the world. This forest was later broken up by continental drift, glaciation, and climate change that left the East Coast species of *Erythronium* (with spotted foliage) far separated from their nearest relatives, which range from China and Japan across the intervening countries to Europe.

The best-known Old World species is *Erythronium dens-canis*, the so-called dogtooth violet, which has spotted leaves and is the only European species. Other common names are trout lily, fawn lily, and adder's tongue. This species is shorter than most of the western North American species and blooms a little earlier. A number of named forms differ in the color of their flowers and to some extent in their blooming date. Among these is 'Snowflake', which is white with blue anthers and is among the earliest to bloom. Other named forms include 'Franz Hals', light reddish violet; 'Lilac Wonder', lavender; 'Pink Perfection', light, clear pink; 'Pink Beauty', slightly darker pink; 'Rose Beauty', rosy pink; and 'Purple King', mid-purple. *Erythronium caucasicum* is a white-flowered plant of the Caucasus and northwestern Iran; *E. sibericum* is found mainly in the Altai Mountains of Siberia. *Erythronium japonicum*, formerly considered a variety of *E. dens-canis*, has for some time been elevated to species status; it has larger flowers which are light purple.

In western North America, some erythroniums have green leaves, but most have mottled foliage. The mottling in some species is very dark and persistent, while in others it fades soon after the leaves emerge. Some authors writing about erythroniums use the terms "spotted," "mottled," and "marbled" interchangeably; this makes their description of the leaf patterns of no practical use for the gardener who is trying to determine in which group of erythroniums an individual plant belongs. Here, therefore, all the eastern North American and Eurasian species that have markings on their leaves are described as having spotted leaves, and all the western North American species with marked foliage are described as having mottled leaves. Spotted leaves often appear to have been splattered with droplets of paint, while mottled leaves have a colored pattern that appears somewhat netted (Plate 55).

The Plant

Erythroniums have a true bulb which is usually elongate and pointed. It is yellow-white in color, with a thin brownish tunic in certain species. Some species (especially eastern American ones) spread by stolons which can extend from the bulb for a considerable distance.

The leaves, which are always basal, are useful in identifying species. The eastern North American species all have spotted leaves, although *Erythronium mesochorum* and *E. propullans* may have green to lightly spotted leaves. The western species with green leaves and white flowers are *E. klamathense*, *E. montanum*, *E. purpurascens*, and *E. pusaterii*; the ones with green leaves and yellow flowers are *E. grandiflorum*, *E. idahoense*, *E. pluriflorum*, and *E. tuolumnense*. Mottled leaves and white flowers with a yellow base are characteristic of *E. californicum*, *E. citrinum*, *E. elegans* (although it varies), *E. helenae*, *E. howellii*, and *E. multiscapoideum*. Also with mottled leaves but having variously colored flowers are *E. hendersonii*, light purple flowers with dark purple centers; *E. revolutum*, pink to rose flowers; and *E. oregonum*, white flowers with dark markings.

The flowers are symmetrical and lilylike, carried outward-facing or nodding. The perianth is composed of six segments: three inner petals and three outer sepals. Because the sepals and petals are so similar in appearance in this genus, all six segments are usually called tepals, as they are in *Lilium*. The tepals of most species are gracefully reflexed. The erect scape (flowering stem) may bear one to many blossoms.

Another distinguishing feature is the auricle, a saccate appendage at the base of the inner petals. These are found on *Erythronium citrinum*, *E. elegans*, *E. grandiflorum*, *E. helenae*, *E. hendersonii*, *E. klamathense*, *E. oregonum*, and *E. tuolumnense*. The shape of the stigma and the color of the anthers are additional diagnostic traits. These structures are illustrated below.

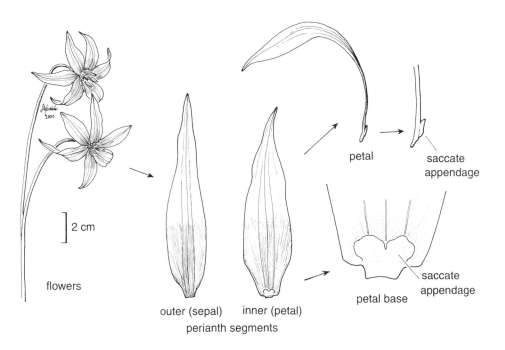

Erythronium flowers and details of perianth segments, showing the saccate appendages characteristic of certain species. Drawing by Linda Vorobik.

Western American Species

Erythroniums are a much more prominent element of the western North American flora than in any other region of the genus' range. Here they have evolved diverse forms and have adapted to habitats other than the woodlands they frequent elsewhere. The botanist Elmer Applegate divided them into two sections, those with mottled leaves (*Pardalinae*) and those with plain leaves (*Concolorae*). Although this characteristic is one of several useful guides to identification, I agree with Mathew (1998: 313) that it "may not be of fundamental significance in the classification of *Erythronium*."

Erythronium californicum Purdy

From the Coast Ranges of northern California, this species favors humus-rich soil in moist woodland. The leaves are mottled in brown, sometimes quite strongly. There may be three or more flowers per stem; these are white with a greenish yellow base marked by a ring of yellow, orange, or brown. The style is moderately clavate with three short lobes, and the anthers white. It is a good garden plant in temperate climates but does not usually produce many offsets, so it is infrequently seen in commerce. An exception is the clone 'White Beauty', a readily propagated plant which most authorities regard as a selection of *Erythronium californicum*, though it is sometimes listed (rather improbably) as a white form of *E. revolutum*. 'White Beauty' was introduced by Carl Purdy, a California nurseryman of the early twentieth century, who selected it from his massive collections of bulbs from the wild.

Erythronium citrinum S. Watson

Native to pine woodland in the border area of southwestern Oregon and northwestern California, this species is named for its yellow-green central zone, which distinguishes it from the similar *Erythronium californicum*. The flowers, one to three on a stem, are otherwise creamy white. There are saccate appendages, or auricles, on the inner petals, and the stigma is almost entire rather than conspicuously lobed. The dark green leaves are mottled. *Erythronium citrinum* var. *roderickii* Shevock & Allen is distinct in having purple anthers, while those of the type are white. This variety was named in honor of Wayne Roderick, who had distributed seeds of it as "*Erythronium hendersonii* var. *album*"—basing that identification on the anther color. The two species, *E. citrinum* and *E. hendersonii*, occur in the same area.

Erythronium elegans Hammond & Chambers

This species is endemic to a few mountaintop sites in the northern Coast Ranges of Oregon, where snow cover is usually present in winter and precipitation is very heavy except in summer. It grows in stony soil among low grasses and at the margins of Douglas fir (*Pseudotsuga menziesii*) forest, flowering particularly profusely on steep, treeless slopes. It was described in the 1970s after being brought to the attention of Oregon botanists by the late Floyd McMullen, a well-known plant explorer and gardener. A protected plant, it may be seen at its best in the preserve on Mount Hebo (Plate 56). Its rarity is undoubtedly due to the limited availability of its preferred open habitat in the mostly forested region where it occurs; it has responded vigorously to garden cultivation in both North America and Britain. The leaves have undulate margins and are usually a uniform deep green, but they may be mottled with a few pale lines and rarely have well-developed brown mottling. The large, substantial flowers are white to pale pink with bright yellow stripes at the base. In most populations the pink forms are rare. There are auricles at the base of the inner tepals. The style is deeply divided into three curved branches.

Erythronium grandiflorum Pursh

This species has an extensive distribution in the West, from the Cascade Range to the Rocky Mountains in open woodland and meadows, often growing in great numbers (Plate 57). It ranges from British Columbia south as far as Humboldt, Siskiyou, and Trinity counties of California; it is the only erythronium found in the central Rockies. Despite this wide distribution, it has proven difficult to grow outside its homeland, especially at low elevations. It is adapted to cold, fairly dry winters, usually under snow cover, and hot, dry summers. At higher elevations, it co-occurs with *Erythronium montanum*, though in slightly different habitats; in the Olympic Mountains of Washington, for example, there are populations of the yellow-flowered *E. grandiflorum* on one slope of a ridge, and colonies of white *E. montanum* on the other.

Botanists have applied a swarm of synonyms to this widespread species, including *Erythronium giganteum*, *E. leptopetalum*, *E. nuttallianum*, *E. obtusatum*, *E. pallidum*, *E. parviflorum*, and *E. utahense*. *Erythronium idahoense* (see below) is sometimes regarded as synonymous with *E. grandiflorum* subsp. *candidum* St. John.

The leaves are plain green. The flower stem bears one to five large, bright yellow flowers with auricles. This is the only plain-leaved, yellow-flowered erythronium with a three-lobed stigma. Three forms have been described based on the color of the anthers, although all three forms may grow together in a single population: *Erythronium grandiflorum* subsp. *grandiflorum* with red anthers, *E. grandiflorum* subsp. *chrysandrum* Applegate with yellow anthers, and *E. grandiflorum* subsp. *pallidum* St. John with white anthers.

Erythronium grandiflorum subsp. *nudipetalum* Applegate is a rare plant found in mixed conifer woods near the snow line in Idaho. Its leaves are plain green. The single flower is small and yellow with greenish veins. The style is not lobed, and the anthers are reddish.

Erythronium helenae Applegate

This species has a limited and local range in four counties near the Pacific Coast in north central California, where it grows in oak and pine woodland and chaparral. In cultivation it responds well to warm, rather dry conditions during its summer dormancy. In the wild it flowers well in considerable shade, but in more northerly gardens it seems to appreciate more sun. It is readily propagated from offsets. The leaves are strongly and darkly mottled. There are one to three large white flowers per stem, with a well-defined yellow base and auricles at the base of the inner petals. The flowers open widely and have a particularly beautiful poise on their stem. On warm days, they emit the fragrance of orange blossom—a characteristic unique in the genus. The stigma lobes are short and stout, and the anthers yellow.

Erythronium hendersonii S. Watson

This beautiful erythronium is native to the Siskiyou Mountains of southern Oregon and northern California, in scrub and woodland. It bears lavender flowers with a purple base and auricles (Plate 58). The leaves are darkly mottled and taper gradually to the base. The anthers and style are also purple. This species is persistent in cultivation, but it does not increase rapidly. It hybridizes readily with *Erythronium oregonum* in gardens, resulting in interesting intermediate forms.

Erythronium howellii S. Watson

This species is found in woodland at higher elevations (above 3000 feet or 900 meters) in the Siskiyou Mountains of southern Oregon and northern California. The leaves are mottled, and the flowers are white with yellow or orange inner markings. The species lacks auricles on the inner segments, and the stigma is nearly entire (clavate, or club-shaped); the latter trait distinguishes it from the closely related *Erythronium californicum*. *Erythronium howellii* does not seem to be cultivated by many gardeners, though it should present no more difficulties than other Siskiyou species.

Erythronium idahoense St. John & G. N. Jones

Some authorities consider this to be a subspecies (*candidum*) of *Erythronium grandiflorum*, but I think it is distinct enough to merit the standing accorded it by others, including Mathew (1998). A plant of pine woods in eastern Washington and western Idaho, it has plain green leaves. The flowers are white with greenish to greenish-yellow centers. The anther filaments are slender, and the stigma is three-lobed. It is only tenuously in cultivation and can be expected to present the same challenge as *E. grandiflorum*: Mathew (1998) reported that in England it took 16 years to flower from seed!

Erythronium klamathense Applegate

Probably the smallest of the western species but quite charming, this erythronium is found in pine woods in southern Oregon and northern California. The leaves are green, and the flowers are usually solitary, white with a yellow throat. The inflated appendages at the bases of the inner petals are well developed.

Erythronium montanum S. Watson

The glacier lily is among the loveliest flowers of the high western mountains—the Cascades, Olympics, and other northwestern ranges in the

United States and Canada. It blooms in masses at the edge of melting snowfields, often on steep, rather open slopes. Like many high-alpine snowmelt plants, it is difficult to grow at lower elevations, especially in regions with mild winters. The plain green leaf blade narrows abruptly to a long, narrow petiole. The flower is white with an orange base and recurves slightly. The anthers are white, and the stigma is deeply lobed.

Erythronium multiscapoideum (Kellogg) A. Nelson & Kennedy

This species comes from wooded slopes in the foothills of the Sierra Nevada of California, generally below 2000 feet (600 meters) elevation. It is an attractive garden plant that increases well by producing new bulbs at the ends of long, slender rhizomes—the only western species with this growth habit. A warm, rather dry summer dormancy suits it. The relatively small leaves are darkly mottled. The large flowers are white with yellow centers; the anthers are also white. The species name means "many-stemmed," but in fact each bulb produces the usual single scape. This flower stem, however, branches almost at ground level, giving the plant the appearance of having as many as a dozen stems. Each stem bears a solitary flower.

A plant under the name *"Erythronium cliftonii"* (or *E. multiscapoideum* 'Cliftonii', though it is not a single clone) is spreading in cultivation, although it has not been validly described. It may bloom as early as December and appears to be a particularly vigorous form of *E. multiscapoideum*. It is native to northern California, growing on serpentine cliffs and screes in full sun.

Erythronium oregonum Applegate

A wildflower familiar to inhabitants of the Pacific Northwest, this species is found at low to mid elevations from British Columbia down through the Willamette Valley to southern Oregon, growing in situations ranging from moist woods to open gravelly prairies (Plate 59). *Erythronium oregonum* is closely related to *E. californicum* but is probably adapted to somewhat colder winters. It is an easy subject for temperate gardens, where it increases fairly well and often self-sows. It hybridizes with several species whose ranges overlap its wide distribution; natural hybrids with *E. hendersonii* are varied and attractive. The leaves are mottled. The medium-sized flowers are white. The tepals are suffused with yellow at the base and usually bear maroon zigzag markings at the throat. The flattened filaments are an important key to identifying the species. The anthers are bright yellow, and the stigma lobes thin and recurved. *Erythronium oregonum* var. *leucandrum* Applegate has white anthers. Pale yellow forms have also been reported in the wild in Oregon and in cultivation in Britain.

Erythronium pluriflorum Shevock, Bartel & Allen

This species from the south central Sierra Nevada in California grows on granitic rocky slopes in subalpine coniferous forest between 3600 and 7500 feet (1080 and 2250 meters). The bright green leaves are not mottled. The nodding flowers, up to 10 per stem, are bright yellow, as are the style, stigma, and filaments (Plate 60). It is a rare plant, and its behavior in cultivation has not been reported.

Erythronium purpurascens S. Watson

In the southern Cascade Range of Oregon and the Sierra Nevada of California, this erythronium grows near the snow line. Its leaves are bright green. The small flowers, as many as eight per stem, are white with yellow centers. They age to pink or purple, the source of the species name, which means "becoming purple." The undivided style is clavate, and the anthers are white. The flowers lack auricles at the base of the petals. This species has not been tried much in cultivation but may be more difficult than species of the same region that grow at lower elevations.

Erythronium pusaterii (Munz & Howell) Shevock, Bartel & Allen

An uncommon plant, this species occurs on rocky outcrops between 7415 and 9450 feet (2225 and 2835 meters) in the central Sierra Nevada of California, blooming at the time of snowmelt. Its range is the most southerly of the western American species in the genus. Its leaves are bright green with undulate margins. The flower stems are tall, up to 45 centimeters. Individual flowers are borne on pedicels of unequal length. The flowers are curved and bicolored, white with a bright yellow center. The inner petals have auricles. The species is absent or rare in cultivation and is likely to be difficult.

Erythronium revolutum Smith

This very pretty plant is found in the Coast Ranges from southern British Columbia south to central California, growing at elevations below 3330 feet (1000 meters). It prefers rather moist but well-drained habitats and can often be seen in woods near streams. It is among the best erythroniums for the garden and increases readily by scattered seed in moist woodland conditions. As might be expected from its extensive range, various forms exist, and gardeners have selected particularly deep-colored and robust strains. A deep pink form, sometimes identified as variety *johnsonii* (not accepted by present authorities), is one of these. The leaves of *Erythronium revolutum* are darkly mottled; it is possible to find remarkable leaf forms (Plate 55). The flowers are various shades of rose pink, with yellow centers. Borne one to three per stem, they are large—up to 4.5 centimeters in diameter. The anthers are yellow, and the style is deeply lobed. There are auricles at the base of the petals. This is the only species besides *E. oregonum* that has broad, tapering filaments.

Erythronium taylori Shevock & Allen

The most recently discovered species in the genus (found in 1995) is a member of the western group with unmottled green leaves. Its only documented site is in the basin of the South Fork of the Tuolumne River in Tuolumne County, California, in the west central Sierra Nevada, at an elevation of 4400 feet (1340 meters). The colony grows in mixed conifer and black oak forest on steep rock outcrops. It is strictly protected, and no material may be collected from it.

Erythronium taylori is most closely related to four other Sierra Nevada endemics: *E. purpurascens*, *E. pusaterii*, *E. pluriflorum*, and *E. tuolumnense*. It resembles the first two in having marked bicolored flowers of white with a bright yellow central zone. Each stem bears one to four strongly reflexed flowers (rarely as many as eight). There are well-defined saccate appendages at the bases of the inner tepals. Like *E. tuolumnense*, it has a clumping habit resulting from the production of numerous offset bulbs.

Erythronium tuolumnense Applegate

Restricted to Tuolumne County, California, this plant grows in the wild in rich, gritty humus in open woodland at around 1670 feet (500 meters) elevation (Plate 61). This area has dry, hot summers, though the erythronium's shaded situation keeps the ground cool and faintly moist. It is the best yellow erythronium for most gardens and is the parent of several popular hybrids. There is also a named selection, 'Spindlestone'. *Erythronium tuolumnense* increases rapidly by offsets. Crowded clumps may fail to bloom well, so they should be divided periodically. The flowers, about 4.5 centimeters in diameter, are borne up to four per stem; they have greenish-yellow centers and auricles at the base of the inner segments. The anthers are yellow. The large, plain green leaves are undulate. The bulb is among the largest in the genus, up to 10 centimeters long.

Eastern American Species

This section includes six species distributed east of the Rocky Mountains. All are woodlanders with relatively insignificant flowers. Their spotted foliage, however, can be a pleasing garden feature, especially since the stoloniferous habit of most of them results in the formation of extensive patches where they are planted in light, leafy soil with ample moisture in summer.

Erythronium albidum Nuttall

This small species comes from the northeastern states, where it grows in forest and scrub. It produces many stolons. The leaves are small, light green, and spotted with reddish brown. The small flowers, borne singly on 10-centimeter stems, are white inside with a yellow throat; there is often a gray tint to the external surface. In our Pacific Northwest gardens—and in Britain, according to Brian Mathew—they seldom open fully. It is shy-flowering in the West, as well. The stigmas have spreading lobes, and the anthers are cream-colored. It is easy to grow in moist woodland conditions, but far from showy; the foliage is its best feature, and even this is best appreciated at close quarters.

Erythronium americanum Ker-Gawler

The most widely distributed eastern North American species ranges from southeastern Canada to Minnesota and southward to Kentucky and Texas in moist woodland and on rocky, wooded hillsides. Like *Erythronium albidum*, it is strongly stoloniferous. The leaves are spotted in two shades of brown. The solitary flowers, on 10-centimeter stems, are yellow inside, often with darker spots at the base; externally, they are yellow flushed with brown (Plate 62). The style is obscurely lobed; the anthers may be yellow, purple, or brown. *Erythronium americanum* subsp. *harperi* (W. Wolf) Parks & Hardin differs in the shape of the seed capsule, which has a long terminal beak. Though this species is small, its color makes it a little more interesting in the garden than *E. albidum*.

Erythronium mesochoreum Knerr

This plant of the Midwest, found from Iowa and Nebraska south to Oklahoma, has sometimes been regarded as a subspecies of *Erythronium albidum*, but *Flora of North America* recognizes it as a separate species. Like the other eastern species, it is stoloniferous. Its narrow leaves vary from plain green to slightly spotted. The small flowers, which tend not to open fully, range from white to pale lavender, with a yellow center. The style has stubby, spreading lobes.

Erythronium propullans Gray

This rare and very local species of moist woods in Minnesota has the smallest flowers in the genus—only 1 to 1.4 centimeters in diameter. The species description calls them rose purple to pink, though Mathew (1998) reports white cultivated specimens with a grayish-blue exterior. The leaves are spotted. The unlobed style is clavate. The plants produce stolons not from the bulb but from the stem below ground level; these then turn downward and away to produce a new bulb. The species name is derived from this characteristic.

Erythronium rostratum W. Wolf

This species is reported primarily from central Alabama north into Tennessee. It is another yellow-flowered plant, very similar to *Erythronium americanum*. It is distinguished by the well-developed auricles on the tepals and by a capsule with a well-developed beak.

Erythronium umbilicatum Parks & Hardin

Native to West Virginia and North Carolina, *Erythronium umbilicatum* is a close relative of *E. americanum* but flowers more freely in West Coast gardens (Plate 63). The typical form is not stoloniferous, but *E. umbilicatum* subsp. *monostolum* Parks & Hardin, from western North Carolina and eastern Tennessee, produces a single stolon from the bulb. The leaves are spotted, and the deep gold flowers are flushed rusty red on the outer petals. There are no auricles, and the anthers are deep red. The specific name *umbilicatum* refers to an indentation at the upper end of the seed capsule which is said to resemble a navel.

Hybrids

Most garden hybrids that are available in commerce have *Erythronium tuolumnense* as one parent, and they have inherited its tendency to offset freely, which makes them attractive to nursery growers. *Erythronium californicum* 'White Beauty' is the other parent of the yellow-flowered 'Pagoda' and 'Kondo'. 'Jeannine', 'Sundisk', and 'Citronella' are also yellow *E. tuolumnense* hybrids with a white parent. The white-flowered 'Jeanette Brickell' and 'Margaret Mathew' are hybrids of *E. tuolumnense* × *E. oregonum*. Another hybrid of *E. oregonum* with *E. californicum* 'White Beauty' is the large, white-flowered 'Minnehaha'.

Cultivation

Most erythroniums thrive in partial shade in light, woodsy soil which has good drainage and is never waterlogged. Some western species grow in rocky, mountainous areas that are quite dry during part of the year. All erythroniums, however, need adequate moisture during the growing season and some moisture even during their dormant period. Bulbs in dry areas in the wild plunge to considerable depths before blooming, so that some coolness and residual moisture is available to them even in an arid summer. This habit of growth may have led to an idea prevalent among gardeners that placing a stone underneath an erythronium at planting time induces it to flower sooner because it prevents it from "pulling" itself deeper into the soil over several seasons;

however, proper management of moisture and nutrition do much more to speed flowering than this practice can.

Erythroniums that grow from seed without transplanting do not begin blooming until the bulbs have pulled themselves down to a depth of 10 to 15 centimeters below the soil surface. The seedlings emerge looking like a tiny blade of grass. Each year they pull themselves down farther and enlarge the size of their single leaf. It may take three to five years before the corm produces a second leaf. The following year, most will bloom. The best germination is achieved by planting the seed as soon as possible after it is harvested. Stored seeds, such as those received from seed exchanges, may not germinate the first year, but if the seed pot is kept from becoming bone dry, many seeds do sprout the second year. In general, the seed of western American species retains its viability better than that of Eurasian species—probably an adaptation to the West's dry summers.

Erythronium bulbs have a very thin tunic and dry out rapidly after digging. They are also very brittle and must be handled carefully. These characteristics make them difficult to market commercially and consequently expensive. The bulbs multiply—rapidly in some species and hybrids—and continue to bloom satisfactorily without being divided. If they need to be lifted, June is the best time, or as soon thereafter as possible.

Bibliography

Anderson, E. B. 1957. "The Genus *Erythronium*." *RHS Lily Yearbook* 1958: 92–100. Kew: Royal Horticultural Society.

Eastman, Donald C. 1990. *Rare and Endangered Plants of Oregon*. Wilsonville, Oregon: Beautiful America.

Grothaus, Molly. 1973. "Notes on Erythroniums in Oregon." *RHS Lily Yearbook* 1974: 66–73. Kew: Royal Horticultural Society.

Mathew, Brian. 1987. *The Smaller Bulbs*. London: Batsford. 69–73.

Mathew, Brian. 1998. "The Genus *Erythronium*." *Quarterly Bulletin of the Alpine Garden Society* 66: 308–322.

Shevock, J. R., J. A. Bartel, and G. A. Allen. 1990. "Distribution, Ecology, and Taxonomy of *Erythronium* (Liliaceae) in the Sierra Nevada of California." *Madroño* 37(4): 261–273.

Wherry, E. T. 1948. *Wild Flower Guide, Northeastern and Midland United States*. New York: Doubleday.

– 6 –

The Genus *Fritillaria*

DAVID KING

Fritillaria is a genus of the Northern Hemisphere, with a world total of 130 to 150 species. There are about 20 American species, all westerners. They occur in British Columbia, Canada, and in 16 U.S. states, from Alaska south to Arizona and New Mexico. In the east they commence at the western edges of the Great Plains in the Dakotas and Nebraska and continue across the Rocky Mountains and the Sierra Nevada to the Pacific Coast. Their ranges are sometimes widely disjunct, or sometimes close and even overlapping. Species distribution gradually coalesces in a center of diversity in California, where, amazingly enough, all but two American species have one or more native localities.

Distant from the rest of the world's *Fritillaria* populations and surrounded by significant barriers of oceans and high mountains, the New World species have long been isolated within the North American landmass. Because of their common ancestry, they are classified botanically as a homogenous group, section *Liliorhiza* (meaning "lilylike, scaly bulbs") within the genus *Fritillaria*.

The two species that occur only outside California are *Fritillaria gentneri* of southwestern Oregon and *F. camschatcensis*, which occupies moist sites in coastal areas of southwestern Alaska, British Columbia, and Washington. Its range continues westward along the Aleutian Islands chain, across Bering Strait to the Kamchatka Peninsula, down the Kurile Islands, and south into Japan; it may represent a link with Old World species that was established in North America before the Bering Land Bridge became submerged.

The western American fritillaries, though few in number compared to the multitude of Eurasian species, combine to exhibit almost as much variety as can be seen in the rest of the world. These differences show up in their size and form, flower color and floriferousness; however, they all display the general traits of nodding, bell-shaped flowers, generally lanceolate or linear leaves, and a single stout stem rising from the bulb.

Their variability continues down to the single species level, where it can be so marked that one is sometimes uncertain whether one is looking at members of one taxon or two. In the wild, only experienced observation and background knowledge can enable one to identify some plants correctly, especially if they are not in flower.

Color is the key factor people look at when plants are in flower. *Fritillaria recurva* is well known for its intense deep scarlet bells, but it can display great color variation, from deep to pale orange-red, while the accompanying checkering (*tessellation*, from the Latin word for "mosaic tile") can vary from barely visible purplish squares to highly defined, intense chrome yellow checkers. *Fritillaria eastwoodiae* has small pendent bells from yellow to the more common reds and brownish reds, while *F. gentneri* flaunts its large and splendid dark red, checkered bells. *Fritillaria striata*, whose name means that it has closely packed, thin, parallel striations on the inside of the flower, has pale brown lines on the normal white form, but plants in the same colony can have pink striations, producing the extremely attractive pink form.

Across the group, physical size varies extremely, from the diminutive yellow-brown *Fritillaria glauca*, not more than 15 centimeters tall, to the wide-ranging *F. affinis*, which attains more than 90 centimeters in prime locations. On other sites, *F. affinis* can be diminutive; for example, a population that grows in stony soil alongside *F. glauca* is barely 5 centimeters taller, and since the two species have similar flower color, they can be told apart only by leaf arrangement and texture. *Fritillaria ojaiensis*, in perhaps its most favored site, can reach 90 centimeters, with an astonishing 26 flowers per stem, far exceeding what may be considered the norm for a fritillary. On other sites, it reaches only 35 to 45 centimeters, with as many as five flowers per stem.

Although *Fritillaria* flowers are generally bell-shaped, their size and the degree of openness can vary widely within a single species. The flowers of *F. affinis*, the largest complex of variable plants under a single species name, range from delicate coolie-hat forms to heavy, square-shouldered blooms; their color varies from deep crimson red through deep browns to pale yellowish green.

Flowering time depends chiefly on elevation and latitude. The season starts by the end of February, when *Fritillaria striata* blooms in Kern and Tulare counties in California. It is followed by the others in a northward progression on the Coast and transverse ranges and the Sierra Nevada foothills. This succession of bloom continues until mid-July, when the loftiest-growing species, *F. atropurpurea*, flowers at 10,500 feet (3150 meters) atop the White Mountains in Mono County, California.

Habitats vary greatly. At the lowest stations near the ocean, fritillaries may grow in turf or coastal prairie among scrub, in sandy or silty soils, and sometimes on serpentine. They climb to valley and foothill grasslands, with more occurrences on serpentine and stiff, black soils that were under the sea long ago. Adobe clay, a stiff, fine-grained clay that bakes brick-hard in summer, is the home of *Fritillaria pluriflora*. All the species growing in these open areas enjoy plenty of sun, and those on the coast can withstand windy conditions. Higher still, the edges of lower montane coniferous forest provide shelter and shade for species like *F. eastwoodiae* and *F. micrantha*, whose bulbs nestle in the soil under the duff. High mountain habitats host species like *F. pudica* and *F. atropurpurea* which are adapted to winter snows, wet clays, and granitic or basaltic soils; they sometimes grow among dwarf shrubs at these elevations. Growing among shrubs helps to protect the plants from browsing deer.

Fritillaries belong to the large plant family Liliaceae, into which fall many other bulbous plants of western North America such as lilies, erythroniums, and calochortus. During my travels to study fritillaries, I have often been fortunate to come across these other plants, making my visits doubly pleasurable, so if you are out on field trips, make sure you don't miss them. Remember that many species are listed as endangered or threatened; their status can be determined from the *Inventory of the Rare and Endangered Vascular Plants of California*, produced by the California Native Plant Society (1994), and from Eastman's (1990) *Rare and Endangered Plants of Oregon*.

The Plant

All fritillaries are perennial and have bulbs with one to several fleshy scales, the number of which increases with age. The bulbs are white to yellow and lack bulb coats (tunics). Many but not all have numerous small bulblets (sometimes referred to as "rice grains") surrounding the bulb. The rice grains develop into bulbs after they have been detached from the parent bulb, usually by foraging animals.

From the bulb emerges one unbranched stem. The leaves, of various shapes according to species, are disposed either in whorls or alternately up the stem. In some short-stemmed species the leaves appear to form a basal rosette. Nonflowering bulbs produce only one leaf, which is often very large the season before the bulb produces flowers. The flowers are borne on pedicels (flower stalks) alternately up the stem in a raceme, often with a leaflike bract at the base of each pedicel. Flower shape can be starry, bell-shaped, or cup-shaped. There are six perianth segments (tepals) in two groups—three inner and three outer. The nectary, a gland that secretes nectar attractive to pollinators, is situated centrally near the base of each tepal. There are six stamens, usually with yellow anthers. The style is either three-branched or entire. The seed capsule is carried upright at the top of the stem and has three compartments, each with two chambers; the brownish, flat, disc-shaped seeds are stacked inside these.

Species

This section contains individual descriptions of the morphology (form and structure) of each species, in alphabetical order, accompanied by its habitat conditions. These descriptions are based on the *Jepson Manual: Higher Plants of California* (Hickman 1993). Where individual variations are known, these too are given, so that plants seen on field trips can be recognized. Additional help can be found in a key in the *Jepson Manual* (pp. 1194–1196) and in the accompanying alphabetical list classifying the plants by botanical characteristics. I also describe the general environment of each plant, so that if you are cultivating them you will be able to devise ways of providing the conditions they like.

Fritillaria affinis (Schultes) Sealy

The checker lily, still widely known by gardeners and wildflower aficionados under its synonym *Fritillaria lanceolata*, is coastally oriented in its distribution, starting in southern San Luis Obispo County, California, and extending north into British Columbia. It reaches about 25 miles (40 kilometers) inland in the southern part of its range, but this increases to more than 125 miles (200 kilometers) in the north. It prefers moister habitats, and its custom of growing under trees or among shrubs lends it coolness during part of the day. Its chosen sites can be sandy loam to heavy clay, flat or sloping but always quite moist in the spring and never baking hot.

Fritillaria affinis is a common species and among the most variable. The average plant can be 38 to 50 centimeters tall, but in more open sites it can be as short as 15 centimeters, and in tall trees it can reach 90 centimeters. The shape of the flowers varies too, from shallow Chinese hats to cup-shaped, to large, heavy, square-shouldered bells. The flower colors run from pale yellowish green and beige through brownish and reddish tints to dark plum red. Some mixed color forms occur, and a form with alternate plum-red and pale green rough stripes has been seen. There are wide variations in the patterns of checkering and speckling. Pale chartreuse forms are not infrequent; one is grown in gardens under the clonal name 'Limelight'.

The leaves are relatively thin-textured on some plants but almost succulent on others. Their disposition is a key element in identification: there are as many as four whorls of two to eight leaves on the lower part of the stem but none at ground level, and above the whorls they are alternate. They are narrowly lanceolate; the lower leaves are 4 to 11 centimeters long and up to 25 millimeters wide. The bulbs are flattened and disclike, up to 75 millimeters in diameter, and are covered by attached small bulblets in a circular arrangement. Flowering time varies with elevation and latitude, and blooms may be seen as early as mid-April until the end of May.

Fritillaria affinis var. *tristulis* A. L. Grant grows on the coast in a limited area north of San Francisco. The sturdy, shorter plant can shrug off the windy conditions common on these bluffs. It is usually found out in the open, sometimes shielded by tall grasses in sandy turf. In the wild it can attain a height of 15 centimeters, but in cultivation it can reach 35 centimeters. The leaf disposition and the bulb are similar to the type. The very large flowers—up to 30 millimeters in diameter—have glands which stand up like raised knuckles on the outside of the tepals, giving them a square-shouldered appearance. They are usually dull mid-brown, sometimes with pinkish tints and a central line of small spots, but they can be much darker, blackish brown. The tepals taper to points of varying angles. There can be as many as six flowers per stem. The epithet *tristulis* suggests that this variety is a little bit sad (or dull-colored), which is not very inspiring, but it is much admired and easy to grow. It is probably a triploid; it has never been recorded as setting seed. It flowers in late March.

Fritillaria affinis 'Wayne Roderick' is a splendid tall form which grows in exactly the same area as variety *tristulis*, sometimes side by side with it. It is also a strong-growing plant, reaching 45 centimeters with 7 to 10 flowers per stem (occasionally 2 flowers per pedicel); these are rich dull brown, densely covered with mid-green checkering and having bright yellow anthers. It presents a wonderful spectacle in the rough, scrubby areas where it survives. The flowers are 25 millimeters in diameter (smaller than those of variety *tristulis*), with rounded shoulders and parallel sides. It flowers at the same time as variety *tristulis*, which it also copies by not setting seed. (Capsules sometimes form, but the seeds lack viable embryos.) It is not difficult in cultivation and can be increased rapidly from its many rice grains.

Fritillaria agrestis Greene

These plants live up to their common name, stinkbells, when they are in flower. The species inhabits grassland areas from near sea level to 3330 feet (1000 meters) elevation in the South Coast Ranges, gets over into the Central Valley, continues north along the Sierra Nevada foothills, and crosses to the North Coast Range in Mendocino County. Its habitats have been seriously diminished by agricultural development, and it is now classified as uncommon. Colonies of more than a hundred plants are the exception rather than the rule. They are found in flat areas, growing 10 to 15 centimeters deep in dark heavy soils or clays that always retain some moisture, but invariably right out in the open, in short grass with no shade.

The bulbs, up to 25 millimeters in diameter, consist of a number of loosely joined scales. Take great care in handling the bulbs in cultivation, because they are fragile and the scales can easily be broken off. Detached scales can be grown on, but the flowering potential of the main bulb may be decreased. It does not produce many bulblets. The flowers are not large but have a wide color range, from brownish greens, to green with brown, to yellowish and even plain green (Plate 64). There can be as many as six bell-shaped flowers per stem, which can reach a height of 38 centimeters in the strongest forms; the norm is 17 to 20 centimeters. The flowers have beautiful internal striations with a dark, prominent gland line inside down the center; they may have slightly recurved tips. The 3 to 10 leaves arise in a cluster at ground level and then are alternate up the stem, oblong-lanceolate to linear, 8 to 15 centimeters long and 15 to 30 millimeters wide. Flowering time varies from mid-March to mid-April, depending on location.

Fritillaria atropurpurea Nuttall

This species has the widest distribution of all the Americans, through 12 or 13 states. It grows in the open or at the edges of shrub and tree shelter at high elevations, from 4,000 to 10,000 feet (1200 to 3000 meters). Here it often has winter snow cover which protects the bulbs from freezing. It is usually found in soils that are a little sandy but have a firm consistency and drain reasonably well but always retain a little moisture in the summer. The conditions of its natural environment are good guidelines for its cultivation, which presents more problems to the gardener than that of many other American fritillaries.

The morphology of this species is inconsistent over its wide range. There can be 6 to 16 leaves, depending on the size of the plant. These are disposed in one or two whorls, the lower of which can be one-sided rather than a complete rosette; above the whorls, the leaves are alternate, singly or in twos or threes. There are no leaves at ground level and all are linear, often pale and glaucous, from 5 to 16 centimeters long by about 8 millimeters wide. The flowers vary widely too, the smallest being 18 millimeters in diameter. They are borne two or three per stem, nodding and flat-faced, with a greenish base color and random red-brown speckles and streaks on the round-pointed tepals. The largest flowers I have observed were outward-facing "coolie hats," one or two per stem and 25 to 30 millimeters in diameter. These had a yellowish base color densely covered with deep red-brown random scribbles, with the yellow showing through as a ring at the center and the glands appearing as red-brown blotches around this zone. Another flattish, nodding form from Arizona, with four or five flowers per stem, had a pale, cloudy yellow ground color with an open pattern of radial brown dots centrally on each tepal, scribbles around the edge, and the yellow glands hardly visible. These two have tongue-shaped tips on the tepals. All have very prominent, deeply divided trifid styles and yellow anthers. The bulbs grow to around 30 millimeters in diameter, with many rice-grain bulblets. Over the species' vast geographic and altitudinal distribution, flowering time runs from late May to mid-July.

Fritillaria adamantina is the name given by Peck to an obscure species from near Diamond Lake, Oregon. It was thought to be extinct until 1976, when it was found again. It is said to reach 60 centimeters in height and to be quite handsome, with large flowers which are red on the outside and yellow internally, with reddish spots; the leaves are narrow. It is clearly related to *F. atropurpurea*, from which Peck separated it on the basis of its stout stem and bulb and many bulblets—probably within the range of variation for *F. atropurpurea*.

Fritillaria biflora Lindley

Although the botanical name of the chocolate lily or mission bells suggests that this Californian species has two flowers per stem, it can be seen right on the Pacific Coast with one flower, and mountain populations can have four or five; the chocolate-brown form can have as many as eight. It is essentially coastal in distribution, inhabiting the North, Central, and South Coast ranges. The bulbs grow to 20 centimeters deep in sunny, grassy areas with heavy soils that protect the bulb from desiccation during hot summers.

The bulbs can attain 30 millimeters at maturity, and most forms never produce bulblets, so all reproduction has to be by seed. The leaf arrangement is fairly consistent, with three to eight leaves forming a ground-level cluster or rosette; if they go higher up the stem, the leaves are smaller and alternate. These upper ones can have fine undulate edges, while the basal leaves are substantial and oblong to narrowly ovate, 5 to 19 centimeters long and 15 to 30 millimeters wide. The stems of plants in exposed coastal sites may be only 10 centimeters tall, but in more sheltered sites they may reach 25 centimeters; the chocolate-brown forms have been seen at a height of 60 centimeters. The flowers vary from yellowish green through mid-green shades with reddish brown or brown markings, to the desirable near-black tall form. This is a good plant to grow under glass because it has no unpleasant odor and flowers dependably.

Several plants with botanical characteristics similar to those of *Fritillaria biflora* have long been recorded in floras and grown in gardens but are not distinguished by the *Jepson Manual*. The earliest published name (1878) is *F. grayana*, which is similar to *F. biflora* var. *ineziana* but is a stronger-growing plant, up to 40 centimeters tall, with broadly linear to narrowly oblong leaves. It can have as many as 10 flowers per stem, with the same striped markings but without any unpleasant odor. It is easily grown in the United Kingdom and makes a fine pot plant.

A smaller plant from the same area was named *Fritillaria roderickii* in 1967. It is of consistent size, not exceeding 15 centimeters, with as many as four flowers per stem. These are of a unique brown color with pale cream tepal tips. When this entity was sunk into *F. biflora*, its discoverer was asked to assign a cultivar name to a form of this plant being grown in England; it is now called 'Martha Roderick' in honor of his mother. The commercial stock offered under this name, however, has variably colored flowers of a much paler, creamy hue—perhaps the result of deterioration through repeated propagation by seed and tissue culture. It would help to keep these two plants on the record if they were referred to as *F. biflora* var. *grayana* and *F. biflora* var. *roderickii*. The state of California has kept the name *F. roderickii* for this form and lists it as an endangered species.

Fritillaria biflora var. *ineziana* Jepson, a very rare plant, occurs on only one site on private land in the western suburbs of San Francisco, close to the ocean. There are two colonies about 1000 feet (300 meters) apart, supporting a total of perhaps a thousand plants. This variety is very slender in stature, with distinctly marked flowers which have an unpleasant odor. It grows in the open on a serpentine barren area, surrounded by rough small grasses against which it does not have to compete strongly to survive. It flowers in mid-March The stems are around 18 centimeters tall, with four to six alternate linear leaves 4 to 10 centimeters long by 6 to 8 millimeters wide, chiefly low on the stem. The flowers are rounded, flared, and bell-shaped, and the outer surfaces have a sheen, while the outer tepals have a wide dark cream-colored stripelike marking sometimes taking up nearly all the surface; there are similar but narrower marks on the inner tepals. This produces a highly decorative striped appearance over the chocolate to red-brown base color.

Fritillaria brandegei Eastwood

As its common name, Greenhorn fritillary, indicates, the home of this plant is the small area of the Greenhorn Mountains, a spur on the west side of the Sierra Nevada that terminates not far from Bakersfield, California. The area is heavily wooded and can receive plenty of snow in cold winters. *Fritillaria brandegei* likes the shelter of trees and grows in the shade of *Cupressus* (cypress) or *Calocedrus decurrens* (incense cedar), where it can dwell in the damp soil it likes, keeping mostly out of the sun. In the wild it is not easy to spot because it generally bears a slim inflorescence and its coloration matches the background. The lanceolate leaves are reminiscent of true lilies in taller specimens, with none at ground level and one or two whorls of four to eight leaves, 4 to 11 centimeters long by up to 20 millimeters wide, with the almost linear bracts becoming alternate above. The large bulbs can attain 50 to 60 millimeters in diameter and produce abundant bulblets. The stout stem can be up to a meter tall, with four or five curiously shaped, 25-millimeter-broad flowers widely spaced at the top. The green tepals are channeled and pointed and change to near black at the center (Plate 65); the style is entire and the anthers maroon. The reverse of the tepals is plain dull green, maintaining its anonymity. Flowering time is around mid-May— if you can find the plant!

Fritillaria camschatcensis (Linnaeus) Ker-Gawler

The black sarana or rice lily is the only New World fritillary that occurs in the Old World as well—one of many plants common to both sides of the Bering Strait. In Kamchatka, British Columbia, and Alaska it was an important food plant for indigenous peoples. This fritillary is widely grown because of its ease of cultivation; a large potful with five or six flowers per stem, each flower 25 to 30 millimeters in diameter, is a splendid sight, especially the very dark, almost black forms, which have a dark purple-red sheen outside. This species is reliable in the garden provided it never dries out, is given shade in warm areas, and is replanted from time to time to prevent overcrowding. It must also be protected carefully from slugs. Various color forms are in cultivation, including a pale greenish-yellow one. Examples from Alaska have greenish blotches on the matt brownish tepals and emit a strong odor. All the flowers have attractive parallel-ridged striations on the inside of the tepals, which are set off by the bright yellow anthers. It is one of the tallest species, reaching 90 centimeters in the moist, rich meadow habitat it prefers. The stout, lanceolate leaves grow in as many as five whorls lower on the stem, 8 to 20 centimeters long and 15 to 30 millimeters wide. Higher on the stem they are alternate, with narrow bractlike leaves subtending the pedicels of the flowers. In the coastal habitats with heavy soils the bulbs can become quite large (50 to 60 millimeters), producing many bulblets, which can be loosely or firmly attached.

Fritillaria eastwoodiae Macfarlane

The Butte County fritillary is among the more northerly Californian species, growing in Butte, Shasta, Plumas, Sierra, and Nevada counties at elevations from 2000 to 4330 feet (600 to 1300 meters) under both deciduous and coniferous trees that shed their leaf litter on the heavy soils the plants like, keeping the surface cool, retaining moisture, and providing shade in the summer. It sometimes grows on serpentine. The *Jepson Manual* lists it as a species, although some earlier authorities considered it a natural hybrid between *Fritillaria micrantha* and *F. recurva*. Its extensive and disjunct range and its fertility lead one to question the assignment of hybrid status. A synonym is *F. phaeanthera*. *Fritillaria eastwoodiae* can be a very elegant, upright plant to 80 centimeters tall, with one to three whorls of more or less glaucous, linear to narrowly lanceolate leaves 5 to 10 centimeters long by 6 to 12 millimeters wide (Plate 66). The leaves are alternate above and enhance the appearance of the small, flared, bell-shaped flowers, which have more or less recurved tips. The numerous flowers, which appear from early April to early May, vary quite a bit in color: scarlet, burnt sienna, orange and marmalade shades, and even yellow, though the paler forms are often weak-growing. Sometimes a single flower displays several shades. These bright and varied colors make it enjoyable to grow, despite the smallness of the

159

individual blooms. The flattish bulbs may attain 40 millimeters in diameter, with many rice-grain bulblets.

Fritillaria falcata (Jepson) D. E. Beetle

This species is among the most difficult to cultivate, but it has been grown from seed and flowered in England several times. The key to this problem is its habitat: stone-covered, sloping sites in full sun on a serpentine soil. These slopes are often referred to as screes, but a scree is strictly composed of a mixture of grit and rock fragments to varying depths, whereas our subject inhabits a slope covered in a layer up to 2 inches (50 millimeters) deep of loose talus, or rocks up to 0.6 inch (15 millimeters) in diameter, over a very fine, open, soft soil that seems to drain well; the bulb sits in this soil about 3 to 4 inches (70 to 100 millimeters) below the surface. Because of their talus mulch, the bulbs never dry out. (Plants with similar habitats have been grown successfully in flue pipes, topped with a deep layer of rocks, and plunged in sand.) *Fritillaria falcata* achieves a height of up to 15 centimeters, with one or two flowers at the top of the stem, and two to six alternate, strongly falcate (sickle-shaped) leaves that are oblong and folded, 4 to 8 centimeters long and 10 to 15 millimeters wide. Externally, the flowers are dull gold with red-brown flecks; the glands are barely visible, shadowy red-brown blotches with small flecks which extend out over the pale, translucent gold base color to the denser red-brown tips (Plate 67). Flowers appear from mid to late March.

Fritillaria gentneri Gilkey

This species is an endemic of southwestern Oregon, where it grows in red clay soils at low elevations in mixed woodland. In form and stature it is very similar to *Fritillaria recurva*, but it differs in having very beautiful large, dark red flowers, 40 millimeters long, with clearly delineated yellow checkers in a broad band down the center of the tepal (Plate 68). The tessellation is stronger on the inner tepals, and the outer are sometimes almost plain. The flowers do not seem to vary over the species' limited range. After the flower opens as a parallel-sided bell shape, the tips of the tepals reflex slightly (not as much as the tepals of *F. recurva*) as the flower ages. The glands show up internally as small, oval yellow pits with tiny brown markings in their centers, while externally they appear as darker red blotches through which shallow ridges run three-quarters of the way to the tips. The plants may attain about 70 centimeters. The bulbs are similar to those of *F. recurva*. The flowers appear in mid to late April. The status of *F. gentneri* as a species is unconfirmed and requires further study; maintaining it as a species is something of a political issue rather than a botanical one, since its rarity makes it a candidate for listing, and its presence would then be grounds for preservation of its habitat. Efforts are being made to preserve at least one colony by protecting the plants from deer, the great foe of American fritillaries.

Fritillaria glauca Greene

This species, called the Siskiyou fritillary in Oregon, grows on high-elevation serpentine slopes from 3000 to 6700 feet (900 to 2000 meters), out in full sun but often beneath a 4-inch (10-centimeter) layer of stony fragments or talus (Plate 69). Depending on elevation, it blooms from the end of April to early June. It is among the shortest American fritillaries, not exceeding 15 centimeters. It is easy to grow in the well-drained standard potting medium recommended in the section on cultivation. *Fritillaria glauca* offers some of the best yellows in the genus in forms found near the southern limit of its range in California. The best ones here have outward-facing, fleshy, unspotted flowers and thick, glaucous, falcate, folded leaves. The more northerly populations are quite variable in flower color, from mixed yellow and brown to deep brown. The flowers are typically nodding and either shallowly saucer-shaped or bell-shaped. The three to six oblong, folded, falcate leaves, 4 to 8 centimeters long by 15 to 30 millimeters, are alternate but sometimes appear in a ground-level cluster. The bulbs are not large—up to 25 millimeters in diameter—with a moderate number of bulblets produced.

Fritillaria liliacea Lindley

This species' common name, fragrant fritillary, signals a trait unusual in its genus: it smells good. The small sites in Marin, Sonoma, Monterey, and San Mateo counties where this relatively uncommon plant grows are not far from the ocean. It inhabits heavy clay soils in full sun (Plate 70). It is easy to cultivate, but its foliage emerges as early as December and must be protected from frost. It produces its beautiful, lightly perfumed blooms in mid-March. They range from almost pure white to very pale greenish yellow and are bowl-shaped or starry, 25 millimeters in diameter. There is a pale greenish-yellow gland line running centrally down the inside of the tepal, with the glands sometimes barely visible or accented by small dark striations at the base. In the wild its stout scape is rarely above 30 centimeters, with as many as eight flowers per stem. The 6 to 14 oblong-lanceolate leaves have dull, pale green, glaucous surfaces; they look almost succulent and are borne in a ground-level rosette, becoming alternate above. The lower leaves can be 5 to 14 centimeters long and 10 to 25 millimeters wide. The bulbs reach 30 millimeters, with plenty of bulblets. The plants show little variation.

Fritillaria micrantha Heller

As the common name, brown bells, and the Latin name (meaning "small-flowered") suggest, this is among the duller species, with small flowers and insignificant leaves, but it is a common plant. It flowers at elevations between 1670 and 6000 feet (500 and 1800 meters) in the foothills of the Sierra Nevada in late April and early May. It is not difficult to cultivate, since it grows on shaded gentle slopes in sandy loam, with a cover of leaf litter or conifer duff, so the bulbs do not get too wet but have some year-round moisture. The 20-millimeter in diameter, round-shouldered, cup-shaped flowers are a dull, pale brownish gray, sometimes enlightened by reddish tints, and sometimes speckled. They are nodding, borne three or four on a stem which can reach 35 centimeters when growing under the canopy of tall conifers. The bulbs may be 25 millimeters in diameter and produce good quantities of bulblets. The narrowly lanceolate leaves grow up the stem in several whorls of four to six; they are 5 to 12 centimeters long by 10 to 15 millimeters wide, becoming alternate above.

Fritillaria ojaiensis A. Davidson

This outstanding plant was considered a variant of *Fritillaria affinis*, but it is recognized as a distinct species in the *Jepson Manual*. It is found in various habitats in the area of Santa Barbara, California, and this may account for the considerable range of size. In flower it can be as short as 35 centimeters, but strong-growing forms at one site have been observed reaching a meter in height. It invariably grows in shade, either from rocky overhangs or dense deciduous trees. The bulbs, which can be as large as 35 millimeters in diameter, grow as deep as 7.5 inches (18 centimeters) in either sandy loam or loose, humus-rich black shaley soils; both of these soils are free-draining and are covered by leaf litter, which retains moisture. The flowers, which appear from mid-March to mid-April, can be described as heavy, with thick tepals that have tongue-shaped tips. They are externally unspotted, green to greenish yellow in color, nodding, large, and deeply saucer-shaped. The gland produces a central ridge extending toward the tepal tip. Internally, the tepals have a random series of dark purple-brown, irregularly shaped spots, denser around the gland and near the base; in some flowers these coalesce as a solid red-brown central ring. The linear to narrowly lanceolate leaves are borne in one to three whorls of three to five, becoming alternate above. They are 6 to 18 centimeters long and 10 to 18 millimeters wide. They may exhibit a characteristic not seen in other *Fritillaria* species: brown-tinted surfaces on the buds and leaves, especially prominent on the large seed leaves.

Fritillaria pinetorum A. Davidson

This fritillary inhabits the high places, commencing at an elevation of 6700 feet (2000 meters) and reaching 9000 feet (2700 meters) in suitable mountain areas, growing in sandy soils which become hard when dry. Consequently, it is not easy to find, and its coloration makes it difficult to see among the low, scrubby plants where it grows. The plants experience harsh extremes of weather and are snow-covered in winter. The one to five outward-facing flowers per stem appear in mid-May. Dark brown markings can be almost absent to very prominent at the center, but they gain in intensity outward and are always prominent at the tepal tips (Plate 71). The patterning is like small circular scribbles which merge to a solid color or thin stripes at the tips. The glands are not obvious, and the anthers are orange when fresh. The reverse of the tepals is pale glaucous green, with some internal marking showing through faintly. The bulbs can reach 30 millimeters in diameter, with plenty of bulblets. The plant is stocky, with the single stem rising to 30 centimeters and bearing 6 to 14 linear leaves; these are alternate above and unevenly disposed low down, and may be folded; they are 5 to 14 centimeters long by 6 to 12 millimeters wide. Dwarf forms can be confused with *Fritillaria falcata*.

Fritillaria pluriflora Torrey ex Bentham

This is the only pink-flowered fritillary in North America, and the color is rare in the genus anywhere (Plate 72); yet its specific name, *pluriflora*, refers not to its striking color but to the fact that it produces several flowers on a single stem. The best stems observed have had 14 flowers. The common name, adobe lily, is more informative: it tells us that this plant grows in a fine-grained, stiff clay that is pliable in winter, allowing root action, but sets hard in summer, protecting the bulb from desiccation. It is very wet in late winter, but it gets baked hard at the surface during the hot summer; however, the bulbs are deep below the surface (as deep as 18 inches or 45 centimeters), protected from the heat. The plant grows out in the open, principally in flat or undulating swales, at 200 to 2000 feet (60 to 600 meters) elevation in valleys of the Coast Ranges west of Sacramento, California, blooming from early to late March. The colonies can be as small as 10 plants, but major spreads can be pink to the horizon, with hundreds of thousands flowering simultaneously. Efforts are now being made to control the timing of cattle grazing on the largest colony to allow the seed to mature. The species is considered difficult to cultivate successfully.

The stem can attain 40 centimeters in height. The 6 to 16 lanceolate leaves, 6 to 15 centimeters long by 8 to 25 millimeters wide, are clustered near the ground; they sometimes have finely dentate margins. The purplish-pink campanulate flowers have prominent internal red-brown gland lines centrally on each tepal, often with short red radial striations at the center; the external color is a shade darker. At maturity the bulbs can be up to 35 millimeters in diameter, with very few bulblets.

Fritillaria pudica (Pursh) Sprenger

The second most widely distributed American fritillary occurs in 10 states. It is common in semiarid steppe habitats at 5000 to 9000 feet (1500 to 2700 meters) on grassy or scrubby slopes in dense soils which are often wet in spring but not in winter. The summers are hot and dry. At high elevations it is late-flowering, emerging after snowmelt in July. At its lowest stations in the Columbia River Gorge, however, it may bloom in March, and it flowers in March or April in most gardens.

This is a variable species: some forms have very small flowers, only 6 millimeters in diameter, while strong-growing forms can have flowers 20 millimeters in diameter. It is worth growing seed from various locations and selecting the more robust plants. The flowers, in the form of conical bells, open medium yellow and turn golden and finally orange as they age (Plate 73). The gland shows externally as a green fleck near the base of the tepal. The flattish, round bulbs are covered in small white rice grains and are particularly hard to handle when repotting because these are easily detached; some growers remove all of them, which does not seem to be detrimental to growth or flowering. There are four to eight leaves in a basal cluster, linear to narrowly lanceolate, 4 to 12 centimeters long by 6 to 10 millimeters wide.

These plants are very attractive and relatively easy to grow if the water regime is controlled. A mature pot containing plenty of bulbs with their pendent yellow bells makes a fine display. Wim de Goede is propagating this species commercially in Holland. It is offered through mass-market bulb catalogs, and one wonders how many of those sold will survive more than a year or two. A large form with dark stems is cultivated by specialist gardeners. Some selections are said to be pleasantly scented, but this is difficult to detect.

Fritillaria purdyi Eastwood

This uncommon species grows from 1670 to 6700 feet (500 to 2000 meters), invariably out in the open. It has a fairly limited distribution in northern California, in the Inner Coast Ranges from Humboldt and Trinity counties south to Napa County. It is almost always found growing alone on serpentine, where it has little competition. Because of the species' wide elevational range and seasonal variation, the flowers can appear from mid-March to June. There is a marked difference between the altitudinal forms. The fleshy tepals of the low-elevation forms have a creamy base color with small, dark red-brown scribbles in the middle, leaving an undulate creamy edge (Plate 74). The glands are not very visible, and when fresh the anthers are dark purplish red. In higher-elevation populations the flowers are borne on longer pedicels, making them more widely spaced and nodding. The marking alters, too, frequently becoming dense at the center with plain edges; the glands are more obvious, making a slight "shoulder," and the outer surfaces of the tepals have a beautiful polished shine. The bells of high-elevation forms are often deeper and the anthers yellow. The bulb, up to 25 millimeters with a moderate number of bulblets, often grows under a generous layer of talus, ensuring that it does not get waterlogged. The 4 to 14 leaves make a dense basal cluster and are oblong, 4 to 10 centimeters long by 10 to 18 millimeters wide.

Fritillaria recurva Bentham

The eye-catching, even spectacular scarlet fritillary grows in nine counties in northern California and Oregon, with an elevation range of 1670 to 6700 feet (500 to 2000 meters). The bulbs are seated as deep as 8 inches (20 centimeters) in stiff clay soils or sometimes in serpentine. The plant usually grows among low shrub oaks or other leafy plants (often, poison oak) that protect it from the sun during part of the day and from deer; at lower elevations it can be in quite moist places during growth, whereas higher up it tends toward somewhat drier sites, and on its highest site it is out in the open. It is not too difficult in cultivation but rather large for a pot. It can remain dormant for an entire season without showing a leaf; in fact, it may do this in the wild, too. A strong stem up to 90 centimeters tall bears the linear to narrowly lanceolate leaves, which are arranged in one to three whorls of two to five below, and alternate above; the leaves are 4 to 14 centimeters long by 10 to 15 millimeters wide. The flowers, which appear from mid-March to early June, are bell-shaped with the recurving tips from which this species takes its specific name and are quite variable in color (Plate 75). The ground color is scarlet, but there is a deeper scarlet form that has been called variety *coccinea*, while some colonies have flowers of pale orange-red or orange. The checkering also varies from site to site, from barely visible purplish marks to intense chrome yellow tessellation. The 30- to 40-millimeter bulbs produce many rice-grain bulblets.

Fritillaria striata Eastwood

The striped adobe lily is the earliest American fritillary to bloom, bringing forth its sweetly perfumed flowers as early as the last week of February in favorable years. Its sites are out in the open, at 1000 to 3000 feet (300 to 900 meters) elevation on the (predominantly western) slopes of the southern Sierra Nevada foothills, in granitic clay soils. It grows among fairly thick grasses which shield the flowers from wind and conceal the seed capsules from predators. The state of California lists it as a threatened species. In cultivation it is the first fritillary to emerge, making foliage growth in December; thus, it is important to protect the plants from frost, though they should not be kept very warm. From the large bulbs, up to 50 millimeters in diameter, the moderate stem (to 40 centimeters) rises carrying 4 to 12 oblong to narrowly lanceolate leaves 5 to 12 centimeters long by 10 to 15 millimeters wide. No leaves are at ground level. The leaves are arranged alternately; they sometimes have very finely dentate margins. The flowers are graceful, of an elongated bell shape with strongly recurving tepals, borne up to five per stem (Plate 76). The usual flower color is white with very fine, dense mid-brown striations internally which sometimes stain the exterior with brown patches; the plant's specific name is taken from these markings. The gland also shows through as a brown stain. Sometimes the striations are deep pink, and the resulting pink form can make up around 10 percent of a population; these show as deep pink patches on the exterior, but the beauty of these flowers is best seen by looking inside them.

Fritillaria viridea Kellogg

The San Benito fritillary is a scarce plant that is not widely grown, but it has great appeal owing to its stature and color. It grows among trees and shrubs and grassy margins, often well shaded, in harsh serpentine soils in the San Benito Range. This is another species that is hard to see against its background. Despite its southerly distribution, it is fairly cold hardy and rather easy to grow. Some writers regard it as a subspecies of *Fritillaria affinis*. The slender plant often bears as many as 7 to 13 small flowers per stem. These appear around mid-April. They have a pale greenish ground color with variable checkering outside, usually in the brownish-red range, but occasionally the tepals have yellowish inclusions. The tepals are generally narrow, producing a star-shaped flower, outward-facing or pendent, saucer- to bell-shaped, sometimes with finely undulate edges. Inside, the gland can show up as a dark brownish oval, pointed at the outer end and becoming yellowish into the fine gland line toward the tip. The bulbs can be up to 30 millimeters in diameter with few bulblets and grow at various depths to 10 centimeters. The lower part of the stem has one to three whorls of three to four leaves that are linear to narrowly lanceolate, 5 to 12 centimeters long by 6 to 12 millimeters wide. The leaves are crimson-tinted when young.

Hybrids

In general, the genus *Fritillaria* does not interbreed freely. The only confirmed American hybrids are between *F. affinis* and *F. recurva* and have been found in several locations in northern California and southern Oregon. The flowers show their parentage in shape and color, being outwardly flared to varying degrees with a little recurving at the tips. Ground colors include pale creamy yellow with light reddish-pink checkering; deeper, cloudy yellow with dense brownish spots; pale scarlet with checkers not unlike those of *F. recurva*; and deep mahogany red, this one with longer flowers. The stems may be shorter than those of the parents.

Cultivation

Fritillaries are not suitable for growing in pots in the house. They are unlikely to take kindly to centrally heated or air-conditioned environments, and in any case their foxy smell makes them unacceptable. They are often grown in specialized greenhouses, called alpine houses, which are kept as cool and well ventilated as possible—just above freezing in winter. They are also very well suited to cultivation in a bulb frame, which is essentially a raised bed covered with a cold frame.

American fritillaries grow in a great variety of habitats, from sea level to high mountains, open grassland to shady forest edge, and in many kinds of soils, from clay to loamy sand and serpentine. Most of them are coastal and experience a Mediterranean climate with cool, wet winters and warm, dry summers, but those from the more inland regions are used to rather dry, cold winters and hot summers, often with monsoon rainstorms in late summer. A new grower might expect to have to duplicate every variation to grow the bulbs successfully, but this is not necessary. There are fairly easy and well-proven methods that produce results, provided the grower gives time, concentration, and understanding to the project. According to the *Jepson Manual*, "most are very difficult" to cultivate successfully, but with good practices they are a growable and rewarding group of bulbs. Success in these circumstances is a state of mind, and the plants do respond to tender, loving care.

Because some species are easy and others difficult outside their native range, the grower needs to know the conditions the bulbs experience in their growth cycle in the wild. This knowledge can then be put into practice, meeting individual needs and giving them all conditions to their liking within an overall growing concept. A regime developed from the following advice can be controlled to bring them eventually into flower. This advice is based on my experience of growing American fritillaries in England at an elevation of 500 feet (150 meters) near the city of Sheffield, approximately 170 miles (270 kilometers) north of London; its climate is locally described as temperate. The 30-year average annual numbers are 33 inches (817 millimeters) rainfall and 1366 hours sun; lowest average minimum temperature is 30°F (1°C) in February, and highest average maximum temperature is 69°F (21°C) in July. The lowest temperature in this period was 16°F (−9°C), in January 1987.

The environmental conditions that vary and the methods of dealing with them are as follows:

- Moisture: Seasonal patterns of alternate moist and dry weather can be imitated by watering at the appropriate times and protecting the plants from natural rainfall at others.
- Soil pH and density: Although wild fritillaries inhabit a very wide range of soils, a basic planting mixture (compost in the United Kingdom) with a few amendments will suffice for all the species, provided temperature and moisture are appropriately managed.
- Temperature: In very cold areas, soil warming cables may be necessary. The species that emerge early must be protected from air frost with overhead cover.

- Humidity: Hot, humid conditions while plants are in growth are conducive to disease; excellent ventilation helps to prevent this.

A good accommodation for fritillaries in pots is a raised bed containing a mixture of half coarse sand and half small grit (that is, 0.25-inch minus crushed rock, washed) to provide good drainage. Into this the pots can be plunged (sunk up to their rims). Alternatively, plant bulbs directly into a raised bed filled with a soil mixture similar to the one described below. Some seeds may drop on this surface, germinate, and grow, but don't disturb them for a year or two.

A structure should be built above the bed to support shading or solid covers for rain protection; these should extend a bit outside the main area of the bed to prevent rain driving underneath. Glasshouses have been used, but an enclosed structure can be unacceptably hot in summer, and an open-sided one provides a more natural atmosphere with little attention. Means of preventing pets or wild animals from getting up onto the bed itself are a must. Lighting for working at night, electricity for watering systems and underground heating cables, and a water supply are all options worth installing.

The next decision to be made is what kind of pots to use. Both clay and plastic pots are used by many growers, but there is a move toward net or mesh pots. Designed principally for pond plants and hydroponic growing, these are rigid, UV-stabilized black plastic and are available in various sizes from water garden specialists. Choose the type in which the sides and base have a regular pattern of small holes (less than 1.5 millimeters) all over them. Bulbs can escape those with larger holes, and those with solid bottoms are not suitable. Both clay and plastic present an unnatural wall around the bulbs, so that the roots follow the pot wall in circles, whereas mesh pots allow a much freer, more natural root run. Clay has been favored in the past because of the capillary action of the material; plastic pots are easy to overwater, with resulting problems. It is difficult to overwater plunged mesh pots, given the right compost.

Although fritillaries grow variously in adobe clay, serpentine, sandy loam, or woodland soils, there is a basic potting medium in which they will all grow perfectly well. The Golden Rule for this compost is that it must be both water-retentive and free draining. This sounds impossible but given the right ingredients it can be done. My recipe is 2 parts sieved loam or fertile garden soil, 1 part fine milled sphagnum peat, and 3 parts coarse sand, washed to remove all fines. All parts are by volume, not packed down. Loam is often found as the 2-inch (50-millimeter) layer immediately underneath the surface of turf or mown grass. The quality of the sand is important: the grain size should be around 0.5 millimeter. Never use the fine sand used in mixing mortar, the silty sand from lowland rivers, or seashore sand. Where it can be obtained, crushed horticultural pumice is a superb amendment and can replace one-third of the sand.

Mixed together, these ingredients create fine interstices which allow water to flow through and carry essential air to the roots. Measure them out in the quantities needed in a heap; before mixing them, sprinkle on a proprietary low-nitrogen granular fertilizer at the manufacturer's recommended rate. Never use dried animal manure. A pH of around 6.5. is quite satisfactory. If the ingredients are very dry, moisten the finished compost before using it to avoid desiccating the bulbs and to keep the compost from running out of the pots.

This standard formula provides a consistent starting compost which can be modified to make it more water-retentive or more freely draining: add fine grit to make a more open compost, or more loam to make it more water-retentive. A very open compost causes the bulbs to dry out and shrivel, and an excessively dense one results in waterlogging and rot. Here is a simple test: take a 3-inch (75-millimeter) plant pot, plastic or clay, and fill it three-quarters full with compost, lightly firmed. Fill the pot to the brim with water. Wait for it to settle and drain; then water it again. If the mix is good, the water drains freely and quickly. If not, modify the compost and test again. Always carry out the test at this stage, before the bulbs are dying of drought or rot.

Everything is now ready to put the bulbs into the pots. The rule is never to overpot, so one bulb about 15 millimeters in diameter should go into a 3-inch (70-millimeter) square pot. The same pot accommodates up to four bulbs of less than mature size. Larger bulbs and greater quantities need progressively larger pots. Fill the pot one-third full and place the bulbs on this surface, making sure that they are right side up. Fill in the remaining two-thirds and rap the pot on the bench to firm the compost, then level it. Don't pack the compost down. Leave about 0.4 inch (10 millimeters) of space below the rim and fill it with grit as topdressing to prevent the compost from drying out on the surface; this will also give a little extra support to the stems. Sink the pot by making a hole in the raised bed, placing the pot in the hole, and filling in around it; be sure the plunge medium is in contact with the sides at all points. It is acceptable to bury mesh pots to the depth the bulbs grow at in the wild but not deeper than 8 inches (20 centimeters).

The time to transplant bulbs is late July or early August, when they are dormant and the roots have completely died back. It is possible to repot fritillaries with root growth, but it is time-consuming and requires care to avoid root breakage. Once the bulbs are in the pots, the growing year has started. The bulbs are now in moist compost plunged in the raised bed and must not dry out, so water the plunge material around each pot to keep it only slightly moist.

A waiting period follows until it is time to give the bulbs their first serious watering. I call this the "first storm," and if you are gardening in the western United States, you can time it by when the real thing occurs. Otherwise, wait until the weather has cooled—in late October or early November in temperate climates. Open the bed to the rain or use a gently running hose to give the plants a thorough soaking. Watch and wait for another four weeks, to early December, and repeat the process, giving them the "second storm." The bulbs are now set up for strong root growth and good flowering. No more water should be needed until early spring.

In climates with freezing winters, plants require protection from frost; if the plunge freezes solid, the bulbs will die. A soil warming cable installed under the pots is the best plan; switch it on when it gets cold. Run the thermostat at 32°F (0°C). An alternative is to use a fleece cover over the bed, but this is not effective over periods longer than a few days. It is best to keep the bulbs barely moist but never dry in the winter; if they are soaking wet, frost is much more dangerous.

Add a low nitrogen / high potassium soluble fertilizer at half the recommended strength to all waterings as soon as the new shoots appear, and keep them watered steadily right up to flowering. Observe the plants daily to eradicate any predatory insects, slugs, snails, and, worst of all, squirrels and mice. After flowering, keep the leaves going as long as possible but reduce watering. When they start to turn yellow, stop watering directly into the pot and just keep the plunge barely moist. (A moisture meter is very handy to get comparative readings at this stage.) Do not dry the bulbs off abruptly; keep them very slightly moist while the roots are dying back—just keep them "ticking over."

Harvest seed, which is frequently set in cultivation, and share it with other growers. The seed is ripe when the capsule is no longer green and splits easily along the seams.

When root growth has ceased, around the end of July to mid-August, turn the bulbs out, clean them up, and start all over. Some growers insist on annual repotting, while others do it only every two or three years. To increase a collection at this time, separate out any loose rice-grains or larger offsets into other pots.

Propagation

Not many American fritillaries are available commercially as bulbs; two that are grown in Holland are *Fritillaria pudica* and *F. glauca*. *Fritillaria affinis*, *F. camschatcensis*, and *F. recurva* are often available on specialist lists. To build a collection, therefore, one must depend on exchanges or grow plants from seed. Fritillary seed is very easy to collect, and a good range of species can be obtained from the suppliers and societies mentioned at the end of this volume. The Alpine Garden Society has a Fritillaria Group which offers a bulb and seed exchange.

The best results are obtained by sowing seed of the current year in fall. Sow the seed thinly on a free-draining soilless mixture and cover it with about 0.2 inch (5 millimeters) of fine grit. Water it well and leave it in cool conditions (outdoors in mild temperate regions). Freezing is not desirable and may kill germinating seed of the coastal and southern species. Germination usually starts in late winter, and the seedlings should be protected from frost. Once they are well developed, they can be given a mild dose of soluble fertilizer to promote bulb formation. If aphids attack, apply a mild granular systemic insecticide to the soil, not to the foliage.

After the cotyledons have withered in late summer, turn out the pot and remove the young bulbs, which are easy to spot because they are white and reflective, like little pearls. Pot and grow them on as described above. Some growers prefer to leave them in the original pot for a second year. Another technique is to transfer the entire soil mass from the seed pot into a larger pot without disturbing the bulbs much, thus giving them more compost and nutrients the next season. Flowering-sized plants of the more amenable species can be raised in three or four years, but some species may take much longer to bloom.

Most American fritillaries produce numerous rice-grain bulblets loosely attached to the main bulb, and these can be removed during repotting (some usually fall off) and treated like first-year seedling bulbs. The orientation of these tiny bulblets in the soil is not important. A few species also increase by natural division, or offsetting.

Bibliography

Beetle, D. E. 1944. "A Monograph of the North American Species of *Fritillaria*." *Madroño* 7: 133–159.

California Native Plant Society. 1994. *Inventory of Rare and Endangered Vascular Plants of California*. 5th ed. Sacramento: California Native Plant Society.

Eastman, Donald. 1990. *Rare and Endangered Plants of Oregon*. Wilsonville, Oregon: Beautiful America.

Hickman, J. C., ed. 1993. *The Jepson Manual: Higher Plants of California*. Berkeley: University of California Press.

Phillips, Roger, and Martyn Rix. 1989. *Bulbs*. New York: Random House; London: Pan.

Rix, Martyn. 1983. *Growing Bulbs*. London: Christopher Helm; Portland: Timber Press.

Turrill, W. B., and J. Robert Sealy. 1980. "Studies in the Genus *Fritillaria* (Liliaceae)." *Hooker's Icones Plantarum* 29, Parts 1–2.

– 7 –

Irids of the Southeast

MICHAEL E. CHELEDNIK

The southeastern and south central United States host several delight-ful members of the family Iridaceae. Even though they are little known even in the areas where they are native, their diminutive stature and jewel-like (if ephemeral) flowers make them interesting and rewarding subjects for cultivation. They are good additions to the rock garden and open woodland garden in hot-summer regions, and they can easily be grown in containers in climates where they are less amenable.

These plants grow in the wild in grassland and pine savanna, usu-ally in soil that remains moist for much of the year. The climate is humid subtropical, with hot summers and cool (occasionally frosty) winters. The ground rarely freezes, but when it does, the frost does not penetrate very deeply and the cold spell is short. Annual rainfall is abundant: most areas receive 40 to 60 inches (1000 to 1500 millimeters) annually. Rainfall decreases as one moves north and west from the Gulf of Mexico, how-ever, and some parts of the Southern Plains receive as little as 25 inches (600 millimeters) annually. Rainfall is heaviest in spring and summer but occurs sporadically throughout the year, including heavy rains from infrequent late summer and fall hurricanes.

Alophia drummondii (Graham) R. C. Foster

Among the more spectacular members of the southeastern Iridaceae is *Alophia drummondii*, the pine woods lily. It grows in moist sandy soils from northeastern Mexico north through Texas, western Louisiana, southeastern Arkansas, and western Mississippi, in grassland and open pine woods. The flowers are large for the size of the plant, up to 5 centi-meters across. They resemble those of the more familiar *Tigridia*. The perianth is composed of three rich violet-maroon segments alternating with three much smaller segments which are spotted with brown, yel-low, and white. They bloom in early summer on stems 15 to 45 cm tall. The foliage is upright, linear, and plicate, and grows from a small, shallow-growing bulb. The small brown seeds are produced in a capsule. Plants thrive in cultivation and can bloom for months when well watered and fed. They do well outdoors in hot-summer climates in USDA Zones 7 to 10 but can be grown in pots in cooler areas. Propagation is by seed, and flowering can occur within one year of germination.

Calydorea coelestina (W. Bartram) Goldblatt & Henrich

The extremely local Bartram's ixia grows abundantly on just a few sites in northeast Florida, in savannas and open pine woods. First discovered by William Bartram (an illustration appears in his *Travels*, published in Philadelphia in 1791), *Calydorea coelestina* has been known as *Sphenostigma coelestinum* and before that was placed in *Ixia*, *Nemastylis*, and *Salpigostyla*.

Blooming in early summer, the flowers are a study in both classical simplicity and intricacy. The perianth is a vivid lavender-violet and is composed of six somewhat spatulate, cupped petals. The small stamens are held perpendicular to the base of the flower, but the curious alpenhorn-shaped style is held below them, presumably to catch the pollen as it is dispersed by insects. A plant blooms for just a few days, with the flowers opening at sunrise and closing by midmorning; the individual flowers last only a day. The plants are 20 to 30 centimeters tall in bloom, and the scant foliage, like that of most members of this family in the Southeast, is linear and plicate. The shallow-growing bulbs are tunicated. *Calydorea coelestina* is winter-dormant. Propagation is by seed, which germinates easily, and seedlings are fast-growing, often blooming within one year of germination. In spite of its southerly distribution this species tolerates a fair amount of cold, at least in hot-summer areas. Pot culture is easy.

Herbertia lahue (Molina) Goldblatt

A charmingly diminutive plant, just 15 centimeters tall, the prairie nymph blooms in late spring to early summer in the coastal savannas where it is native. This species occurs in heavy soils of coastal prairies in Louisiana and Texas but also in southeastern South America, a curious distribution shared by a number of bulbous plants including *Habranthus tubispathus* and *Zephyranthes chlorosolen*; it has been speculated that all these were introduced from South America, possibly by early Spanish missionaries. The flowers are large for so small a plant, sometimes approaching 7 centimeters in width. They are composed of six segments, three large ones and three that are much smaller. The segments are clear lavender-blue with deeper violet blotches near the bases of the petals. They last for only a few hours each morning before being shriveled by the sun's rays. After blooming and setting seed, the plants go dormant, with nothing above ground until the foliage (a basal whorl of plicate, lax leaves) reappears in autumn. Propagation is by seed or division of the small bulbs.

Nemastylis

Four species of this genus inhabit the southern tier of the United States: three in the southeastern and south central states, and one in the arid Southwest. All have deeply set, tunicated bulbs up to 2.5 centimeters in diameter, and upright, linear, plicate foliage (which has given rise to one of the common names, pleatleaf). The flowers are short-lived, often for no more than a few hours, and are produced from spathes on stems which overtop the foliage. The flowers are composed of six tepals of more or less equal size which open flat. The generic name refers to the slender erect styles (from the Greek *nema*, "thread," and *stylos*, "column"). The anthers are yellow or golden and contrast vividly with the blue or lavender of the tepals. The yellowish to brownish seeds are borne in capsules. All the U.S. species are winter-dormant. They are uncommon in cultivation but worth growing for their ethereal if short-lived blooms. They are easily cultivated outdoors in warm-summer climates and can be grown in pots in climates less to their liking. Propagation is by seed, which is slow to germinate. Once up, however, plants can bloom in as little as two years.

Nemastylis floridana Small

Once widespread throughout much of the pinelands of central and southeastern Florida, the Florida pleatleaf is now threatened by urban development and suburban expansion. The giant of the genus, this species can grow to nearly 100 centimeters tall and produces its dark blue flowers in fall (August and September). The flowers also differ from those of most species in that they open in the afternoon rather than the morning.

Nemastylis geminiflora Nuttall

Ranging from Tennessee and Mississippi west through Texas and north to Kansas and Missouri, the prairie iris is the most widespread and best-known nemastylis. This species is a grassland and prairie plant in most of its range but occurs in open pine woods in the range's eastern periphery. The small bulbs can be set remarkably deeply; I once found plants in a Kansas meadow growing almost 35 centimeters down. Plants grow 20 to 40 centimeters tall and bloom in late spring and early summer, bearing large flowers (to 6 centimeters across) of a remarkably rich blue or sometimes blue-lavender. The tepals open out flat, recurving slightly and becoming cupped toward the tips. They are white or pale blue at the base and are further enhanced by a column of yellow anthers. The flowers open in the morning and shrivel by midday.

Nemastylis nuttallii Pickering ex R. C. Foster

Nuttall's pleatleaf occurs in scattered sites in Texas, Oklahoma, Arkansas, and Missouri. Plants grow on open wooded slopes and clearings and tend to occur on circumbasic soils with granitic outcroppings. The flowering stems reach 40 centimeters in height. Flowering is in late spring to early summer. The flowers are pale blue to blue-lavender and have petals that are more spatulate than those of the preceding species. They open in the late afternoon for a few hours and last for just a day.

Nemastylis tenuis var. *pringlei* (Watson) Goldblatt

Nemastylis tenuis is primarily a Mexican species, but one form of it, var. *pringlei*, crosses the border into the United States and occurs in western Texas, southern New Mexico, and southeastern Arizona. It grows at higher elevations and is not a desert-floor species. The flowers are pale, watery blue, and like those of the preceding species, they have rather narrow-based tepals. This species blooms in late spring (April to May), opening its flowers for a few hours each morning.

Bibliography

Atlas of Florida Vascular Plants. Institute of Systematic Botany. University of Florida. Updated 12 October 2000. <http://www.plantatlas.usf.edu/>.

Bartram, William. 1980 [1792]. *Travels*. [facsimile London edition] Charlottesville, Virginia: University of Virginia Press.

Dormon, Caroline. 1958. *Flowers Native to the Deep South*. Baton Rouge: Claitor's Book Store.

Innes, Clive. 1985. *The World of Iridaceae*. Ashington, United Kingdom: Holly Gate.

Ogden, Scott. 1994. *Garden Bulbs for the South*. Dallas: Taylor.

Small, John K. 1931. Bartram's *Ixia coelestina* rediscovered. *Journal of the New York Botanical Garden* 32: 155–161.

1. *Allium cernuum*, various color forms (Mark McDonough)

2. *Allium cernuum* 'Rich Mountain', the smallest form of this species (Mark McDonough)

3. *Allium stellatum*, fall-blooming deep pink form (Mark McDonough)

4. *Allium plummerae* (Mark McDonough)

5. *Allium eulae* (Mark McDonough)

6. *Allium zenobiae* (Mark McDonough)

7. *Allium perdulce* (Mark McDonough)

8. *Allium textile* near Sun Valley, Idaho (Mark McDonough)

9. *Allium douglasii*, Wenatchee Mountains, Washington (Mark McDonough)

10. *Allium pleianthum* (Mark McDonough)

11. *Allium robinsonii* (Mark McDonough)

12. *Allium sanbornii* var. *sanbornii*, Sierra Nevada foothills, Yuba County, California (James Robinett)

13. *Allium howellii* var. *howellii*, east of Bakersfield, Kern County, California (James Robinett)

14. *Allium cratericola* near border of Lake and Colusa counties, California
(James Robinett)

15. *Allium falcifolium* near Rough and Ready Creek, Oregon (Jay Lunn)

16. *Allium platycaule*, Cedar Pass, Modoc County, California (James Robinett)

17. *Allium crispum*, San Benito County, California (James Robinett)

18. *Allium amplectens* (James Robinett)

19. *Allium serra*, Colusa County, California (James Robinett)

20. *Allium haematochiton*, Santa Barbara County, California
(James Robinett)

21. *Allium hyalinum* on damp granite slab, Fresno County, California (James Robinett)

22. *Allium validum* (James Robinett)

24. *Hymenocallis palmeri* (Alan Meerow)

23. *Crinum americanum* (Alan Meerow)

25. *Hymenocallis coronaria*, Florida (Alan Meerow)

26. *Hymenocallis duvalensis* (Alan Meerow)

27. *Zephyranthes simpsonii*, Gainesville, Florida (Alan Meerow)

28. *Brodiaea elegans*, Sonoma County, California (James Robinett)

29. *Brodiaea minor*, east of Redding, California (James Robinett)

30. *Brodiaea terrestris*, San Mateo County, California (James Robinett)

31. *Dichelostemma congestum*, Siskiyou Mountains, Oregon
(Jay Lunn)

32. *Dichelostemma ida-maia*, northern California (David Hale)

33. *Triteleia grandiflora* subsp. *howellii*, Siskiyou Mountains, Oregon (Jay Lunn)

34. *Triteleia hyacinthina*, Skamania County, Washington (Jay Lunn)

35. *Triteleia ixioides* var. *scabra*, northern California (Jay Lunn)

36. *Calochortus amabilis* (John Erwin)

37. *Calochortus elegans* var. *nanus* (John Erwin)

38. *Calochortus westonii* (Frank Callahan)

39. *Calochortus nudus* (John Erwin)

40. *Calochortus coxii* (Frank Callahan)

41. *Calochortus eurycarpus* (John Erwin)

42. *Calochortus howellii* (John Erwin)

43. *Calochortus flexuosus* (John Erwin)

44. *Calochortus syntrophus* (John Erwin)

45. *Calochortus aureus* (John Erwin)

46. *Calochortus kennedyi* (John Erwin)

47. *Calochortus obispoensis* (John Erwin)

49. *Calochortus ownbeyi* (Frank Callahan)

48. *Calochortus ghiesbreghtii* (Frank Callahan)

50. *Calochortus pringlei* (Frank Callahan)

51. *Calochortus venustulus* (Frank Callahan)

52. *Calochortus balsensis* (Frank Callahan)

53. *Calochortus nigrescens* (Frank Callahan)

55. *Erythronium revolutum* with mottled leaves, *E. dens-canis* with spotted leaves (Molly Grothaus)

54. *Calochortus hartwegii* (Frank Callahan)

56. *Erythronium elegans*, Mount Hebo, Oregon Coast Range (Jay Lunn)

57. *Erythronium grandiflorum*, Columbia Gorge, Oregon (Jay Lunn)

58. *Erythronium hendersonii* (Molly Grothaus)

59. *Erythronium oregonum* with heavily mottled leaves (Molly Grothaus)

60. *Erythronium pluriflorum* (Molly Grothaus)

61. *Erythronium tuolumnense* (Molly Grothaus)

62. *Erythronium americanum*, Winterthur Gardens, Delaware (Molly Grothaus)

63. *Erythronium umbilicatum* (Molly Grothaus)

64. *Fritillaria agrestis*, San Benito County, California (David King)

65. *Fritillaria brandegei*, Kern County, California (David King)

67. *Fritillaria falcata*, Stanislaus County, California (David King)

66. *Fritillaria eastwoodiae*, northern California (James Robinett)

68. *Fritillaria gentneri*, Jackson County, Oregon (David King)

69. *Fritillaria glauca*, Josephine County, Oregon (David King)

70. *Fritillaria liliacea*, Marin County, California (David King)

71. *Fritillaria pinetorum* (David King)

72. *Fritillaria pluriflora*, Colusa County, California (David King)

73. *Fritillaria pudica*, Skamania County, Washington (Jay Lunn)

74. *Fritillaria purdyi*, Lake County, California (David King)

75. *Fritillaria recurva*, Lake County, California (David King)

76. *Fritillaria striata*, Kern County, California (David King)

77. *Lilium canadense* var. *rubrum* (Edward McRae)

78. *Lilium michiganense*, Wisconsin (Edward McRae)

79. *Lilium superbum*, Perth, Scotland (Edward McRae)

80. *Lilium bolanderi*, Siskiyou Mountains, Oregon (Jay Lunn)

81. *Lilium kelloggii* near Arcata, California (Edward McRae)

82. *Lilium maritimum* (Edward McRae)

84. *Lilium rubescens*, northern California
(Billie Mathieu)

83. *Lilium pardalinum* 'Sunset' (Herman von Wall)

85. *Lilium washingtonianum* near Mount Jefferson, Oregon Cascades (Loren Russell)

86. *Camassia leichtlinii* near Roseburg, Oregon (Loren Russell)

87. *Clintonia uniflora*, central Oregon Cascades (Loren Russell)

88. *Leucocrinum montanum* near Sisters, Oregon (Loren Russell)

89. *Scoliopus bigelovii* in cultivation, Tilden Park, Oakland, California (Loren Russell)

90. *Veratrum californicum* with variegated foliage, Steens Mountain, Oregon (Loren Russell)

91. *Xerophyllum tenax* near Mount Jefferson, central Oregon Cascades (Loren Russell)

92. *Zigadenus elegans*, Mount Townsend, Washington (Loren Russell)

93. *Hesperocallis undulata*, Mohave Desert, California (David Hale)

94. *Arisaema triphyllum*, form with four stripes (Jim McClements)

95. *Arisaema dracontium* (Tony Avent)

96. *Chamaelirium luteum* (Jim McClements)

97. *Clintonia borealis* (Tony Avent)

98. *Aletris farinosa* (Tony Avent)

99. *Helonias bullata* (Jim McClements)

100. *Hypoxis hirsuta* (Jim McClements)

101. *Veratrum viride* (Tony Avent)

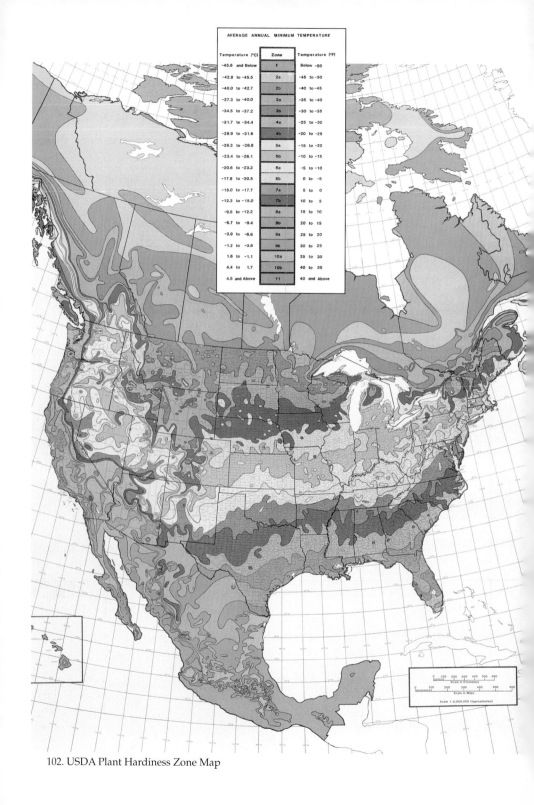

102. USDA Plant Hardiness Zone Map

AVERAGE ANNUAL MINIMUM TEMPERATURE

Temperature (°C)	Zone	Temperature (°F)
-45.6 and Below	1	Below -50
-42.8 to -45.5	2a	-45 to -50
-40.0 to -42.7	2b	-40 to -45
-37.3 to -40.0	3a	-35 to -40
-34.5 to -37.2	3b	-30 to -35
-31.7 to -34.4	4a	-25 to -30
-28.9 to -31.6	4b	-20 to -25
-26.2 to -28.8	5a	-15 to -20
-23.4 to -26.1	5b	-10 to -15
-20.6 to -23.3	6a	-5 to -10
-17.8 to -20.5	6b	0 to -5
-15.0 to -17.7	7a	5 to 0
-12.3 to -15.0	7b	10 to 5
-9.5 to -12.2	8a	15 to 10
-6.7 to -9.4	8b	20 to 15
-3.9 to -6.6	9a	25 to 20
-1.2 to -3.8	9b	30 to 25
1.6 to -1.1	10a	35 to 30
4.4 to 1.7	10b	40 to 35
4.5 and Above	11	40 and Above

– 8 –

The Genus *Lilium*

EDWARD AUSTIN McRAE

The North American lilies are a varied group within the great genus *Lilium*, whose members occur throughout the Northern Hemisphere, primarily in cool temperate regions. The current botanical view of the genus *Lilium* recognizes about 25 American species and at least 17 subspecies and varieties. These are conveniently divided according to their geographical distribution to the east and west of the Rocky Mountains.

Eastern Species

The eight eastern species occur primarily along the Atlantic Coast, from Florida north to Nova Scotia and New Brunswick, and west through the Appalachian Mountains to the Great Lakes and central Great Plains. *Lilium philadelphicum* crosses the northern Great Plains and reaches the eastern slope of the Rockies, from New Mexico into southern Canada; this species has the greatest areal extent of the eastern lilies.

The climatic variability experienced by the eastern lilies is enormous, from the warm southeastern states to the chill continental winters of Canada. In general, however, eastern lilies are species of wetlands, meadows, ditches, streams, and lakesides. Their bulbs usually grow in free-draining acid soils, never in stagnant conditions. They may grow in full sun in the company of coarse grasses and other perennials, partly shaded at the edge of woodlands, or under a light canopy of deciduous trees.

The majority of eastern lilies have stout stems with leaves arranged in whorls and pendent flowers. Two species have upright flowers: *Lilium catesbaei* and *L. philadelphicum*. These two species also differ in the scattered arrangement of their leaves and in their immediate epigeal germination pattern (that is, the germinating seed produces a cotyledon immediately, rather than forming a bulb before any aboveground growth emerges). The bulbs of eastern species are mostly stoloniferous. The parent bulb produces one or more stout, fleshy stolons 5 to 10 centimeters long, with new bulbs at the tips, resulting in what growers sometimes call "dumbbell" bulbs. The parent bulb then withers away, leaving the new bulbs to grow on.

Many plants of eastern North America seem unable to adapt to the sparse rainfall and low atmospheric humidity of West Coast summers, even in irrigated gardens. They tend to decline gradually in the West.

Lilium canadense Linnaeus

The first American lily introduced to Europe ranges from 35° to 50° north latitude, roughly from North Carolina to southern Quebec and Ontario. It grows in moist meadows, ditches, and roadsides, on the edge of woodlands, or among shrubs where it is safe from grazing and mowing. In cultivation it requires an acid, moist, very well drained bed prepared with sand, loam, and peat. It is important to provide a constant moisture level, perhaps with drip irrigation. Very susceptible to virus, *Lilium canadense* should be grown in isolation from other lilies.

This is an elegant, graceful plant. Its fleshy stolons produce scaly annual bulbs. The stem, 60 to 150 centimeters tall, in early summer bears an umbel of as many as 20 flowers. These are usually yellow with dark purple spots. They are of "turk's-cap" form, with the tepals reflexed halfway into an exquisite bell shape. The species has many distinct variants over its extensive range. *Lilium canadense* var. *coccineum* Pursh has dark brick-red flowers with yellow throats, heavily spotted. *Lilium canadense* var. *editorum* Fernald grows in drier sites in the Appalachians and is distinguished by its broader leaves and more delicate red flowers. *Lilium canadense* var. *flavum* Pursh, with chocolate-spotted yellow flowers, is the most widely distributed taxon of the species. *Lilium canadense* var. *immaculatum* Jenkinson has unspotted cadmium-yellow flowers. *Lilium canadense* var. *rubrum* hort. ex T. Moore is still another variety (Plate 77).

We have recently raised considerable populations of seedlings from this species in the Pacific Northwest. They have many subtle variations in flower form, color, and spotting patterns. The bulbs are fragile, losing scales easily if not handled with care. Smaller bulbs have been stored successfully over winter, packed in sphagnum peat. Some of the larger bulbs produced four short stolons apiece; the new bulbs can be separated with a sharp knife.

Lilium catesbaei Walter

The pine lily is native to the U.S. Southeast in Alabama, Florida, Louisiana, Georgia, Mississippi, North Carolina, South Carolina, southern Virginia, and southern Illinois, growing in open pine woods and marshlands. It is demanding to cultivate. Feldmaier (1970) suggested planting it in sandy, peaty mud on a substrate of sphagnum in a pot, then standing the pot in shallow water. Samuel Emsweller lifted bulbs with a ball of soil and potted them in sphagnum moss, then plunged the pots in a greenhouse bed that was kept constantly moist. I was able to flower bulbs using Emsweller's method but was not able to maintain them in Oregon for the long term. The bulbs are small, with tiny, loose, whitish scales. The persistent leaves are very small and narrowly lanceolate. The scape attains 30 to 50 centimeters, with scattered leaves. The flower, usually borne singly, is an upfacing starry bowl, scarlet or yellow, speckled with heavy brown spots. The tepals with their long petioles are almost unique in the genus. This species can be distinguished from the somewhat similar *Lilium philadelphicum* by its scattered rather than whorled leaves.

Lilium grayi Watson

Named for its first collector, the famous botanist Asa Gray, this lily is native to North Carolina, Tennessee, and Virginia. It grows on slopes at 3000 to 5900 feet (900 to 1770 meters) in the Allegheny Mountains of Virginia, where it is uncommon. It is no more difficult to grow than *Lilium canadense* and has flourished in the cool summers of Scotland as well as the hot ones of Massachusetts. We grew it well in Oregon in full sun, with liberal applications of horse manure as a mulch; one large stem produced 30 flowers. *Lilium grayi* is closely related to *L. canadense*, but it differs in its flowers, which are glossy trumpets with tepals that are not reflexed. The flowers are usually dark carmine externally and orange within, strongly spotted in red-purple. The bulb produces short, fleshy stolons with new bulbs at the ends; these have yellowish white scales.

Lilium iridollae M. G. Henry

This is a southerner, native to southern Alabama and northwestern Florida in peaty soils and sphagnum bogs. It is uncommon in cultivation and may be assumed to have requirements similar to those of *Lilium catesbaei*. Related to *L. canadense* and *L. superbum*, it has small white bulbs produced on short stolons. It grows 90 to 150 centimeters tall, with lanceolate leaves arranged in whorls; the upper half of the stem is often leafless. The flowers are typically borne singly, but robust plants may bear as many as eight. These are of martagon-lily form, reflexed and pendent, and warm golden yellow in color, heavily spotted toward the base with brown; the nectaries are green.

Lilium michauxii Poiret

First described under the name *Lilium carolinianum*, this species is native to Virginia, the Carolinas, Georgia, Alabama, Louisiana, and Florida. It grows in dry, well-drained soils from sea level to 2490 feet (745 meters). It is rarely seen in cultivation, but this has been due more to lack of availability than to any difficulty in growing it. It should be planted 5 inches

(12 centimeters) deep in acid sandy loam with sufficient moisture in the growing season. It may not be winter hardy in cold regions.

The stoloniferous bulbs produce stems 30 to 100 centimeters tall with broadly lanceolate, usually undulate leaves arranged in whorls. The inflorescence is an umbel of one to five strongly scented, pendent turk's-cap flowers, gleaming orange-red with yellowish white at the throat. It produces roots from the stem as well as the bulb.

We recently grew an interesting group of *Lilium michauxii* seedlings at Parkdale, Oregon. We were intrigued by several qualities observed. It was much later flowering than all other American species. The foliage was especially attractive—dark, almost blue-green. The rich red flowers were exceptionally large, and on warm days they emitted an intense and delightful fragrance.

Lilium michiganense Farwell

Named for Michigan, this species is found there and in Wisconsin, and along the Mississippi drainage in Ohio and Kentucky. It prefers moist soils and is often seen by roadsides. In cultivation its soil must be mildly acidic and moist but never stagnant. It is not especially shade-tolerant and enjoys full exposure in a continental climate. Good plants have been grown in both humus-enriched sand and stiff clay. I have found it to detest dry conditions at any time.

The bulb produces long stolons (15 centimeters or more). The 60- to 150-centimeter stem bears elliptical leaves in whorls, and one to eight flowers on long, upright pedicels. The flowers themselves are pendent, of graceful turk's-cap form, and broadly reflexed like those of *Lilium canadense*. They are red-orange with copious red-brown spotting at the base, and reddish yellow pollen (Plate 78).

This has been the most difficult of all East Coast lilies I have tried. Calvin Helsley (personal communication) of Missouri has grown this species successfully among masses of perennials and grasses. He has demonstrated the wide variation in its flower forms, color, and spotting patterns, and he has identified a tetraploid form.

Lilium philadelphicum Linnaeus

The city of Philadelphia, Pennsylvania, was a center of natural science in eighteenth-century America, so it gave its name to this species, which does not grow wild anywhere nearby. It is native farther west. The type grows from the eastern slope of the Rocky Mountains to the juncture of the Ohio and Mississippi rivers, and variety *andinum* Ker-Gawler is found from the Missouri River north to eastern British Columbia and in the mountains of North Carolina and Virginia. It is thus the westernmost of the eastern species, and indeed has the widest distribution of the American lilies. It is said to flower best following prairie fires. It can be grown in well-drained, sandy loam enriched with leafmold and peat;

it should be covered to keep it from rotting where winters are wet. The bulbs have short stolons. The lanceolate leaves of the type are arranged in several whorls on a stem 45 to 90 centimeters tall. Variety *andinum* is distinguished by its linear leaves scattered along the stem. The wide, upfacing, bowl-shaped flowers, borne in an umbel, are a lively orange-scarlet, often spotted within with dark brown. The tepals are small and claw-shaped at the base, much like those of *Lilium catesbaei*. A yellow form has been reported from the prairies of Saskatchewan.

Lilium superbum Linnaeus

Most common on the Atlantic seaboard, this lily is native from Massachusetts west to Indiana and south to Alabama and Florida. It grows in rich humus on moist slopes and in acid bogs and marshes. It grows best in the garden if planted 6 to 12 inches (15 to 30 centimeters) deep among small shrubs (such as rhododendrons), with the upper part of the lily in the sun. I once viewed an excellent planting in Perth, Scotland: the plants were 200 centimeters tall, in light shade (Plate 79). This is probably the strongest growing and most dependable of the eastern species—the *Lilium pardalinum* of the East Coast! I have seen it growing well in many places and climates, with never a report of viral disease.

The bulb is round, sharply pointed, whitish, and stolon-forming. The lanceolate leaves are arranged in whorls. The purplish scape can reach 3 meters in cultivation. It bears a pyramidal inflorescence of as many as 40 long-petioled, large, pendent turk's-cap flowers, which are orange-yellow, flushed carmine red at the tips. In the center is a green star, and the throat is brown-spotted. Yellow and true red forms have been found.

Lilium superbum var. *mary-henryae* Henry was found near Marianna, Florida, by its namesake, growing on riverbanks and in woodland. It was separated as a species for a while. It bears up to 15 pendent flowers with reflexed tepals, orange with wine-red spots and green nectaries.

Western Species

Fifteen species are found west of the Rockies, from the crest of the Sierra Nevada to the Pacific Coast. (One of them, *Lilium philadelphicum*, is described above; although it is primarily eastern, it has a disjunct range in British Columbia.) Nine of these are native to California alone, while six others occur in the Pacific Northwest of the United States and Canada. The region of northwestern California and adjacent southwestern Oregon has been called lily heaven because of the remarkable variety of native lilies there. They are also quite varied: dryland and wetland dwellers, various plant habits, and many colors and patterns of spotting in the flowers. *Lilium columbianum* is the northernmost-ranging of the westerners, in Washington and British Columbia; it also extends east to the Rockies, by far the most extensive range of the western lily species.

The region these lilies inhabit is primarily a long, narrow strip adjacent to the Pacific Ocean, where warm ocean currents meet and mix with the colder Arctic waters. Subregions include a narrow coastal zone, the interior high desert, and high mountains. Four major mountain ranges and several minor ranges divide this land throughout its length. Snowpack, rainfall, erosion, fog, and humidity are the factors that influenced the evolution of western lilies. Different species are adapted to dry or moist situations, and all are vastly different from the eastern group.

Two types of bulbs are found in this group. Unique to the West are the rhizomatous species that grow along streambanks or in bogs and swamps. As long as the water is moving, they thrive in very wet soils. In winter these rhizomatous bulbs can lie dormant under several inches of water without harm. All the rhizomatous bulbs are quite fragile. Many have jointed scales and therefore must be handled carefully. They also deteriorate very rapidly if allowed to dry out.

The dryland species have the concentric or subrhizomatous (slightly bulging on one side) bulbs common to the genus, with large scales. They grow only in well-drained soils that dry out during summer. All receive ample moisture during the rainy season, which usually lasts from early November to late March or April. This group of lilies is considered difficult in cultivation, possibly because the plants receive too much moisture late in the season in most other parts of the world.

The majority of western species have stout stems with leaves arranged in whorls, and pendent flowers. An exception is *Lilium rubescens*, which has upright flowers. Like the eastern species, the western ones grow among grasses and other perennial herbs; they are also frequently seen growing up through shrubs, which protect them from deer and other grazing animals. The seed of most species germinates hypogeally (that is, the germinating seed produces a radicle but no cotyledon) when fall brings cool, moist conditions, and the first true leaf emerges above ground in spring.

Lilium bolanderi S. Watson

This species is native to the Siskiyou Mountains of southern Oregon and northern California at subalpine elevations from 3000 to 5900 feet (900 to 1770 meters). It inhabits rocky soils and screes where the climate is moist in fall and spring, with snow cover in winter, and very hot and dry in summer. It is one of several western species that require extreme drainage to survive, but the soil beneath the bulb should not be allowed to dry out completely. It is rather easily grown from seed, typically flowering in three years. Outside its native range, it succeeds best in the bulb frame where the moisture regime can be managed. The typical dryland lily bulb has loosely attached scales. The sturdy plants grow 30 to 120 centimeters tall. The waxy, blue-green, lanceolate leaves are arranged in three to eight whorls on the stem, which carries as many as nine delicate, upfacing flowers of a true bell shape (Plate 80). These are various shades of red—brick, wine, crimson, and true red. The species flowers in July in nature.

Lilium columbianum Hanson ex Baker

Distributed very widely through the Pacific Northwest from northern California to southern British Columbia, and from the Pacific Coast to western Idaho, the Columbia tiger lily is found from sea level to 5900 feet (1770 meters). It grows in moist meadows and woodland margins and openings, preferring sites where ground moisture persists some time into the normally dry summer. As its wide range would suggest, it enjoys many different climates and aspects and is quite easy in most gardens, where it requires a leafy, acid loam and does best in light shade. It needs plenty of moisture during the growing season but if possible should be dried off for a month or two after flowering.

The bulbs are small and white. They produce a slender stalk that often leans at a graceful angle, from 60 to 150 centimeters tall; plants in shade grow tallest, while those near the summit of Saddle Mountain in northwestern Oregon are less than 30 centimeters tall. The broadly lanceolate, bright green leaves are ranked in whorls. The inflorescence is a raceme of 2 to 10 or more small, pendent flowers. The tepals reflex sharply at about the halfway point. The flowers may be bright gold to red-orange, with purple spots in the throat. The spots are usually small, but populations have been found where they are so large that they almost constitute a solid zone.

This species hybridizes readily with many other western species in cultivation. Natural hybrids with *Lilium occidentale* have been reported in the wild. *Lilium columbianum* var. *ingramii* Anderson is a robust plant that is suspected of being a natural hybrid.

Lilium humboldtii Duchartre

The Sierra Nevada of central California is the home of this lily, which frequents open woodland, growing in loam soils at 1950 to 3900 feet (585 to 1170 meters). It is quite variable: among a thousand seedlings, hardly two are exactly identical. Of the western dryland lilies, this is probably the least fastidious and easiest to manage in cultivation, as long as it has perfect drainage and dry conditions from July to November. It loves full sun and a warm position.

The large bulb is subrhizomatous, with yellowish-white scales. In nature it grows very deep. The stem is 120 to 180 centimeters tall, with undulate, shiny, oblanceolate leaves in whorls. The pyramidal inflorescence is made up of 10 to 15 turk's-cap flowers of bright orange, spotted with chestnut brown or purple. The pollen is dark orange. Plants from southern populations may produce leaves immediately after germination, rather than waiting until spring.

There are two varieties in addition to the typical plant. *Lilium humboldtii* var. *bloomerianum* (Kellogg) Jepson (synonyms *L. ocellatum* var. *bloomerianum*, *L. fairchildii*) is shorter, with narrower leaves, and is restricted to San Diego County in far southern California. *Lilium humboldtii* var. *ocellatum* (Kellogg) Thorne (synonyms *L. bloomerianum* var. *ocellatum*, *L. ocellatum*), from Santa Barbara County, is distinguished by its eyelike maroon spots or blotches with red margins.

Lilium kelleyanum Lemmon

One of the moisture-loving westerners, this species is found in California's Sierra Nevada from Tulare County north to Siskiyou and Trinity counties, in moist places in montane coniferous forest. It is one of a rather confusing group of lilies related to *Lilium pardalinum*; its synonyms have included *L. nevadense*, *L. pardalinum* var. *nevadense*, and *L. parviflorum*. This taxon now includes the entities formerly known as *L. shastense* and *L. inyoense*. It is not too difficult to grow and enjoys conditions similar to the more familiar *L. parvum*. The bulbs should remain moist, while the foliage is warm and dry—a regime not easy in most gardens. It wants a fairly acid loam, rich in humus, and an exposed situation with excellent air circulation; a bit of shade in the afternoon will be welcome.

This lily grows to 200 centimeters tall and can produce as many as 70 sweet-scented flowers in its pyramidal inflorescence. These are cadmium yellow, lightly spotted with purple, and with a greenish tint at the base. They are a modified turk's-cap shape; the tepals do not turn completely under, so that they resemble a crown. The bulb is rhizomatous, with many small, close-set scales.

Some populations I have grown from seed have shown enormous variation in flower form, color, spotting patterns, height, and foliar habit; others have been remarkably uniform, with small, soft orange flowers. The former, though from wild-collected seed, resembled a group of hybrids more than a population of a true species. In fact, *Lilium kelleyanum* is known to hybridize in the wild with *L. parvum*, and in cultivation it crosses readily with *L. parryi* and *L. pardalinum*.

Lilium kelloggii Purdy

This fragrant lily has a very narrow distribution in the coastal redwood belt from northwestern California to southwestern Oregon, where the otherwise arid summer climate is cooled and moistened by ocean fog. It does not grow close to the ocean but on high ridges some distance inland. It has been observed at 3000 feet (900 meters) elevation, growing in heavy, yellow, gravelly clay soils and brownish-red loose loam. The drainage is excellent in these dry, rocky places, and the soil has little humus. The grower must provide the difficult combination of perfect drainage and sufficient moisture, and a site that is not too shaded or too exposed to blazing sun.

Despite its limited range, *Lilium kelloggii* exhibits enormous variation in flower color (Plate 81). The pendent turk's-cap flowers—to 30 on a stem—are typically ivory-white with pink spots, turning pink to magenta as they age. The spots also darken. Each tepal usually bears a yellow central stripe. The bulbs are small and concentric. The plant grows 45 to 120 centimeters tall; individuals to 240 centimeters have been seen. The light green leaves are arranged in four to eight whorls.

Lilium maritimum Kellogg

The coast lily is native to the Pacific counties of California from Marin to Mendocino, in habitats well described by Munz and Keck (1968, p. 1343): "sometimes in sandy soil, usually on raised hummocks in bogs, also in brush and woods, at low elevations." A dwarf form grows in the dry, sandy barrens among ferns on the forest margin, in a soil rich in leafmold and peat. In cultivation it does not demand as much water as its wild habitat would suggest, but adequate moisture and good drainage are essential. I have succeeded with it on a north-facing slope. Young bulbs should be planted 2.5 to 3 inches (6 to 8 centimeters) below the surface and progressively mulched with leafmold as they mature. This lily has a long growing season, making it unsuitable for northern gardens. It has little rhizomatous bulbs which do not branch and therefore do not form clumps. Depending on the habitat, the stem can be from 10 to 200 centimeters tall. The narrowly lanceolate leaves are usually scattered along the stem from the base, but taller plants may carry some leaves in whorls. The small, bell-shaped flowers (one to eight per stem) are various shades of orange-red (Plate 82).

Lilium occidentale Purdy

The Eureka lily derives its common name from a city in its range, and its scientific name (*occidentale* means "western") from its distribution. It occurs in the coastal zone from northern California to southern Oregon, growing in the drier parts of sphagnum bogs. It may be submerged during the wetter months but dried out to some extent in mid to late summer. The water in these bogs is moving, not stagnant. Cultivation can be attempted in lime-free loam enriched with leafmold and peat. I feel strongly, however, that many lily species cannot be saved from extinction merely by maintaining them in botanic gardens. They demand their own natural environment, and this applies particularly to *Lilium occidentale*. Research has found that this species is threatened in the wild by the encroachment of trees, which shade it excessively. It is listed as an endangered species by both state and federal authorities. This rare plant has a short rhizomatous bulb and a 60- to 180-centimeter stem with small, elliptical leaves in whorls. There may be up to 15 small, pendent turk's-cap flowers. The rich red-orange tepals are green at the base, with brown spots in the throat and carmine tips. The anthers are purple, with red-orange pollen.

Lilium pardalinum Kellogg

The conspicuously spotted leopard lily is native to the Pacific Coast from southern Oregon to San Diego County, California. It is usually seen in woodland, growing near streams. It is the hardiest and easiest to grow of the western forest lilies, as well as one of the most desirable. Leafy, well-drained soil with adequate moisture permits it to flourish in most temperate gardens. The plant prefers shade at its base and sun above, conditions found among low shrubs. The rapidly multiplying bulbs should be dug, divided, and replanted every three or four years.

A stout, branching rhizome bears several bulbs with many yellow, brittle, jointed scales. Scapes may be 120 to 200 centimeters tall, with lanceolate leaves in whorls. The flowers are borne on elegantly arching stalks and are strongly reflexed, around 5 centimeters in diameter. They are usually gleaming orange-red tipped in carmine, with prominent brown spotting and green nectaries. The pollen is orange.

Lilium pardalinum subsp. *vollmeri* Eastwood (synonym *L. vollmeri*) is native to Del Norte County, California, and Josephine County, Oregon, growing along watercourses. It is distinguished from the typical species by its unbranched rhizomes and multiply rather than singly jointed scales. *Lilium pardalinum* var. *fragrans* Purdy is a sweetly scented form (the typical plant is scentless) found by Carl Purdy in the Cuyamaca Mountains of San Diego County. It may be a natural hybrid with the fragrant *L. parryi*.

A popular cultivar of this species, known as 'Red Giant' or 'Giganteum', was formerly called *Lilium harrisianum*. It arose from a wild population on the banks of Van Duzen Creek in northern California, where the lilies were often inundated by flash floods and deeply buried in gravel and sand. This magnificent plant grows 150 to 200 centimeters tall and has large flowers (8 to 10 centimeters wide); they are brilliant carmine-red from the tip to the midpoint, and chrome yellow from the midpoint to the base, slightly green in the throat, with large spots of gold ringed in brown. This cultivar is particularly amenable to cultivation. Another selection which we grew at Oregon Bulb Farms for many years was 'Sunset', a huge rich red flower with a gold center (Plate 83).

Lilium parryi S. Watson

This species is native to the Southwest, in the San Gabriel Mountains of southern California and in Arizona, at 5900 to 9800 feet (1770 to 2940 meters), where it experiences some winter snowfall. It inhabits granitic soils. It has proven difficult in cultivation outside its range. Perfect drainage is necessary, and this can be provided by a planting mixture of two to three parts leafmold and peat to one part grit, with some charcoal added. It should not be planted too deep, and the base should be shaded. It needs plenty of water during the summer growing season, but after flowering it should be protected against rain.

Lilium parryi has an erect habit and can be 60 to 180 centimeters tall. The leaves are arranged in whorls, though this characteristic can vary, especially in cultivation. The rhizomatous bulb has numerous jointed white scales which yellow with age. The trumpet-shaped, partially reflexed flowers, as many as 50 on a stem, are borne horizontally on obliquely ascending pedicels. They have an exquisite fragrance and are pale to bright yellow, spotted with light brown. *Lilium parryi* var. *kessleri* Davidson, from the San Gabriel Mountains, is more robust in all respects than the type.

I grew a considerable population of *Lilium parryi* in western Oregon in 1998. The young plants charmed all who saw them, and we were fascinated by the natural variations. The colors included bright lemon yellow and rich golden yellow in almost equal numbers. Flower form, intensity of fragrance, and especially spotting patterns varied too: unspotted, lightly or heavily spotted, some with blotches and speckles.

Lilium parvum Kellogg

This small alpine species is native to the Sierra Nevada of California and the Cascade Range of southern Oregon, at 4900 to 9800 feet (1470 to 2940 meters). It grows along riverbanks and in snowmelt areas—damp sites in an otherwise dry zone. I was delighted to view several hundred plants in the northern Sierra, where they were growing on the banks of a running stream near woodland. I was told that the color variation in this population was enormous. In many ways it looked like a higher-elevation form of *Lilium maritimum*.

Lilium parvum is readily increased from seed or bulb scales and can be obtained from commercial growers. It requires good drainage in a sandy humus soil, with plenty of moisture in the growing season and protection against excessive wet in winter, when it would be under snow in nature. It produces a small, flattened bulb on a short rhizome. The stem rises 90 to 120 centimeters and bears small (hence the name *parvum*), outward-facing, bell-shaped flowers with brown spots. The tepal color is quite variable—yellow, orange, pink, or red—a character that seems to be associated with the elevation of the population.

Lilium pitkinense Beane & Vollmer

This plant has puzzled taxonomists since it was discovered in Pitkin Marsh in Sonoma County, California—its only wild site. Munz and Keck (1968) considered it to be closely related to *Lilium occidentale*, but it has since then been referred to *L. pardalinum*, which it resembles in appearance. In fact, seedling populations I have grown show enormous variation in height, flower size, color, and flowering time, much as a hybrid population would. This observation, coupled with the plant's singular wild locality, suggests that it is a fertile natural hybrid population—a step in the ongoing evolution of lily species in America's lily heaven. Nonetheless, it has been listed as an endangered species (both state and federal) under the name *L. pardalinum* subsp. *pitkinense*. I have found it vigorous and easy to grow, given plenty of moisture. The large, stout, stoloniferous rhizome produces a stem to 180 centimeters tall, resembling that of *L. pardalinum*. The reflexed turk's-cap flowers are usually strong cinnabar or scarlet red with a yellow throat; a pink form has been called variety *fiski*.

Lilium rubescens Watson

This species, clearly related to the larger *Lilium washingtonianum*, ranges along the Pacific Coast from San Francisco Bay north to Siskiyou County, Oregon. It grows on north-facing slopes (often in redwood [*Sequoia sempervirens*] forest), in rather dry soils at elevations to 3000 feet (900 meters). Its cultivation is difficult. In nature it experiences high rainfall from autumn to spring, with a very dry period from flowering time in June through late autumn; the aridity is mitigated, however, by frequent fogs. In northern Oregon it has been most successful in a bulb frame in stony, gritty clay loam.

The bulb is described by several authorities as subrhizomatous, but in cultivation it is concentric. It is white, with broad scales firmly attached. The slender stem rises 60 to 180 centimeters, with many whorls of broadly lanceolate, stiff leaves. The raceme is made up of 3 to 30 (sometimes more) obliquely upfacing, narrow trumpets whose tepals reflex strongly for the outer third of their length. The flower opens white, lightly spotted in purple, and gradually ages to rose purple or wine red (Plate 84). It is very sweetly scented.

Lilium washingtonianum Kellogg

This large, showy lily is found in inland mountain ranges from the Sierra Nevada around Yosemite National Park in central California to the Cascades of Washington State. It grows on slopes (often quite steep) high in the subalpine zone, frequently among conifers and sometimes in rather dense shade. The soils here are stony and acidic. This stately species has proven difficult to grow, but in the Pacific Northwest it can become established in gardens and grow beautifully for many years. It resents transplanting, and its bulbs deteriorate quickly when exposed to air.

The subrhizomatous bulb is white. The flowering stem is 120 to 200 centimeters tall, with light green, broadly lanceolate leaves. In early to midsummer it bears as many as 30 horizontally poised, slightly reflexed trumpet flowers. These are pure white with purple spots in the throat and darken to purple as they age (Plate 85). They have a strong, spicy fragrance.

Lilium washingtonianum var. *purpurascens* Stearn, the Cascade lily, extends from northern California to Mount Hood in northern Oregon. It is distinguished by the fact that the its flowers open already lavender and age to dark purple.

In the late 1970s, we grew several hundred seedlings which produced first-year bulbs measuring 8 to 10 millimeters in diameter. We planted them in late September in their native habitat on the slopes of Mount Hood. The following summer, few could be found; most had been devoured by deer. We then understood perfectly why so many plants of *Lilium washingtonianum* are seen growing among dense shrubs, which protect them during their vulnerable youth.

Lilium wigginsii Beane & Vollmer

This rare lily, not described until 1955, is endemic to higher elevations in the Siskiyou Mountains in southern Oregon and northern California. Its habitat preferences are similar to those of *Lilium pardalinum*, and its cultivation should be similarly unproblematic. In place of a bulb it has a thick rhizome covered with small scales. The stem produces stem roots, an unusual feature in western lilies. The leaves are either scattered or arranged in two to four whorls on the 120-centimeter scape. The flowers have a broadly open turk's-cap form and are pure yellow with dark purple spots. They are borne on upright petioles 15 to 30 centimeters long.

Conservation

We must work fervently to preserve threatened species before mankind bulldozes them into oblivion. It is impossible to determine the extent to which lily populations in North America have been reduced, because their original distributions were not accurately recorded. Many human activities have forced them from places where they were formerly abundant: intensive and uncontrolled livestock grazing, farming, urban development, and draining of wetlands are significant among these practices. Logging sometimes stimulates lily populations, but its long-term results are mostly detrimental. Fire suppression in the West has reduced the habitat available to these plants, which depend on periodic opening of the forest cover to flourish. Finally, humans have killed off the large predators that once controlled populations of deer, which love to eat the plants, buds, and seedpods of lilies and other native bulbous plants.

Hybrids

A multitude of hybrids has been raised from the western American species but very few using the eastern ones. *Lilium* ×*burbankii* was shown in 1901 at the first Lily Conference in England and received an Award of Merit. It was mentioned by Gertrude Jekyll in *Lilies for English Gardens* (1901); she gave its parentage as *L. pardalinum* × *L. washingtonianum*, but this seems very unlikely!

The early twentieth century produced the Bellingham hybrids, bred from *Lilium humboldtii*, *L. pardalinum*, and *L. parryi*. Many of them still grow profusely, especially in English gardens; the cultivar 'Shuksan' is close to 80 years old and still thriving. Many enthusiasts worked with western American lilies in England, notably Oliver Wyatt, who introduced the Maid series. *Lilium parryi* figured prominently in these hybrids, and in some the fragrance was almost anesthetizing. The finest American hybrid I have ever known is 'Lake Tahoe', bred by Derek Fox from *L. kelloggii*—a fitting monument to a fine gentleman.

Oregon Bulb Farms produced a series of excellent clones in the 1960s, including 'Afterglow', 'Buttercup', and *Lilium pardalinum* 'Sunset'. The nursery's 'Bunting', 'Nightingale', 'Robin', and 'Snowgoose' were hybrids of *L. kelloggii*. These remained reliable and vigorous in the garden, which is more than can be said of *L. kelloggii* itself, whose attractions they mirror and surpass.

There was no more suitable cross to be made than that of a dryland lily with a wetland one, which realized many happy and harmonious results. I made a series of such crosses in the late 1960s, using the dryland *Lilium kelloggii* and such hybrids as 'Afterglow', 'Buttercup', 'Shuksan', and *L. pardalinum* 'Sunset' as the wetland partners. The first generation in all these crosses produced strong seedlings with somewhat muddy coloring. The second generation, however, had a startling array of clear colors, including soft pink, rich wine, cream, and pure white. A wonderful adventure awaits those who breed using western American lilies. The species *L. humboldtii*, *L. kelloggii*, *L. pardalinum*, and *L. parryi* are the choice keys and carry the genes for vigor, color, form, and fragrance. Interesting hybrids have also been bred using *L. bolanderi*, which imparts unusual coloring and spotting and almost unrecurved tepals.

Cultivation

The most suitable method of propagating American lilies is unquestionably by seed. The vast majority of these species (including all the western natives) exhibit hypogeal germination, a pattern in which the young plant spends its first season underground, forming a tiny bulblet before producing a true leaf after a winter's dormancy. The seed is best sown in late summer or early fall in cool conditions: 60°F (16°C) for three months, followed by 32° to 36°F (0° to 2°C) until transplanting, is a good average recommendation. Southern species may not require a cold period before growth, since their tiny bulblets form leaves immediately after development. Flowering plants may be raised from seed in three or four years. Vegetative methods of propagation such as scaling and tissue culture can also be used; these techniques are described in detail in my book, *Lilies* (1998).

Species lilies are not common in the bulb trade, but several of the more easily grown American natives are sometimes offered. *Lilium columbianum*, *L. pardalinum*, and *L. parvum* are most likely to appear on lists. The Lily Species Preservation Society, a group affiliated with the American Lily Society, has begun to offer many species from around the world on their annual list for members. Seed from wild populations is offered on society exchange lists and by commercial collectors.

Three problems trouble species under cultivation: virus disease, drought, and alkaline soils. Seed propagation and controlling aphids, the vectors of plant viruses, help to keep disease at bay. An adequate supply of moisture in combination with good drainage is essential in a garden setting. I have seen these lilies thrive in full sun, light shade, and filtered light. At the Edinburgh Botanical Garden, several North American species were grown to perfection in the woodland garden, which had areas of considerable shade. It must be appreciated, however, that many West Coast species prefer nearly dry conditions from late July to November, so drainage must be excellent. At the same time, the bulbs must not become desiccated; in nature, they are deep in clay soils and often shaded by shrubs, so that they retain some coolness and a trace of moisture despite the arid summer.

It is important to select superior forms from within a population of any species, especially in terms of vigor and adaptability. Mary G. Henry collected many distinct and beautiful variants of the eastern American lilies, especially *Lilium canadense* and *L. superbum*. Her work revealed the wealth of material available for those who wish to search anew for similar variants. Remember, however, that it is illegal to dig bulbs of rare and endangered species, so selections must be made from populations in cultivation. Growing large numbers of seedlings is the best guarantee of discovering good forms.

Bibliography

Feldmaier, Carl. 1970. *Die neuen Lilien*. Stuttgart: Verlag Eugen Ulmer; trans. as *Lilies*. Batsford.

Fox, Derek. 1985. *Growing Lilies*. London: Croom Helm.

McRae, Edward Austin. 1998. *Lilies: A Guide for Growers and Collectors*. Portland: Timber Press.

Munz, Philip A., and David D. Keck. 1968. *A California Flora*. 4th ed. Berkeley: University of California Press.

– 9 –

Bulbs of the Northwest

LOREN RUSSELL

The species described in this chapter are a mixed bag in terms of both taxonomy and garden value; of the genera discussed here, only *Camassia* is really well known and often grown as a garden plant. These plants are as ecologically diverse as is the U.S. Northwest, with habitats ranging from coastal rain forest to alpine meadow to desert steppe. All but one of the genera discussed belong to the Liliaceae in the broad, traditional sense (the exception is *Olsynium*, of the Iridaceae), but these represent several of the new families into which Liliaceae has been split by some botanists (see Dahlgren et al. 1985). Several are rhizomatous or fibrous-rooted, and therefore bulbs only by courtesy: monocotyledonous perennials that go dormant soon after flowering, and some that are close relatives of truly bulbous species.

To the adventurous grower, familiarity is not necessarily a virtue in plants, and difficulty of cultivation is merely a challenge. I hope that some of the plants discussed will be tested more widely in gardens. Though few of these species can presently be obtained from commercial nurseries, nearly all are frequently available as seed from society exchanges and commercial seed collectors.

Environment

The Pacific Northwest comprises the U.S. states of Washington and Oregon with adjacent parts of northern Idaho and northwestern California, and the Canadian province of British Columbia. This is a region of great ecological diversity, largely because of the rain-shadow effect of the Cascade Range. The region west of the Cascades has a quasi-Mediterranean climate: winters are wet and mild, with average January low temperatures near 32°F (0°C); summers are dry and warm, with July mean highs ranging from about 73°F (23°C) in the north to 86°F (30°C) or above in the south. Annual precipitation is highest near the coast and at middle elevations in the western Cascades, ranging from 60 to 120 inches (1500 to 3000 millimeters). In the Puget Sound lowlands and the interior valleys of western Oregon, precipitation (almost all as rain) is usually 32 to 48 inches (800 to 1200 millimeters); it decreases to 20 inches (500 millimeters) in the Rogue Valley of southern Oregon. Throughout the western region there is a pronounced summer drought, so that 10 percent or less of the annual precipitation occurs from June through August. On the West Coast, annual precipitation is sometimes expressed in terms of a "rain year," 12 months beginning in October, and this figure is a useful guide to the relationship of moisture and plant growth in a given year.

East of the Cascades, rainfall is much lower, winters are much colder, and the frost-free season is shorter. Precipitation generally ranges from 20 to 32 inches (500 to 800 millimeters) annually on the eastern slope of the Cascades and on interior mountain ranges; it decreases to 8 to 16 inches (200 to 400 millimeters) in the plateaus and basins of eastern Washington and Oregon. Although summer thunderstorms are common, most of the precipitation falls in the winter months, usually as snow. Average January minimums range from about 9° to 21°F (–6° to –13°C), and July highs are 82° to 90°F (28° to 32°C).

The surface geology of the Pacific Northwest is dominated by recent volcanic activity, and most soils in the region are directly or ultimately derived from basalt, andesite, and volcanic ash. The few areas of limestone in the region are not well populated by bulbs, but large areas of ultramafic (serpentine) soils in the Siskiyou Mountains are noted for their endemics, including many bulbs. Soil pH in this region is affected more by rainfall than by parent material: the leached soils west of the Cascades are usually acidic, while most soils in the drier areas are slightly to strongly alkaline.

At the time of initial European settlement, dense coniferous forests predominated west of the Cascade crest, along with large areas of oak savanna and grassland near Puget Sound, in the Columbia River Gorge, and in the Willamette, Umpqua, and Rogue valleys of western Oregon. Considerable expanses of alpine and subalpine vegetation exist in the northern Cascades and Olympic Mountains of Washington and in British Columbia, but these communities are rarer in the Oregon Cascades, Coast Ranges, and Siskiyous.

East of the mountain spine, communities include coniferous forest (particularly pines), grassland, juniper woodland, sagebrush (*Artemisia*) shrub steppe, and cold desert. Here there are significant areas of alpine and subalpine vegetation, both in the eastern Cascades and in interior ranges such as the Wallowa Mountains. The extensive grassland and shrub steppe communities of the inland Northwest are climatically comparable to areas of western Asia. It is remarkable, therefore, that so few species of true bulbs have evolved in these American communities. The majority of the species described in this chapter occur in wet or forested regions on both sides of the Cascades. Many of them have a wide boreal distribution and occur at high elevations in the Rocky Mountain region and north to Alaska.

Camassia (Liliaceae: Scilloideae)

Four species of this genus occur in the Northwest. (A fifth, *Camassia scilloides*, is described in chapter 11, "Bulbs of Eastern North America.") Camases (*camas* comes from a Shoshonean word and is sometimes spelled *camass*) are perennials of moist open habitats, where they often grow in great local abundance. They have bulbs with a dark brown or black tunic. The bulbs are edible, though unpalatable in one species, and they were a staple food for aboriginal peoples throughout the range of the genus. The abundance and cultural importance of camases in the Pacific Northwest are evident in the frequency of geographical names like Camas Prairie and Camas Creek.

Camassia is the only Northwest American genus placed in the scilla-hyacinth alliance. It can be distinguished from other American Liliaceae by the following traits: bulbs with dark tunics; several narrow, keeled leaves, all basal; and large flowers (usually 4 to 5 centimeters across) with six similar tepals, borne in unbranched racemes. The flowers are usually blue or purple but sometimes cream or white. The inflorescence is usually dense, with as many as 100 flowers, each subtended by a linear floral bract. The scape elongates and the bracts wither as the flowers open. The oblong to round capsules contain numerous shiny, black, ovoid seeds about 3 millimeters in diameter.

All species of camas are easily grown, long-lived bulbs. They are commonly planted in perennial borders and in open woodland or meadow situations. *Camassia quamash* and *C. leichtlinii* can sometimes be found in rocky crevices, suggesting their use in planted rock walls and in large rock gardens. These two common western American species are grown commercially in large quantities, and *C. cusickii* is also available from specialty nurseries. In nature, camases usually grow on heavy soils that are wet in the winter and spring and dry in summer, but in the garden they can thrive in a wide range of climates, exposures, and soils. All three species mentioned above are considered hardy in USDA Zones 3 to 8. Propagation is by seed, which should be sown outdoors in autumn, or by the very numerous offset bulbs.

Camassia cusickii S. Watson

Cusick's camas is native to northeastern Oregon and central Idaho, where it is locally abundant on grassy slopes and in open ponderosa pine (*Pinus ponderosa*) forest. It is a large plant, generally similar in appearance to *Camassia leichtlinii*, with radially symmetric, pale grayish blue flowers. In this species, however, the tepals are relatively narrow, and they wither and drop separately as in *C. quamash*. The bulbs are 3 to 5 centimeters in diameter, larger than those of other camas species, and tightly clustered; they have an unpleasant odor and taste. *Camassia cusickii* is the only camas to form large clumps in nature, and it generally grows in drier sites than do other camases. The numerous leaves reach 90 centimeters long, and flower stalks are up to 140 centimeters high. This is an easy garden subject, rapidly forming large clumps with many flowering stems. An established clump in full bloom is showy, but the abundant, coarse foliage of this species can make it hard to accommodate in mixed plantings. 'Zwanenburg' is a Dutch selection (by Michael Hoog) with deep blue flowers and relatively broad tepals.

Camassia quamash (Pursh) Greene

Common camas ranges from southwestern British Columbia to northern California, and inland to Montana, Wyoming, and Utah. This species is distinguished from *Camassia leichtlinii* by a number of characteristics: smaller size (less than 80 centimeters tall in flower, in most forms); the usual bilateral symmetry of the flowers, with the lower tepal widely separated from the other five; and tepals that persist as the capsule forms and usually dry up separately, rather than twisting around the capsule. The flower color in common camas is usually rich purple-blue, whereas flowers of *C. leichtlinii* are duller, grayish blue.

Several subspecies of *Camassia quamash* have been recognized on the basis of variations in plant stature and flower size, structure, and color. The following are recognized in the *Flora of the Pacific Northwest* (Hitchcock and Cronquist 1973) and are distinct enough to be of interest to gardeners. *Camassia quamash* var. *azurea* (Heller) Gould, a small form with lighter blue flowers, is local in gravelly meadows on glacial outwash in southwestern Washington. *Camassia quamash* var. *breviflora* (Gould) C. L. Hitchcock is a montane form in the Cascade Range from Washington to California; it is of interest to rock gardeners because of its small size and its occurrence in subalpine meadows, in low, rocky swales, and in crevices at the base of outcrops. It is shorter than the typical species with somewhat smaller flowers in dense racemes. Confusingly, the drying tepals twist together, as in *C. leichtlinii*; this trait also occurs in *C. quamash* var. *utahensis* Gould from Idaho, Utah, and Wyoming. *Camassia quamash* var. *maxima* Gould is a robust form with deep purple-blue flowers which grows on heavy soils in the Puget Sound and Willamette Valley lowlands.

Several named forms of *Camassia quamash* are in cultivation, sometimes as seed strains and sometimes as vegetatively propagated clones. The best-known is 'Orion', a short-growing plant with deep blue flowers. 'Blue Melody' is a clone in which the leaves have distinct cream-colored margins, particularly effective early in its growth period; the flowers are mid-blue.

Camassia leichtlinii (Baker) S. Watson

The great camas and common camas (*Camassia quamash*) often occur together in low-elevation wetlands on the Pacific Slope. Both species are highly variable, and some treatments, notably the *Jepson Manual* (Hickman 1993), regard the two as synonymous. Great camas, however, can usually be distinguished from common camas by several characteristics, although each of these is variable in both species. *Camassia leichtlinii* can usually be recognized by its larger size and its regular flowers with evenly spaced tepals, which twist together and wrap around the developing capsule as they shrivel; the dried tepals typically remain twisted together until they are shed as the capsule expands. In addition, wild forms rarely have the brilliant floral color of *C. quamash*. *Camassia leichtlinii* usually has only two or three flowers open at a time, and the flowers tend to open less widely than those of *C. quamash*. Most cultivated forms of *C. leichtlinii* are robust and clumping, typically with leaves 50 centimeters long, and a scape between 100 and 140 centimeters in height; they have also been selected for more widely open flowers.

Camassia leichtlinii var. *leichtlinii* is a distinctive form restricted to the area around Roseburg, Oregon, in the Umpqua River Valley (Plate 86). It can be seen blooming in masses along the right-of-way of Interstate 5 in April. This variety is distinguished from *C. leichtlinii* var. *suksdorfii* by its cream-colored flowers. Although a few albinos can be observed in any large population of either *C. quamash* or *C. leichtlinii* var. *suksdorfii*, most pale-flowered camases in cultivation probably were derived from variety *leichtlinii*.

All other populations of great camas are normally blue-flowered and are referable to *Camassia leichtlinii* var. *suksdorfii* (Greenman) C. Hitchcock. (Pale variants in these populations usually constitute far less than 1 percent of individuals.) This variety is commonest in western Oregon but ranges north to northern Washington, and southern British Columbia, and south to California in the interior valleys and lower slopes of the Cascades, Siskiyous, and Sierra Nevada. *Camassia leichtlinii* var. *suksdorfii* is adapted to a wide range of habitats and soils. In the Oregon Cascades and Siskiyou Mountains, compact forms only 15 to 40 centimeters high can be found in vernally moist areas at the base of outcrops at 3000 to 5000 feet (900 to 1500 meters) elevation. The stature varies with soil depth, suggesting that planting in a rock garden might maintain the dwarf habit.

Several named forms of *Camassia leichtlinii* are available commercially, for the most part differing only in flower color. The most distinctive cultivar is 'Semiplena', a semidouble whose creamy white flowers have been compared to those of a double tuberose. It can attain 120 centimeters in fertile soil, and its long season of bloom makes it a showy specimen once it forms a good clump. The extra petals are modified stamens, and pollen-bearing anthers sometimes form at their tips, so the plant is not quite sterile; however, double forms are not to be expected from seed. Blue-flowered cultivars include 'Blauwe Donau' and 'Caerulea'. A white form received the Royal Horticultural Society's Award of Garden Merit under the name "forma *alba.*" "Var. *coerulea*" and "var. *alba*" have no standing either botanically or as cultivar names; the former designates the usual blue cultivated forms of variety *suksdorfii*, while the latter denotes any pale form of either variety.

Camassia howellii S. Watson

This species is restricted to southwestern Oregon, where it is locally abundant in wet meadows and seeps in serpentine soils. Howell's camas often grows with *Camassia leichtlinii*, from which it is distinguished by the capsules, which are smaller in *C. howellii*—less than 1 centimeter in diameter—and smooth, shining, and nearly globose. *Camassia howellii* also has smaller flowers and blooms somewhat later than *C. leichtlinii*. This species can occasionally be found in seed lists, but it is probably not in general cultivation, and it has little distinct garden value.

Clintonia (Liliaceae: Convallariaceae)

The basal foliage, deciduous habit, and erect flower stalks of the so-called bead lilies make them bulbs in a garden sense only: they actually grow from slender horizontal rhizomes. These branching rhizomes, together with the fleshy fruit and the woodland habitat, suggest a relationship with such genera as *Disporum* and *Maianthemum*.

Clintonia is best recognized by its leaves, which are all basal, broadly ovate, smooth, and unmottled. The flowers have six similar tepals, pure white or red in the two western American species. (Two eastern species are discussed in chapter 11, "Bulbs of Eastern North America.") They are borne on a leafless stem, either solitary or in one or more umbels. The fruit is a blue berry (the source of the common name, bead lily) with several to many seeds. The seeds are rounded, with one or more flat facets, about 3 millimeters in diameter. Clintonias generally grow in deep shade in acid soils under conifers.

Both *Clintonia* species are candidates for moist woodland gardens or for peat beds. *Clintonia uniflora* requires well-drained, moist, acid woodland conditions. Gardeners can simulate these conditions by amending the soil with coniferous leafmold and coarse woody debris, such as well-rotted logs. The plant should be tried in garden conditions where *Cornus canadensis* (bunchberry) already grows well. *Clintonia andrewsiana* has similar requirements but tolerates open shade and heavier soils. Neither species tolerates dry shade, and both are most successfully grown in maritime climates with relatively cool summers. In the Pacific Northwest, protection from slugs is advisable. *Clintonia uniflora* is hardy in USDA Zones 5 to 8; *C. andrewsiana* is somewhat less hardy, perhaps to USDA Zone 7, since Phillips and Rix (1989) noted that it grows well at the Edinburgh Botanic Garden. Sheltered planting sites and mulch protection may extend the hardiness of both species.

Both western American species are occasionally available from wildflower specialists and can also be found in seed lists. *Clintonia uniflora* when offered for sale may be wild-dug or direct divisions of wild stock, but this is not a great concern: it is very abundant in the wild and has a limited market. *Clintonia andrewsiana*, however, is nowhere abundant and should be purchased only from nurseries the buyer is sure are propagating it ethically.

Plants can be propagated by division of rhizomes in early spring, with the growth tips set just below the surface. Seed should be cleaned of pulp and sown fresh, or stored moist for autumn planting. It takes at least four years from sowing to bloom.

Clintonia uniflora (Menzies ex J. A. & J. H. Schultes) Kunth

Queen-cup is well loved as one of the most conspicuous summer-blooming plants in Douglas fir (*Pseudotsuga menziesii*) forests in the Pacific Northwest. The effect of the gleaming flowers strewn across a mossy carpet in the cathedral lighting of old-growth forest floor is memorable; the botanist and author Arthur Kruckeberg (1982) has called it "angelic." The porcelain-blue berries are also beautiful and among my earliest botanic memories from childhood.

This species occurs inland, with other elements of the Pacific coastal forests, as far east as Alberta and in Glacier National Park. In California queen-cup grows in fir (*Abies*) forest along the western slope of the Sierra Nevada. The pure white flowers, 3 to 5 centimeters in diameter, are solitary (rarely, paired) and face upward on 8- to 15-centimeter pedicels (Plate 87). The two or three leaves are broad and hairy, about 10 to 15 centimeters long. Queen-cup is a diagnostic species of moist understory communities, often in association with *Anemone deltoidea*, *Cornus canadensis*, *Disporum* spp., *Oxalis oregana* (redwood sorrel), and *Vancouveria hexandra*. The rhizomes can be long and often form a ground cover; they sometimes run through old rotten logs, so that the plant can surprise hikers by blooming near eye level on an ancient conifer stump.

Clintonia andrewsiana Torrey

Red bead lily is an unmistakable and impressive species. The pink to purplish-red flower color is unique in the genus. The flowers are bell-shaped, about 15 millimeters long, in umbels of 20 or more on 30- to 50-centimeter stems. Often there are one or two smaller umbels lower on the stem in an arrangement reminiscent of candelabra primulas. The leaves are usually five or six in number, broadly ovate and hairy, 15 to 25 centimeters long and 5 to 10 centimeters wide.

Red bead lily occurs only in the coastal fog belt of the northern two-thirds of California, and in a small area of southwestern Oregon. It is restricted there to coast redwood forest, usually on stream terraces in rich, moist alluvial soil. It often grows in the deeply shaded understory, where it may be among the few flowering plants present. It can also be found in more open stands of redwood, along with trilliums and other forest herbs, and at the forest edge. It blooms in midspring, usually early April in coastal California.

Leucocrinum (Liliaceae)

The monotypic genus *Leucocrinum* is native from north-central Oregon to the Modoc Plateau of northeastern California, and eastward to the Dakotas, and to the southern Rockies. Populations are often very local, perhaps as the result of degradation by grazing.

Leucocrinum montanum Nuttall ex A. Gray

Sand lily is a stemless dryland perennial which grows from a short, very deeply buried rhizome with several fleshy storage roots; the leaves are grasslike, 10 to 15 centimeters long, and usually numerous (Plate 88). The glistening white flowers are starlike and usually abundant. The six similar tepals are united in a long floral tube, with the ovary below ground level. The exposed stamens with conspicuous yellow anthers are attached at the apex of the floral tube. Excavation of the plant reveals that the flowers originate from an umbel; the capsules also form underground, each with several shiny black seeds.

Leucocrinum montanum grows in sagebrush steppe and semiarid grasslands, and in openings in juniper or ponderosa pine forest. In the Pacific Northwest this species is usually found in sandy or pumice soils but also in heavy loams and in rocky sites.

The habit of sand lily is ideal for cultivation in the rock garden, bulb frame, and alpine house, but few gardeners seem to grow it. Dry-sand beds, kept barely moist at depth, are a good situation for this species; Norman Deno (1986) reported success in a sand bed in his Pennsylvania garden, where the plants increased in size over several years. Sand lily would be an extremely attractive subject for the alpine house, but its extensive root system requires the use of very deep containers and a medium of nearly pure pumice or grit. The pot should be kept plunged and nearly dry during dormancy.

Propagation is normally by seed, sown outdoors in autumn. Division of the rootstock is also possible, but the plant is slow to recover from disturbance. Nursery-grown plants may be available, especially from growers in the Rocky Mountain region.

Lloydia (Liliaceae)

The small genus *Lloydia* has a single American species, usually a diminutive perennial of alpine and subalpine grassland.

Lloydia serotina (Linnaeus) Reichenbach

The alp lily grows from a fibrous-coated, bulblike rhizome. The two to four basal leaves are thick, linear, and usually longer than the stem. The starry white or creamy flowers, about 15 to 20 millimeters in diameter, are borne singly on leafy stems. The seeds are numerous.

This circumboreal species has an extraordinarily wide and disjunct range in the mountains of Europe, Asia, and North America. In the Pacific Northwest it is known from the Olympics and the North Cascades in Washington, Saddle Mountain in the northern Coast Ranges (where it occurs at only 3330 feet or 1000 meters elevation), the Wallowas, and Steens Mountain in Oregon. It grows at higher elevations in the Rocky Mountains from Colorado north into Canada, and in mountains throughout Alaska.

Alp lily is well known and well loved by rock gardeners who view it in the wild; however, they are rarely successful at growing it. Its requirements are suggested by its typical habitat in alpine turf: bright but cool sites in gritty acid loam, probably with protection against winter wet. American forms of the species are unlikely to adapt well to the heat of most American gardens, and in any case, their modest beauty gives little reward for the gardener's effort. Those who wish to attempt it can start with seed, which germinates well if sown outdoors in early winter.

Olsynium (Iridaceae)

The species of *Olsynium* have been segregated from *Sisyrinchium* on the basis of the only partly connate (arising together) stamen filaments, and by stems that are rounded, not winged. There are two intergrading geographic races.

Olsynium douglasii (A. Dietrich) Bicknell

This plant, called grass widows by local people, is still better known to gardeners under its former botanical name, *Sisyrinchium douglasii*; it has also been called *Olsynium grandiflorum*. Grass widows signal the arrival of spring in many areas of the West. Each March, great displays of *O. douglasii* can be seen in vernally moist rocky grassland at the eastern end of the Columbia River Gorge in Washington and Oregon, often growing with bright pink *Dodecatheon* species and golden *Fritillaria pudica* (yellow fritillary).

Grass widows are small estivating herbs that die back after flowering to clusters of fleshy storage roots, then resume growth in late fall. The bractlike leaves ensheathe the fleshy cylindrical stem at the base. The conspicuous flowers, in shades of purple to pink, have a satiny texture and an open bell form. They are borne in small umbels surmounted by a leafy spathe. The globular, black seeds are finely pitted, about 2 millimeters in diameter.

Olsynium douglasii is an excellent subject for troughs or small planters, and perfect for the alpine house. In the open, garden plants require vernally moist loamy soil and dry summer conditions. They are usually more persistent in containers than in the rock garden, even in gardens within their natural range. Some gardeners have reported grass widows sowing into gravel paths, suggesting that scree and dry-sand beds are possible sites for this species. Slug damage to the flowers and new foliage can be a problem. Propagation is easy from seed sown in midwinter. Germination occurs in about eight weeks at 40°F (4°C). The seedlings should be kept in growth as long as possible. The rootstocks may be divided either in growth or when dormant.

Olsynium douglasii var. *douglasii* (synonym var. *grandiflorum*) is found from southern British Columbia south to the Klamath Ranges of northern California, from sea level to about 6700 feet (2000 meters), in grassland and openings in pine and oak forests. In the northern part of its range it is most frequent east of the Cascade Range, but there are isolated populations on southern Vancouver Island and near Eugene, Oregon. The scapes are usually less than 15 centimeters in height, with deep purplish-red flowers. White, pink, bicolored, and striped flowers can be found in most populations. There are usually three flowers per scape, held horizontally or nodding on short pedicels, and opening in succession. The tepals are 15 to 20 millimeters long, broadest near the apex.

Olsynium douglasii var. *inflatum* (Suksdorf) Cholewa & D. Henderson has also been known as a distinct species, *O. inflatum*. It is widely distributed east of the Cascades and Sierra Nevada, from southeastern British Columbia to the Modoc Plateau of California, and eastward to Idaho and Utah, often in moist meadow openings in sagebrush, ponderosa pine, and juniper communities. It can usually be distinguished from the typical variety by the swollen base of the filament tube. In addition, its flowers are usually paler, from pink to light purple, and have narrower tepals with a pointed apex.

Scoliopus (Liliaceae)

The genus *Scoliopus* (slinkpods or fetid adders-tongues) includes only two species, both native to cool, moist woodland in Oregon and California. *Scoliopus* is not closely related to any other genus, but it has some traits reminiscent of *Trillium*. The resemblance between its seed dispersal mechanism and that of *T. rivale* is probably coincidental. Slinkpods grow from short underground stems with numerous fleshy storage roots. There are generally two leaves, each broadly ovate and attractively mottled with brown. The several flowers, borne on naked peduncles, are somewhat similar to trilliums.

Slinkpods bloom in late winter or early spring and soon go dormant for the summer. The flowers have a fetid scent and attract small carrion beetles, the presumptive pollinators. The broad, recurved outer tepals are yellow with brown spots. The brownish inner tepals are linear and erect, and curve inward over the stamens. The capsules are fleshy and do not split open at maturity. Instead, the capsules self-plant by growing downward into the duff, where they decay to release the seeds. The seeds are curved and elliptical, with a fleshy appendage (an elaiosome).

Although slinkpods are quite restricted geographically and ecologically, their apparent rarity is also in part due to their very early bloom period and to their inconspicuousness during, and especially after, flowering. In western Oregon, *Scoliopus hallii* usually blooms in late February and early March. Seeds are shed a month later, and the leaves disappear by late spring. Both species do best in cool acid woodland and have been grown in peat beds, where they may self-sow. They are attractive to slugs, and protection is advisable. The larger and more attractive *S. bigelovii* tolerates warmer temperatures than does *S. hallii* and is the easier species in cultivation. *Scoliopus bigelovii* is grown in a partially shaded bulb bed at Tilden Botanic Garden in Berkeley, California, and it is also a rather popular subject for alpine house cultivation in the British Isles. (It has received the Alpine Garden Society's Award of Merit.) Neither species tolerates dry, warm conditions, and they should be grown in full shade with fairly moist soil during the summer dormancy. Container-grown plants are typically kept in a cool, shaded plunge during summer. Both species are hardy to about USDA Zone 6 and benefit from mulch in cold winters.

Propagation is by seed, which, however, rarely appears on seed lists, no doubt because of its early disappearance in nature. In cultivation, seed set is improved by hand pollination. The seed should be treated similarly to trillium seed: either sown fresh, or stored moist and given warm stratification before autumn sowing. Growth is fairly rapid from seed. Division of the rhizomes is also possible.

Scoliopus bigelovii Torrey

Larger in all parts than *Scoliopus hallii*, this species has tepals 14 to 20 millimeters long, leaves 15 to 25 centimeters long, and pedicels up to 20 centimeters long (Plate 89). *Scoliopus bigelovii* is endemic to the northern coast of California from Humboldt County south to Marin County. It grows in moist, shady forest, usually under coast redwoods, and on mossy streambanks from sea level to about 1670 feet (500 meters) elevation.

Scoliopus hallii S. Watson

This species has the typical characters of the genus. Its perianth segments are smaller than those of *Scoliopus bigelovii* at 7 to 8 millimeters long, and the leaves are 10 to 15 centimeters long. It is restricted to Oregon, where it is found along the coast and the lower slopes of the Coast Ranges, Siskiyous, and western Cascades. *Scoliopus hallii* ranges from sea level to about 3330 feet (1000 meters) elevation. It inhabits open to moderately dense forest in very cool, moist sites with rapidly draining, acid soils composed of rock fragments, well-rotted coniferous wood fragments, and humus. It is likely to be seen growing among *Maianthemum bifolium* (false lily of the valley), *Oxalis oregona* (redwood sorrel), and mosses near a stream flowing through a narrow canyon.

Stenanthium (Liliaceae)

Stenanthiums have no widely used common name. The two American species are woodland perennials very closely related to *Zigadenus*, with small tubular flowers (a trait for which the genus is named) and small tunicate bulbs. (*Stenanthium gramineum* is discussed in chapter 11, "Bulbs of Eastern North America.")

Stenanthium occidentale Gray

The western species, *Stenanthium occidentale*, is found from British Columbia to northern California, and east to Glacier National Park. This quiet little lily is fairly common, though rarely noticed, in moist meadows and shaded, mossy rock faces, often along streams and in the spray of waterfalls. It is much smaller than *S. gramineum*, with solitary flowering stems about 25 centimeters in height. The several lanceolate leaves, each about 20 centimeters long, are arranged as in *Zigadenus*: apparently basal at first, but one or two clearly attached to the lower stem as this elongates in fruit. The slender, tubular flowers are arranged in a narrow raceme, each with a small subtending bract; the flowers have six similar tepals about 20 millimeters long which are usually greenish, mottled with purple or brown and spreading at the tip. In the most attractive forms, the flowers are glossy reddish purple, individually similar to those of *Allium falcifolium*. Fine forms can be seen on Saddle Mountain in the Coast Ranges near Seaside, Oregon. The flowers and inflorescences of this species are rather similar in appearance to those of *Tolmiea menziesii* (Saxifragaceae); since the two plants often grow together, they may share a common pollinator. The seeds of stenanthium are well adapted for wind transport: they are about 3 millimeters long, pale and elongate, with a loose netted outer coat that acts as a sail.

Cultivation is easy in well-drained crevices of shaded rock walls. I have grown *Stenanthium occidentale* among small ferns and mossy saxifrages in the rockwork of a shaded artificial waterfall. Propagation is from seed, sown fresh in fall. Examined closely, *S. occidentale* is attractive, but it is too inconspicuous to be of much interest outside native-plant collections. Since *Stenanthium* is closely related to *Zigadenus*, both species of the genus should be presumed to be toxic in all parts.

Veratrum (Liliaceae)

The false hellebores (which are not related to *Helleborus*) are imposing deciduous perennials with tall, leafy stems and large paniculate inflorescences. As in related genera, many flowers on their lateral branches are staminate, while those of the main axis are perfect (possessing both male and female reproductive parts). The plants grow from the bulblike apex of a stout horizontal rhizome with several fleshy storage roots. The flowers are white or green, with six similar tepals that open flat and expose fleshy glands at the base of the ovary. The seeds are large and flattened, easily dispersed by the wind. The general habit of veratrums, with tassel-like inflorescences and broad, boldly veined leaves, suggests the alternate common name of corn lily.

Despite their very different appearance, veratrums are rather closely related to death camas (*Zigadenus*) and, like the latter, are extremely toxic in all parts. The alkaloids of veratrums were valued tools for ancient and medieval poisoners in Europe. Alaskan natives used the root as a topical medicine, but they respected the plant's toxicity so much that they left a gift in the hole when they dug it, to avoid offending its spirit.

These imposing perennials are long-lived and mostly pest-free, and they deserve more use in the garden. The strikingly pleated foliage is extremely attractive as it emerges in midspring, and the tall, leafy stems (1.2 to 2 meters high in the western American species) with huge panicles of long-lasting summer flowers are unusual among temperate-zone plants. Unfortunately, few nurseries offer them, and where offered, the rhizomes may have been collected from the wild. This, however, is unlikely to threaten populations of the very abundant *Veratrum viride* and *V. californicum*. Plants that have been disturbed usually respond with vigorous increase the following season. It is often possible to salvage rhizomes from pastureland, where farmers destroy the plants to keep them from poisoning livestock.

Veratrums may be used as architectural specimen plants among lower perennials in sunny perennial borders or in mixed borders. They do well in deep, rich loam soils, which should be moist through the bloom period. The widespread *Veratrum viride* is the commonest species on the Pacific Slope, but *V. californicum* and the similar *V. insolitum* are more attractive, and the latter, especially, tolerates drier soils.

Propagation is easiest by late-summer division of the dormant rhizomes, which are so large and deeply rooted that this is not a task for the puny. Seed is produced in vast quantities and should be sown in fall. Norman Deno (1993) reported obtaining germination by treating seed with gibberellic acid, followed by moist chilling at 40°F (4°C) for three months before germination at 70°F (21°C). The seed can also be sown in situ, where it will produce flowering plants in five to seven years.

Veratrum californicum Durieu

This species is distinguished by its white flowers with glabrous ovaries and unfringed perianth segments, and its large size (usually 2 meters in flower). The flowers are large for the genus at 20 to 30 millimeters across, in a crowded inflorescence. The tepals are entire, and sometimes woolly beneath. The seed is oblong and flattened, with marginal wings, 10 to 12 millimeters long. *Veratrum californicum* is very widespread in mountain meadows in the western United States, from Washington to southern California, and eastward to Montana and Colorado. Habitats range from sunny marshes to well-drained mesic meadows. In the interior mountains of the Pacific Northwest, stands of this species often outline streams and underground seepages. It also occurs at lower elevations in western Oregon and Washington, usually growing in roadside ditches and other open, marshy sites.

Veratrum californicum var. *caudatum* (Heller) C. Hitchcock, which has a narrower inflorescence, is common in western Washington. Variants with distinct white leaf margins are sometimes seen, and out of flower, these look oddly similar to variegated hostas (Plate 90). Such variants do not appear to be caused by virus and should be prime candidates for cultivation.

Veratrum fimbriatum Gray

This species is also similar to *Veratrium californicum*, but the ovary is glabrous, and the tepals are fringed even more deeply than those of *V. insolitum*. The foliage is less hairy than in other species. This is a very local plant, endemic to wet coastal meadows in Mendocino and Sonoma counties of California. Judging by its natural distribution, it may be less hardy than the other American species. This species is not attractive, though it is quite similar in appearance to the two more common white-flowered veratrums, and it might be tried from seed, when available.

Veratrum insolitum Jepson

Similar to *Veratrum californicum*, this white-flowered species is distinguished by the conspicuous white tomentum (felted hairs) over the inflorescence, densely tomentose ovary, and fringed perianth segments, which are oddly reminiscent of *Parnassia*. It is smaller than *V. californicum*—usually 1.2 to 1.5 meters in bloom—and the flowers are somewhat smaller too at 15 to 20 millimeters across. Seed is larger than that of other western American veratrums, to 15 millimeters long. *Veratrum insolitum* is most abundant in the Cascades and Klamath Ranges of southern Oregon and northern California, but it has also been reported from Washington. It grows in mountain meadows, often on serpentine soils but also in open forest and clear-cuts, typically on ridgetops.

Veratrum viride Aitken

This widespread species is the largest and coarsest of the western false hellebores, and also the most toxic. It can be easily distinguished by its drooping panicles of green flowers. The flowers are 15 to 20 millimeters across; the tepals are hairy and often coarsely toothed. The winged seed is smaller than that of *Veratrum californicum*, usually 8 to 10 millimeters long. Green hellebore has a transcontinental, boreal distribution, including populations in the eastern United States and Canada. On the Pacific Slope, it is very abundant from Alaska to California's Klamath Ranges, usually in very wet subalpine meadows. In the western Cascades of Oregon, *V. viride* sometimes grows with *V. californicum* in more mesic sites on deep, well-drained loamy soils. This species is not quite as amenable to cultivation in lowland gardens as the others discussed here, nor does it have quite as much aesthetic appeal. It should be a good choice, however, for mountain and far northern gardens.

Xerophyllum (Liliaceae)

Like *Stenanthium*, this is a genus with two members—one in the West, and one in the East. (*Xerophyllum asphodeloides* is discussed in chapter 11, "Bulbs of Eastern North America.")

Xerophyllum tenax (Pursh) Nuttall

The western representative is a long-lived, evergreen, perennial herb with several densely leaved crowns growing from a large, woody rhizome (Plate 91). The linear leaves are tough and wiry (hence the name *tenax*, or "tough"). Only a few crowns produce flowering stems each year, and these crowns die after seed is set. The stems are leafy, with the leaves gradating upward into green bracts. Each stem bears a large, showy raceme composed of hundreds of small, fragrant white flowers. The stems elongate as the flowers open on long pedicels, giving a characteristic clublike shape to the inflorescence. The black, angular seeds are 4 millimeters long.

Xerophyllum tenax, popularly known as beargrass, is distinguished from the eastern American *X. asphodeloides* by its greater size, usually 100 to 150 centimeters tall in bloom, and its longer racemes, usually at least 50 centimeters when fully developed. Beargrass is common on dry open slopes and ridges, and it often forms much of the understory in open montane coniferous forest in the Cascades and Coast Ranges from British Columbia to California, eastward to the northern Rocky Mountains of Montana and Wyoming. Beargrass survives removal of the forest canopy and burning in clear-cuts, and when exposed thus to more sunlight, it often blooms in spectacular mass displays.

Xerophyllum lacks the toxic alkaloids of *Zigadenus* and other related genera. The rhizomes were roasted and eaten by aboriginal peoples. The foliage was also valued for basketry, and today it is collected in great quantities for use by florists; some populations have been damaged by unscrupulous cutting for this purpose.

Xerophyllum tenax is so similar in garden effect to *X. asphodeloides* that most gardeners have no reason to grow both. The two are adapted to quite different climatic areas, and beargrass can be expected to do better in areas with summer-dry rainfall patterns. Seed- or cutting-grown plants are available from several nurseries specializing in Pacific Northwest natives.

Beargrass is usually recommended for use as a specimen plant in partial shade on sloping ground, but it has also grown well and flowered on a sunny, east-facing slope in the Sebring Rock Garden in Eugene, Oregon. Good drainage is necessary, and at least the base of the plant should be protected from hot afternoon sun. Beargrass is highly drought-tolerant when established. In good conditions, with at least half a day of sun, a gallon-sized (about 4 liters) plant may bloom in its second year. More frequently, offsets require several years to build up to blooming size. This species is hardy to about USDA Zone 4; in mild climates, it should be protected from winter wet, since it grows in the snow zone in its native range.

Beargrass is best propagated from small offsets, taken in autumn or early spring and rooted uncovered in ground pumice or sand. Seed sown outdoors in autumn germinates well, but obtaining flowering plants from seed can take 10 to 12 years.

Zigadenus (Liliaceae)

About six species of death camas occur in the Northwest. They are perennials of open, moist to semiarid habitats which grow from brown-coated bulbs. There are several narrow, keeled leaves at the base, and one to several progressively smaller leaves on the stem which grade into membranous floral bracts. The foliage is hairy and rough to the touch. The greenish-white to cream, cup-shaped or starry flowers are numerous in simple or branched racemes. Each of the six similar tepals has a yellowish nectary at its base, which gives the genus its name. The seeds are rather large, elongate, flattened, and twisted.

It is easy to imagine that the unpopularity of this genus derives in part from its ominous common name, which arose because it often grows with edible species of *Camassia*. Bulbs of these two genera are similar, so indigenous harvesters had to distinguish them carefully to avoid poisoning their families. Both *Zigadenus venenosus* and *Z. elegans* sometimes cause livestock poisoning, and both appear in the official list of noxious weeds in Canada. The former appears to be much more toxic than any other species, but other garden bulbs (for example, *Colchicum*) are at least as toxic and far more popular. Many death camas species lack star quality and are perhaps best suited for mass plantings, but they are easily grown from seed and deserve more garden use. Three species —*Z. elegans*, *Z. fremontii*, and *Z. micrantha*—have received the Alpine Garden Society (AGS) Award of Merit. Most species are variable in flower size and habit and would reward selection.

Zigadenus venenosus and *Z. paniculatus* are suitable for crevices in the rock garden, rocky pasture, or alpine lawn. The narrow, relatively sparse foliage makes death camas easier than many other bulbs to place among small alpine plants. The cream-colored *Z. venenosus* often blooms in masses among purple *Delphinium menziesii* in rocky meadows in the Cascade Range, and this association would be worth trying in the rock garden—if nothing else, this pairing should be invulnerable to deer and rabbits.

Zigadenus elegans and the larger forms of *Z. fremontii* are showier plants with more open, elegantly formed flowers, and these may be suitable as specimen plants in the rock garden or informal border. Small forms of *Z. fremontii* are suitable for bulb frame or alpine house culture. Only *Z. elegans* is commonly sold by bulb suppliers, but seed of most species is often available and germinates readily when planted outdoors in midwinter. These are normally cold-germinators, although Deno (1986) indicated that cold stratification is not required. As is often the case with dryland bulbs, it is critical to maintain first-year seedling bulbs with a trace of moisture.

Zigadenus elegans Pursh

This is a widely distributed boreal species with two geographically separated subspecies which are sometimes treated as separate species.
Forms east of the Rocky Mountains are considered subspecies *glaucus*
(Nuttall) Hultén (synonym *Z. glaucus*), which ranges through most of
the eastern United States and Canadian provinces; curiously, this is the
subspecies found in Alaska, where it can be a very showy element of
subalpine meadows. Subspecies *elegans* is a smaller plant with a less
open inflorescence, found at higher elevations in the Rockies and the
Pacific Coast states (Plate 92). It often has green rather than glaucous
foliage. In the Pacific Northwest *Z. elegans* has a discontinuous distribution in the subalpine meadows and moist screes of the Olympics, Wallowas, and Steens Mountain.

Plants are handsome and compact, usually 20 to 50 centimeters
high, exceptionally to 80 centimeters, with flowers 20 to 25 millimeters in
diameter, well-spaced in the raceme. The flower structure of *Zigadenus
elegans* differs from that of the other species: the flowers open widely, the
stamens are much shorter than the tepals, and the ovary is partly inferior. The greenish glands at the base of each tepal are bilobed and contrast nicely with the cream tepals. *Zigadenus elegans* is rather similar in
appearance to *Z. fremontii*, but they can be distinguished by the fully
exposed ovary of the latter species.

The Pacific Northwest forms of *Zigadenus elegans* subsp. *elegans* are
among the most attractive in the genus and are particularly suitable for
cool situations in the larger rock garden or at the woodland edge. Collected seed is regularly available for gardeners interested in exploring its
adaptability to lowland gardens.

Zigadenus exaltatus Eastwood

Giant death camas is a distinctive and imposing Californian species from
moderate elevations on the western slope of the Sierra Nevada. The
numerous flowers are borne in open panicles on 60- to 100-centimeter
stems from very large, often clustered bulbs. Leaves are also large and
broader than they are in other species in the genus. *Zigadenus exaltatus*
can be expected to be less hardy than most species mentioned, perhaps
to USDA Zone 7. It certainly merits garden use and selection for forms
with larger, denser panicles. Collected seed is sometimes available, and
established clumps can be divided.

Zigadenus fremontii (Torrey) Torrey ex S. Watson

This is a widespread and variable plant distributed through much of
western California; it also occurs near the coast in southern Oregon. *Zigadenus fremontii* varies in height from 20 to 80 centimeters. The flowers
are broadly open, about 25 millimeters in diameter, with the stamens
much shorter than the tepals. The typical forms of this species are showy

plants with many flowers in open panicles. Low-growing plants known as *Z. fremontii* var. *minor* (Hooker & Arnott) Jepson occur near the Pacific Coast. These bear only a few large flowers in a corymbose (flat-topped) raceme. Both forms are attractive and worthy of cultivation. General habit and flower structure are rather similar to *Z. elegans*, but in *Z. fremontii*, the ovary is completely superior. Molecular studies suggest that these two species are not closely related.

Zigadenus micranthus Eastwood

Limited to serpentine soils in southwestern Oregon and northwestern California, this small species is similar to *Zigadenus venenosus*, differing in the usually smaller flowers (tepals generally 3 to 5 millimeters long) and more conical raceme, with the pedicels of the lower flowers much longer than those at the apex. Most forms of this species are of little garden value, but plants grown from seed collected in California by Wayne Roderick received an AGS Award of Merit. The award plants were very compact and may have been artificially dwarfed, since several bulbs were grown together in a clay pot.

Zigadenus paniculatus (Nuttall) S. Watson

Common east of the Cascade Range from Washington to California, and eastward to Montana and New Mexico, this dryland death camas is easily distinguished from other western species by its small flowers (tepals generally less than 5 millimeters long), borne in open panicles. The stamens protrude and are usually longer than the tepals. Flowers on the lateral branches of the inflorescence are frequently staminate, so that seed is commonly set only on those of the main axis. *Zigadenus paniculatus* ranges in height from about 30 to 70 centimeters.

Zigadenus venenosus S. Watson

The most deadly species of the genus occurs through most of the western half of North America. The distinguishing characteristics of *Zigadenus venenosus* are its generally small size and its small flowers in unbranched racemes. The stems are 5 to 25 centimeters tall in flower, then elongating in fruit. The flowers are cream-colored, and all are perfect, with both stamens and pistils. The tepals and stamens are both about 5 millimeters long. The tight spacing of the flowers on the raceme and conspicuous stamens create an attractively fuzzy inflorescence.

In nature, and probably in gardens, this is probably the most adaptable species of the genus. Although it is commonest at moderate elevations on open hillsides and in rocky meadows and vernal seeps, it is also locally abundant in grassland on coastal headlands, and in the heavy wet soils of low-elevation camas meadows. It would probably be much more abundant in these habitats today if it had not been rogued out for centuries by Native Americans. It blooms later than *Camassia*, usually

211

appearing during late May and early June at low elevations in western Oregon.

Bibliography

Dahlgren, R. M. T., H. T. Clifford, and P. F. Yeo. 1985. *The Families of Monocotyledons: Structure, Evolution and Taxonomy*. Berlin: Springer.

Deno, Norman C. 1986. "In Dry Sand." In Jean Williams, ed., *Rocky Mountain Alpines*. Portland: Timber Press. 252–255.

Deno, Norman C. 1993. *Seed Germination Theory and Practice*. State College, Pennsylvania: Privately printed.

Elliott, Jack G. 1978. "Successes and Failures in a New Garden, Part 1." *Bulletin of the Alpine Garden Society* 46(3): 204–211.

Franklin, Jerry F., and C. T. Dryness. 1988. *Natural Vegetation of Oregon and Washington*. Corvallis: Oregon State University Press.

Gorer, Richard. 1972. "Award of Merit: *Zigadenus venenosus* var. *micranthus*." *Bulletin of the Alpine Garden Society* 40(4): 318, 321.

Halliwell, Brian. 1981. "Award of Merit: *Scoliopus bigelowii*." *Bulletin of the Alpine Garden Society* 49(4): 345–346.

Halliwell, Brian. 1983. "Award of Merit: *Zigadenus fremontii*." *Bulletin of the Alpine Garden Society* 51(4): 298.

Hickman, James C., ed. 1993. *The Jepson Manual: Higher Plants of California*. Berkeley: University of California Press.

Hitchcock, C. Leo, and Arthur Cronquist. 1973. *Flora of the Pacific Northwest*. Seattle: University of Washington Press.

Kingsbury, J. M. 1964. *Poisonous Plants of the United States and Canada*. Englewood Cliffs, New Jersey: Prentice-Hall.

Kruckeberg, Arthur R. 1982. *Gardening with Native Plants of the Pacific Northwest*. Seattle: University of Washington Press.

Phillips, Roger, and Martyn Rix. 1989. *Bulbs*. New York: Random House; London: Pan.

Saunders, D. E. 1965. "Award of Merit: *Zigadenus elegans*." *Bulletin of the Alpine Garden Society* 33(4): 355.

Schmidt, Marjorie G. 1980. *Growing California Native Plants*. Berkeley: University of California Press.

– 10 –

Bulbs of the Southwest

MARY IRISH

The southwestern United States includes the states of New Mexico and Arizona, neighboring western Texas and southeastern California, and the southern portions of Nevada, Utah, and Colorado. Here most bulbous or rhizomatous plant species are found in the hills and mountains which interrupt the low, arid plains and are a prominent physical feature of the region. The low deserts, arid shrublands, and sparse grasslands are generally at elevations below 4000 feet (1200 meters). These habitats contain a varied and highly ornamental though poorly known assortment of species.

The low-elevation areas of the arid Southwest may be divided into three (or four) climatic and physical regions. The Chihuahuan Desert region penetrates the United States in far western Texas, southern New Mexico, and a small corner of southeastern Arizona. This area has a base elevation of around 2500 to 4000 feet (750 to 1200 meters), but there are high mountains throughout. Rainfall is split between thunderstorms in summer and longer, gentler winter rains; it averages 20 to 30 inches (508 to 762 millimeters) annually. Summer highs can be well over 100°F (38°C), and freezing temperatures are common in winter. Most of this area falls into USDA Zones 8 and 9 in terms of average annual low temperatures. The Edwards Plateau area of Texas occurs east of the Chihuahuan Desert; the South Texas Plains are south of this plateau. Both share its high summer temperatures and intermittent freezing winter temperatures. In the Edwards Plateau the highly alkaline soils are generally very thin. Most of this area is in USDA Zone 8 or 9.

The Sonoran Desert region encompasses all of southern Arizona and continues into Mexico in the states of Sonora, Baja California, and part of Sinaloa. This area is hot in summer—average highs are well above 105°F (41°C)—but winter freezing temperatures are infrequent and of short duration. Although numerous high hills or mountains are in the area, most are not high enough to offer more than a fleeting respite from the heat. Soils are alkaline and may be rocky on the slopes or heavy clays in the lower areas. Rainfall occurs in both winter and summer; annual ranges are from 7.5 or less to 12 inches (191 to 304 millimeters). This region falls into USDA Zone 9, with a few areas in Zone 10.

The area of southwestern Arizona and southeastern California that borders the Colorado River and continues into northern Mexico and Baja California is among the driest parts of North America. Rain occurs only in winter and is generally 3 to 4 inches (76 to 102 millimeters) a year. Infrequently, summer rains occur as the result of Pacific hurricanes, but they can never be relied on. This region is generally frost-free, and high temperatures are well above 108°F (42°C) for much of the summer. Soils are often deep and sandy, with some alluvial or clay soils in the valleys. This region is in USDA Zone 10, with a few areas in Zone 9.

The Mohave Desert of eastern California and western Nevada is equally dry. Rainfall is in the winter and amounts to less than 3 inches (76 millimeters) per year. It can, however, be quite cold on winter nights in this region, with freezing temperatures brief in duration but common over the season. Snowfall occurs occasionally. The soils are varied: rocky hillsides, sandy lenses in the valleys, and heavy clays in old lakebeds and rivercourses. These areas fall into USDA Zones 7, 8, and 9.

The implications of the Southwest's climate for its plants' growing preferences are obvious. Few species here, particularly the bulbous ones, tolerate permanently moist soils. Less obviously, many of them are intolerant of atmospheric humidity; even during the rainy season, their natural environment dries out rapidly between storms. Deciduous Southwest plants, especially those of the true desert, tend to grow rapidly when moisture is present, flower quickly, and retreat into a long dormancy soon thereafter. In years that are drier than average they may fail to flower or even to emerge above ground.

Androstephium (Liliaceae)

Androstephium is a small genus of two species in the family Liliaceae (or Alliaceae, in the new system). The genus is restricted to the American Southwest from southern California east to Kansas and south to Arizona. The plant grows from a fibrous-coated corm. The leaves are thin, channeled, rough, and completely basal. The scape is erect and leafless. The flowers are held in an umbel and may be blue, mauve, or white. The filaments of the stamen are fused into a crownlike tube or corona.

Androstephium breviflorum S. Watson

This is the only *Androstephium* found in desert regions. It occurs at elevations of 2000 to 7000 feet (600 to 2100 meters) in southeastern California, Arizona, and western Colorado, growing in open desert scrub and sandy soils. This species is rarely seen in cultivation. Propagation is by either division or seed. The leaves are 10 to 39 centimeters long and rough in texture. The scape grows up to 39 centimeters tall and bears funnel-shaped flowers that are whorled and open above the tube and about 1.2 centimeters long. The perianth segments are white to light lavender, drying to yellow or brown; they open in March and April.

Androstephium caeruleum (Scheele) Greene

The blue funnel lily, or blue Bethlehem lily (synonym *Androstephium violaceum*), ranges from eastern Texas north to Kansas. It is distinguished from the previous species by its azure blue flowers. It grows in deep, well-drained sandy loam and undisturbed prairie soils. This species is hardy to at least 14°F (–10°C).

Behria (Liliaceae)

Behria is a small genus of primarily Mexican species.

Behria tenuiflora Greene

This species (synonym *Bessera tenuiflora*) is found on rocky hillsides and sandy plains in Baja California and blooms from September to October. The plants form a dark red-brown, membranous corm. The leaves are narrow and linear, to 12 inches (30 centimeters) long. The flowers are held in an umbel, each floret on a slender pedicel to 4.5 centimeters long. The perianth segments are bright orange-red with yellow veins, and the stamens are somewhat exserted.

Bloomeria (Liliaceae)

This small genus of two species occurs from central California to northern Baja California. Plants form a fibrous corm. Leaves are basal and flowers are held in an umbel. (See chapter 3 "The *Brodiaea* Alliance" for more information.)

Chlorogalum (Liliaceae)

Chlorogalum is a small genus of five species distributed from southern Oregon to northern Baja California. The plant forms a bulb with a tunic which is fibrous or membranous. The leaves are basal and undulate. Flowers are held in a terminal panicle.

Chlorogalum parviflorum S. Watson

Chlorogalum parviflorum is the only species in the genus that occurs in the desert parts of North America. It is found in dry, coastal sage scrub from central and southern California to northern Baja California, usually on the western sides of hills at elevations of 2500 feet (750 meters) or lower. Its leaves emerge in early spring and die back before blooming. Bloom occurs from May to July in nature, but in cultivation it is more likely in late spring. Plants should be kept entirely dry during summer dormancy. This species has a broadly ovate bulb, 4 to 7 centimeters long, with a dark brown, membranous coat. The plant with its scape is 30 to 90 centimeters tall. The leaves are narrow and undulate. The tiny, spreading flowers, white or pink with a dark rose midvein, are held on slender pedicels with two or more per node and form a delicate spray of bloom. They open at dawn but last only one day. The flowers have an unpleasant aroma consistent with fly pollination.

Echeandia (Liliaceae)

This small genus comprises species formerly included in the genus *Anthericum*, which is now restricted to Old World plants. *Echeandia* species occur in western North America in Texas, New Mexico, and Arizona, and south into Mexico. The plants grow from fleshy roots and rhizomes. The leaves occur in loose, open rosettes and are sessile and grasslike. The slender inflorescence may be a raceme or a panicle. Stamens may be naked or bearded and are half the length of the perianth segments.

Echeandia chandleri (Greenman & C. H. Thompson) M. C. Johnston

This species, known in Spanish as *lila de los llanos* (lily of the plains), occurs in the Rio Grande Valley and on the southern coast of Texas, extending south into northeastern Mexico. It is found in clay soils in chaparral, thickets, and prairies. This species is evergreen in warm areas and blooms throughout the year in nearly frost-free zones. Outside those climates, it blooms in the fall. The plants are erect and 30 to 90 centimeters tall when in flower. The leaves are held in a loose rosette and are 1.2 centimeters wide or more, flattened and with visible veins. The pale yellow to yellow-gold flowers are held in a loose panicle; individual blossoms are as much as 4 centimeters across. Several slender stems bloom at once, and the loose raceme makes them attractive in mass.

Echeandia flavescens (J. A. & J. H. Schultes) Cruden

The amber lily, or crag lily, is similar to *Echeandia chandleri* in most respects, but its leaves are narrower than those of the latter and do not have distinct cross veins. *Echeandia flavescens* is now considered to include two formerly distinct taxa, *Anthericum flavescens* and *A. torreyi*. This species occurs in far western Texas and in the mountains of Arizona, New Mexico, and northeastern Mexico. In Arizona and New Mexico it is found at 5000 to 9000 feet (1500 to 2700 meters) on rocky hillsides in pine forests. It also grows in the canyons and hillsides of western Texas east onto the Edwards Plateau. In cultivation *E. flavescens* must be prevented from becoming too wet, so a loose, gravelly medium is advised. The leaves are up to 18 centimeters long. The flowers are generally dark orange-yellow with a greenish medial stripe, and about 1.2 centimeters long; they are borne in a loose raceme up to 51 centimeters tall. *Echeandia flavescens* blooms from June to November; the mountain populations bloom in August.

Hesperocallis (Liliaceae)

Hesperocallis is a monotypic genus. The beauty of *Hesperocallis* tempts many to try growing it. Seed germinates easily in the late winter or very early spring when temperatures are relatively cool. Following germination, it is important not to let the young plants go dormant, or they are unlikely to recover. It can be two years or more before the bulb is large enough to endure dormancy and grow more than one or two leaves. It has not been reported how many years *Hesperocallis* takes to flower from seed. Some authors write that it is cold-intolerant, but it is more likely to be intolerant of cool, wet conditions, considering its natural distribution. In nature, bulbs may plunge 20 feet (more than 6 meters) below the dunes, and it is advisable to give cultivated bulbs plenty of room.

Hesperocallis undulata A. Gray

This species, commonly known as ajo lily or desert lily, is found in deep sandy soils in some of the most arid regions of North America: the deserts of southeastern California, Baja California and Sonora in Mexico, and southwestern Arizona, at elevations below 800 feet (250 meters). The bulb is large, pale, and ovoid. The leaves are gray-green, undulate, basal, and 20 to 50 centimeters long. The flowers are large (4 to 5 centimeters in diameter) and held in a raceme on a tall scape (Plate 93). They are white with a silver or green midstripe and are delicately fragrant. Flowering is from February to May; it is erratic from year to year but appears to follow a wet winter.

Hymenocallis (Amaryllidaceae)

Hymenocallis is a genus with about 40 species of bulbous plants. (The remainder of the North American species are discussed in chapter 2, "Amaryllidaceae of North America.") The species *H. sonorensis* is found along streams and valleys throughout Sonora, Mexico, and is among the few plants discussed in this chapter that prefer moist habitats.

Hymenocallis sonorensis Standley

This species has an ovoid membranous bulb that is white or pink. The leaves generally are basal, large, and evergreen, to 25 centimeters long and about 1.2 centimeters wide. The flowers are held in an umbel on a scape 20 to 30 centimeters tall, three to six flowers on a stem. They are sessile on the scape and are pure white, appearing in July in nature. In cultivation this species is evergreen in warm climates and does best with regular summer watering. It may bloom in late summer but more commonly in the fall and, like many *Hymenocallis* species, it blooms in considerable shade. In cultivation it often does not bloom every year. It may be grown from seed or division.

Hypoxis (Hypoxidaceae)

Hypoxis is large genus of about 150 species in the Hypoxidaceae (formerly considered part of the Amaryllidaceae), distributed through North America, Africa, Australia, and tropical Asia. Plants form a corm and have basal leaves that are sometimes ridged, often hairy. The inflorescence is a sparsely flowered raceme, or solitary.

Hypoxis mexicana J. A. & J. H. Schultes

The only species reported for the desert areas of the West is *Hypoxis mexicana*, documented only from a collection made by Lemmon in the Huachuca Mountains of southern Arizona. It has not been reported in cultivation.

Milla (Liliaceae)

Milla is a genus of about six species. The plants have small corms with a thin coat, linear leaves, and flowers held in an erect umbel.

Milla biflora Cavanilles

This species is the only one in the genus reported to range north of Mexico. It occurs on hills, rocky slopes, and grasslands from 4000 to 7000 feet (1200 to 2100 meters) in Arizona, southern New Mexico, and western Texas, as well as in Mexico from Baja California and Sonora south to Oaxaca. The Mexican star is a charming summer-blooming bulb with narrow, channeled, basal, blue-green leaves which appear round in cross section. The flowers are bright white with a green midstripe on the outer surface; they are funnel-form with a long tube and are held in an open umbel of two to six flowers. Individual flowers are up to 4 centimeters in diameter, and the scape is 15 to 40 centimeters tall. The flowers are delicately fragrant and bloom from August to September.

Muilla (Liliaceae)

Muilla is a genus of about five species; they resemble *Allium* but lack the characteristic odor. The plants have corms with fibrous coverings, few leaves, and numerous flowers in umbels. The genus occurs in the southwestern United States and Mexico.

Muilla clevelandii (S. Watson) Hoover

The San Diego golden star (synonym *Bloomeria clevelandii*) is quite rare, found only in southwestern San Diego County and northern Baja California in grasslands and scrub edges below 150 feet (45 meters). Its leaves are 6 to 15 centimeters long. The flowers are yellow striped with green, and the filament appendages are entire. The scape is less than 30 centimeters tall, with 20 to 30 flowers in an umbel.

Muilla coronata E. Greene

The crowned muilla, an uncommon species, is found in open desert scrub and woodland in heavy soils at elevations of 3000 to 5000 feet (900 to 1500 meters) in the Mohave Desert of eastern California and southwestern Nevada. It has leaves that are less than 18 centimeters long, narrow, and basal. The flowers are small—less than 1.2 centimeters long—and green outside, white or light blue inside. The filaments are petal-like, wide at the base and fused into a crown, hence the specific name. The anthers are yellow. The scape is 3 to 15 centimeters tall and ends in an umbel.

Muilla maritima (Torrey) S. Watson

The common muilla (synonyms *Muilla serotina*, *M. tenuis*) is found in the eastern deserts of California and Baja California in alkaline, granite, or serpentine soils from sea level to 7500 feet (2250 meters). The leaves are basal, narrow, and to 60 centimeters long. The flowers are greenish white with a brown midrib; the anthers are remarkably colored in purple, blue, or green. The scape rises to 50 centimeters and ends in an umbel of 4 to 70 flowers.

Muilla serotina Greene

This species is similar to *Muilla maritima* but has more scabrous (rougher) leaves. It is found along the coast of northern Baja California almost to Rosario.

Muilla transmontana E. Greene

This species strongly resembles *Muilla maritima,* but the flowers open white and age to lilac, and the anthers are yellow. It occurs in the desert scrub of the Great Basin and western Nevada from 4000 to 7500 feet (1200 to 2250 meters).

Schoenocaulon (Liliaceae)

Schoenocaulon is a genus of about 10 species. The plants have ovoid bulbs and basal, grasslike leaves with serrulate margins. The flowers are held in a raceme or spike. The genus occurs from western North America south through Mexico to Peru.

Schoenocaulon drummondii Gray

The coconut lily occurs along the coastal prairie and South Texas Plains of southern Texas and into northeastern Mexico. It may form large colonies of plants with numerous flowering stalks. It has evergreen leaves to 50 centimeters long. The tiny flowers are creamy white, thin, with irregularly toothed margins and stamens that reach well beyond the perianth. The scape is 60 centimeters tall. It blooms in fall. The flowers smell strongly of coconut, hence the common name.

Schoenocaulon texanum Scheele

Known as green lily, this species occurs on limestone in canyons, bluffs, and outwashes from the South Texas Plains through the Edwards Plateau into western Texas, southeastern New Mexico, and adjacent Mexico. Its leaves are similar to those of *Schoenocaulon drummondii.* The flowers are pinkish green, with no scent, fleshy—even leathery—and have stamens which extend well beyond the perianth segments. Bloom is from March to July.

Sisyrinchium (Iridaceae)

This large genus of about 90 species occurs throughout the Americas, and some species are widely naturalized elsewhere. The plant arises from a rhizome with prominent stems that are generally flat but may be winged or rounded. Leaves are narrow and grasslike. The inflorescence is an umbel. Flowers may be purple, blue, violet, or yellow, or rarely white. Though not bulbous, *Sisyrinchium* is so prominent in the monocot flora of the American Southwest that its representatives are discussed here. In addition to the species described below, three others are in the region, all from higher elevations. *Sisyrinchium arizonicum* Rothrock is a mountain plant of Arizona and New Mexico, at elevations of 6000 to 9500 feet (1800 to 2850 meters). *Sisyrinchium cernuum* (Bicknell) Kearney occurs in southeastern Arizona and Mexico along streams at about 4000 feet (1200 meters) elevation. *Sisyrinchium longipes* (Bicknell) Kearney & Peebles is found in Arizona and northern Mexico at elevations of 5500 to 9000 feet (1650 to 2700 meters).

Sisyrinchium demissum Greene

This species is found along streams in Oregon to California, Arizona to western Texas, and in the mountains of northern Mexico at elevations of 5000 to 9500 feet (1500 to 2850 meters). It has erect stems 22 to 72 centimeters tall. The leaves are narrow and less than half the height of the flowering scape. The flowers, small and blue, appear from June to August.

Sisyrinchium dimorphum R. Oliver

Found along streams in the Edwards Plateau and far western Texas into northern Mexico, this species has numerous stems which are spreading to erect and 9 to 32 centimeters tall. The flowers are violet-purple to dark blue and appear from April to July.

Sisyrinchium ensigerum Bicknell

This species is found in clay, limestone, or sandy soils in the Edwards Plateau and South Texas Plains south into northern Mexico and north to Oklahoma. It is known to hybridize naturally with the more eastern *Sisyrinchium pruinosum* where their ranges overlap. The western Texas population may be similar to the Mexican species *S. scabrum* Schlechtendal & Chamisso. *Sisyrinchium ensigerum* produces numerous or few erect stems 15 to 47 centimeters tall. The flowers are purple-blue. In cultivation *S. ensigerum* is evergreen if kept watered through the summer. It blooms over a long period in midspring and does not tolerate being dry when in bloom. It is wonderful when massed.

Sisyrinchium funereum Bicknell

This species (named for its locality, not its appearance) grows only along the alkaline margins of wet areas below 2800 feet (840 meters) in the Death Valley region of California into Nevada. It has tufted stems to 70 centimeters tall and pale blue flowers.

Zephyranthes (Amaryllidaceae)

In Mexico the rain lilies, as a group, are generally referred to as *las flores de mayo* (the flowers of May), suggested by their popping up following spring rains.

Zephyranthes longifolia Hemsley

This rain lily is a resident of the desert areas of northern Mexico, western Texas, and parts of Arizona and New Mexico. It blooms in June and July in southern Arizona, and earlier in Mexico, where it is known from the high plateau region on the Tropic of Cancer, growing up to an elevation of 6000 feet (1800 meters). In Arizona it grows among oaks, junipers, *Dasylirion*, and *Nolina*. The oval bulb is tunicated and bears a single flower stalk with one small, cup-shaped golden-bronze flower. The leaves are slender, linear, and up to 25 centimeters long (hence the specific epithet *longifolia*) and emerge at the same time as the flowering stem (in botanical terms, they are *synanthous*). The plant is quick to shed its black seed, which often germinates the same season rather than remaining dormant until the next annual rainy season. Occasionally there is a second bloom season in September.

Zigadenus (Liliaceae)

Zigadenus is a genus comprising about 18 species of both bulbous and rhizomatous plants. Stems are erect with or without a few small leaves. Leaves are linear and basal, and the scape may be with or without leaves. Flowers are held in panicles or racemes. The genus occurs mostly in North America, with one species in northern Asia; most North American species are found within or near our area of interest. All species contain toxic alkaloids that may cause serious to fatal symptoms if ingested; all parts are lethal to cattle and other herbivorous animals. *Zigadenus elegans*, *Z. fremontii*, *Z. paniculatus*, and *Z. venenosus*, described in the chapter on the Northwest, also occur at higher elevations in the Southwest.

Zigadenus brevibracteatus (M. E. Jones) H. M. Hall

This species is found on rocky hillsides and in sandy deserts of California and Baja California at elevations from 2000 to 6000 feet (600 to 1800 meters). It forms an ovoid bulb with a dark brown to black coat. The leaves are up to 25 centimeters long, and rough. The flowers are yellowish with a short claw and are held in an erect, open raceme on a scape to 60 centimeters tall. The stamens are not exserted beyond the tepals. Bloom is in May.

Zigadenus virescens (Humboldt, Bonpland, & Kunth) Macbride

This plant inhabits coniferous forests of New Mexico and Arizona south through Mexico to Central America, at 6,500 to 10,000 feet (1950 to 3000 meters) elevation. Its bulb has a dark tunic. The flowers, held in a loose panicle, are greenish white, often with a purple tint.

Acknowledgment

Helpful information was provided by Mark Dimmitt, Mary Sue Ittner, Michael Mace, Shawn Pollard, and Russell Stafford.

Bibliography

Hickman, James C., ed. 1993. *The Jepson Manual: Higher Plants of California.* Berkeley: University of California Press.

Kearney, Thomas H., Robert H. Peebles, and collaborators. 1960. *Arizona Flora.* Berkeley: University of California Press.

Martin, William C., and Charles R. Hutchins. 1980. *A Flora of New Mexico.* Vaduz: J. Cramer.

Ogden, Scott. 1991. "Bulbous Plants of the Edwards Plateau." *Proceedings of the Native Plants Society of Texas Symposium.* 37–43.

Ogden, Scott. 1994. *Garden Bulbs for the South.* Dallas: Taylor.

Shreve, Forrest, and Ira L. Wiggins. 1964. *Vegetation and Flora of the Sonoran Desert.* Stanford: Stanford University Press.

Walker, Sally. 1999. "Rainy-season Plants of the Southwest." *Rock Garden Quarterly* 57(3): 191–210.

Wasowski, Sally, and Andy Wasowski. 1988. *Native Texas Plants: Landscaping Region by Region.* Austin: Texas Monthly Press.

Welsh, Stanley L., N. Duane Atwood, Sherel Goodrich, and Larry C. Higgins, eds. 1976. *A Utah Flora.* Great Basin Naturalist Memoirs, 9. Salt Lake City: Brigham Young University.

– 11 –

Bulbs of Eastern North America

C. COLSTON BURRELL

Like a prophet, a good bulb is seldom recognized in its native land. In our quest for the unusual we often overlook the obvious. The native flora of North America east of the Rocky Mountains contains a great diversity of easily cultivated, garden-worthy bulbs. They originate in woodlands, meadows, prairies, and wetlands. Many of these overlooked species lack the splashy flowers of trilliums and lilies, but they have a quiet charm and an ethereal beauty. A few, like the spider lily (*Hymenocallis*), are stunning in both flower and fragrance. A little extra attention to soil and moisture conditions gains experienced gardeners a few additional species whose beauty repays the effort tenfold.

Many American flowering bulbs are ephemeral: the plants use the energy stored within their bulbs to put on a quick spurt of growth in the early spring. They flower, set seed, and disappear underground before the forest canopy—mostly deciduous, in the area discussed in this chapter—closes in or summer dryness makes leaves a liability. Summer moisture is preferable for most of these species, but once they are dormant, they tolerate some drying. Summer-flowering species and certain spring bloomers that remain in growth after flowering require consistent moisture throughout the growing season. In addition, the later-blooming species invariably require some direct sunlight, and many thrive in full sun.

The plants are categorized here by their habitats: forest-dwellers first, then bulbs of grassland and wetland.

Forest Species

Arisaema triphyllum (Linnaeus) Torrey

The genus *Arisaema* (Araceae), largely distributed in eastern Asia, contains two American species that are of interest to gardeners for their attractive foliage and intriguing floral structures.

Some botanists elevate the different color forms of *Arisaema triphyllum* to species status, but I have retained them as one species. In the arum family, flower petals and sepals are replaced by a fleshy hood (spathe), familiar as the white part of the calla lily (*Zantedeschia*); it surrounds a central reproductive column (spadix). This variable plant has many local English names but is best known as Jack-in-the-pulpit. It is native to low woods, forested swamps, and deciduous or mixed forests throughout the East and Midwest. The leaves are divided into three broad leaflets borne on a fleshy, spotted stalk 30 to 90 centimeters tall. Young plants have a single leaf, while older plants produce a pair. The showy green spathe, appearing in April and May, may be striped with purple, brown, or light green (Plate 94). Some showy forms have a rich purple blaze on the spathe.

"Jacks" have an interesting reproductive biology. The young plants, usually those with a single leaf, produce only pollen-bearing flowers. As they mature and presumably become able to expend enough energy to ripen seed, the flowers switch sex to female. The oldest plants are presumed to be bisexual, producing male flowers at the apex of the spadix and female flowers toward the base—a characteristic seen in most arums.

Jack-in-the-pulpit is so easy to grow, it seems to thrive wherever planted. In the wild it prefers rich, seasonally wet to moist soil in light to full shade. In the garden, plants produce the best flowers and lushest foliage in deep, humus-rich, evenly moist soil. Plants increase in size with each passing season, and old patriarchs may stand 1 meter tall. In the garden combine them with low ephemerals and ground covers, so the stately stems and curious flowers will stand out above a flowered carpet. Good companions include spring beauty (*Claytonia virginica*), bloodroot (*Sanguinaria canadensis*), toothwort (*Cardamine dentata*), and Virginia bluebells (*Mertensia virginica*). In wetter sites they are found with skunk cabbage (*Symplocarpus foetidus*), marsh marigold (*Caltha palustris*), and golden groundsel (*Senecio aureus*).

Jacks have showy, orange-red fruits which tend to flop over from their own weight as they ripen. Remove the pulp and sow the cleaned seeds outdoors, or indoors with six weeks of cold, moist stratification. Tubers should be transplanted while dormant.

Arisaema dracontium (Linnaeus) Schott

Known as green dragon, *Arisaema dracontium* is showier in foliage than in flower, though the curious dragon-shaped blossom has its own charms. The large, single leaf with 7 to 15 leaflets arranged in a semicircle around the central stalk is reminiscent of maidenhair fern (*Adiantum* spp.). A long, awl-like spadix protrudes majestically from the inconspicuous hooded green spathe (Plate 95). Mature plants may reach 120 centimeters in height, with a 60-centimeter spread. Green dragon needs moist to wet soil—it does not tolerate drying out—and prefers full to partial sun in cooler climates. Use this stately species as an accent plant. The persistent foliage is useful in the summer garden swaying above a delicately textured carpet of astilbe, tassel rue (*Trautvetteria carolinensis*), brook saxifrage (*Boykinia aconitifolia*), and violets. Primroses, iris, sedges, and ferns are additional good companions. This species is propagated as described for *A. triphyllum*.

Amianthium muscaetoxicum (Walter) A. Gray

A member of the Liliaceae (Melanthiaceae) and the only species in its genus, fly poison is a handsome plant of acidic woodlands and savannas from New York south to Florida and west into Missouri and Oklahoma. Plants are found above granitic rocks, usually on south-facing or west-facing slopes under oaks, often in the company of mountain laurel (*Kalmia latifolia*) and rhododendrons. The poisonous bulb produces a mound of attractive straplike foliage and a single 60-centimeter flowering stalk bearing a dense, elongate cluster of creamy white flowers that fade to green and persist long after pollination. The flowers open in late spring or early summer.

Somewhat finicky, the plants like humus-rich, sandy soil that is evenly moist but well drained. They tolerate considerable summer dryness once established. Give them a spot in a rock garden or peat bed in light to partial shade; in warmer zones, full shade is acceptable. Plants are often single-stemmed in the wild, but in cultivation they may form many-stemmed clumps. Fly poison shares its upland habitats with small-flowered veratrum (*Veratrum parviflorum*), galax (*Galax urceolata*), wintergreen (*Gaultheria procumbens*), and partridgeberry (*Mitchella repens*), all of which make good garden companions. Contrast the strappy leaves with airy ferns, and bold textures from sarsaparilla (*Aralia nudicaulis*) or hostas.

Propagate *Amianthium* by sowing seed outdoors when ripe or indoors, alternating warm moist and cold moist periods. Bulbs can be divided when dormant.

Chamaelirium luteum (Linnaeus) A. Gray

Another monotypic genus of the Liliaceae (Melanthiaceae), *Chamaelirium* has a fascinating variety of common names: devil's bit, fairy wand, and shooting star. This charming but rarely encountered plant has a long history of medicinal use but is almost unknown in horticulture. Plants grow wild in open dry to mesic woods, sunny serpentine barrens, and low, sandy meadows from Massachusetts and Michigan, ranging south to Florida and Arkansas. Powders and teas made from the root have been used to treat colic, worms, indigestion, and maladies of the male and female reproductive systems.

In bloom in late spring, *Chamaelirium luteum* stands 30 to 75 centimeters tall, with a densely packed wand of small flowers that often droops at the tip, giving rise to the name fairy wand (Plate 96). This plant is unusual among members of the lily family because it is dioecious, having male and female flowers on separate plants. Male flowers are a bit showier owing to the protruding stamens. The bright evergreen basal leaves are narrow to broadly oval, and widest at the tip.

Plants are easy to grow in humus-rich, well-drained, slightly acidic soil in partial to full shade. In the wild they grow as scattered individuals or small clumps, and they perform similarly in the garden. In my experience *Chamaelirium* does not bulk up fast, and self-sown seedlings are rare. Contrast is the key to exciting garden combinations: choose maidenhair fern (*Adiantum* spp.), rue anemone (*Anemonella thalictroides*), *Iris cristata*, and tall arching stems of Solomon's seal (*Polygonatum* spp.). Multicrowned plants can be divided in spring or autumn.

Clintonia borealis (Aiton) Rafinesque

Two species of this ornamental genus in the Liliaceae (Convallariaceae) are found in eastern North America. Additional species are native to the west coast of North America and to Asia. Plants produce two or three broadly oval, satiny leaves from a small crown with spidery, succulent roots. The flowers have three petals and three petal-like sepals and are followed by large, spherical fruits.

Called bluebeard for its fruits, *Clintonia borealis* is a denizen of rich, acidic northern coniferous and mixed deciduous woods and bogs from Labrador and Manitoba in Canada south to Minnesota and Pennsylvania; it also occurs in the mountains south to North Carolina. Plants produce a lush pair or triad of glossy, flat, oval deciduous leaves that emerge like a cylinder around the bloom stalk (Plate 97). Each single, slender, naked stalk is topped by a cluster of four to eight 2-centimeter, nodding chartreuse bells. The glossy berries turn deep blue in late summer. Plants spread by underground stolons to form broad, dense clumps.

Clintonias are not for every garden. They demand cool, humus-rich acidic soil in partial to full shade with consistent summer moisture. Do not attempt to grow plants in less than optimal conditions, or they will perish. They are difficult to establish, and it has been suggested that they require associations with soil fungi or other microorganisms. Try them in a rotted pine stump, which will also raise the foliage and flowers to eye level. Their northern companions include *Mitchella repens*, bunchberry (*Cornus canadensis*), *Gaultheria procumbens*, starflower (*Trientalis borealis*), false lily-of-the-valley (*Maianthemum canadense*), and ferns. Choose ericaceous shrubs such as rhododendrons as a backdrop. Clintonias have no serious pests, though excessive heat may promote leaf and root rots.

Plants slowly form broad clumps that can be divided in fall. Pull the individual, discrete crowns apart. Store seed refrigerated in moist sphagnum moss for six to eight weeks; it has a complex dormancy. When seed is sown outdoors, germination occurs the following summer. Seedlings develop slowly.

Clintonia umbellulata (Michaux) Morong

The speckled wood lily is found in rich woods, moist, sheltered cove forests, and mountain slopes from New York and Ohio, south to North Carolina and Tennessee. This species differs from bead lily in having 10 to 30 upfacing white flowers with flat, open faces. The berries are black. The plants are similar in other respects. Plant *Clintonia umbellulata* in moist, well-drained, humus-rich acidic soil in partial to full shade. Combine this mat-forming beauty with red trillium (*Trillium erectum*), mountain bellwort (*Uvularia pudica*), liverleaf (*Hepatica americana*), Allegheny spurge (*Pachysandra procumbens*), Fraser's sedge (*Cymophyllus fraseri*), and ferns. Propagation is the same as for *Clintonia borealis*.

Stenanthium gramineum (Ker-Gawler) Morong

Look for the airy flowers of feather-fleece or feather-bells (Liliaceae [Melanthiaceae]) on seepage slopes in the mountains, and in low wet meadows and bogs in the coastal plain and Piedmont from Pennsylvania and Indiana south to Florida and Arkansas. (*Stenanthium occidentale* is discussed in chapter 9, "Bulbs of the Northwest.") This late-summer bloomer sports slender stems 60 to 120 centimeters tall, topped by a cluster of creamy white flowers. *Stenanthium* means "narrow flower," referring to the narrow segments that look like they never fully open. The grasslike foliage is attractive from spring onward.

Stenanthium gramineum var. *robustum* (S. Watson) Fernald is a superior garden plant for any deep, rich soil that retains moisture all summer. It may reach 1.6 meters, with stout stems bearing branched panicles of nodding, feathery flowers in mid to late summer. Found from Maryland and Pennsylvania west to Indiana, this form has been distributed by the New England Wildflower Society.

Perennial pundit Alan Armitage calls this genus "unknown, unused, and unloved." *Stenanthium* is quite ornamental and should be more widely grown. Give it rich, wet to constantly moist acid soils in full sun for best growth. Plants form full, multistemmed clumps in time. Propagate them by dividing the bulbs when dormant. Fresh, stratified seed gives slow but reliable results.

Veratrum parviflorum Michaux
Veratrum woodii J. W. Robbins ex Wood

The small-flowered veratrum is found in rich woods, on rocky slopes, and around seeps in the mountains from Virginia to North Carolina and

Tennessee. (The western species are discussed in chapter 9, "Bulbs of the Northwest.") It is a diminutive species by comparison with its giant relations, the so-called false hellebores. In fact, some botanists place this species in the genus *Melanthium* as *M. parviflorum* (Michaux) S. Watson. Distinctive, basal rosettes of three to five broadly oval, pleated leaves form a low skirt for the tall (to 1 meter) leafless stalks. The 1-centimeter lime-green flowers are carried in open panicles in summer. Flowering is sporadic, and basal leaves are a more common sight than flower stalks. Plants may bloom one year and rest the next.

Veratrum woodii is similar to *V. parviflorum*, but its larger flowers are carried on stalks to 1.6 meters tall, and it is Midwestern in distribution, in dry woods and savannas from Ohio and Iowa south to Missouri and Oklahoma.

Plant the two eastern forest-dwelling veratrums in humus-rich, moist acidic soil in light to full shade. Though native to dryish woods, cultivated plants prefer consistent moisture through the growing season. In the wild, plants occur with fly poison (*Amianthium muscaetoxicum*) and speckled wood lily (*Clintonia umbellulata*), which make good garden companions. Extend the blooming season and add textural interest with plants like *Uvularia*, gaywings (*Polygala pauciflora*), evergreen wild ginger (*Asarum* spp.), Oconee bells (*Shortia galacifolia*), and yellow-root (*Xanthorhiza simplicifolia*). Sow fresh seed outdoors as soon as it is ripe. Seedlings develop slowly and take at least five years to reach blooming size.

Grassland and Wetland Species

Aletris farinosa Linnaeus

The pencil-thin spikes of colicroot or unicorn-root (Liliaceae [Melanthiaceae]) are seen waving in sandy ditches, savannas, pine flatwoods and bogs from Maine and Wisconsin, south to Florida and Texas. The curious, inflated tubular flowers with five starry lobes have a mealy appearance, hence the name *farinosa* (Plate 98). I can't help thinking of sea cucumbers when I look at them through a magnifying glass. They are borne in mid to late spring in unbranched spikes 30 to 90 centimeters above a basal rosette of smooth, bright green, lance-shaped leaves. This plant has a long history of medicinal use for treating colic, indigestion, and rheumatism; its active ingredient, diosgenin, is an anti-inflammatory.

Aletris lutea Small

The yellow colicroot resembles *Aletris farinosa* in most respects but is slightly shorter and has bright yellow flowers. It is restricted to the coastal plain from South Carolina to Texas, growing in pine savannas, flatwoods (low-lying forests, often poorly drained in winter), and bogs on sterile, acidic soils.

Colicroot likes sterile, dry to seasonally wet sandy soil in full sun or light shade. It can withstand summer drought. Plants are easy to grow in a sand or peat bed, or in a bog garden. Colicroot shares its native habitat with milkworts (*Polygala*), Virginia chain fern (*Woodwardia virginica*), cinnamon fern (*Osmunda cinnamonea*), white-bracted sedge (*Dichromena* spp.), and pitcher plants (*Sarracenia*). Other good garden companions include golden asters (*Heterotheca* spp.), *Hypoxis hirsuta*, turtlehead (*Chelone* spp.), *Zephyranthes atamasca*, and *Iris prismatica*.

Divide the dense crowns in spring or after flowering. Norman Deno (1993), in his compendium on seed germination, recommended sowing fresh seed uncovered at 70°F (21°C) or moist chilling at 40°F (4°C) for several weeks, then germinating it at 70°F (21°C). Seedlings are slow to reach flowering size.

Camassia scilloides (Rafinesque) Cory

Wild hyacinth (Hyacinthaceae) is a lovely denizen of low meadows, prairies, seeps, and wet woods from Pennsylvania and Missouri, south to Georgia and Texas. Plants are found in various situations, from deep, rich loam to the thin soil atop limestone outcrops. The common denominator in all sites is wet to moist soil in winter and spring. The bulbs of the eastern species, like the western native species (described in chapter 9, "Bulbs of the Northwest"), were eaten by Native Americans.

The pale to mid lavender-blue, starry, fragrant flowers are produced in open, elongate clusters on 30- to 60-centimeter stalks in early to mid-spring. Albino forms are scattered throughout most populations, but rich blue flowers are extremely rare. Narrow, weak foliage emerges with the flowers and persists for a month or more if the soil remains moist. Plants are summer-dormant.

This lovely but hard-to-find species can be a little tricky to cultivate. Plants require constant moisture in winter and spring, but once dormant, they tolerate some drought. For optimal growth, plant the bulbs in rich circumneutral to alkaline soil in full sun or light shade. In warmer areas provide afternoon shade and a cool root run. Where plants are well sited, they spread quickly to form scattered individuals or small clumps. Combine the pale blue spires with *Zephyranthes atamasca*, skunk cabbage (*Symplocarpus foetidus*), golden ragwort (*Senecio aureus*), violets, astilbes, primulas, and water-loving irises. Additional companions include ferns, sedges, and ornamental grasses which fill the void left when plants go dormant.

Propagate *Camassia* by division when plants are dormant. Seeds germinate readily with cold, moist stratification but require many years to flower.

Helonias bullata Linnaeus

Swamp pink (Liliaceae [Melanthiaceae]) has a curious, disjunct distribution: coastal pine barrens, and mountain seepage slopes and bogs from New York south to North Carolina. This showy species has long been exploited for its beauty as well as for its purported medicinal value. Never plentiful in the wild, it is rare throughout its range and is federally listed as threatened; it is listed as endangered in many states.

The new foliage emerges wrapped around the elongating, naked flower stalk, which reaches 30 to 60 centimeters. A terminal, elongated oval cluster of small, tightly packed pink flowers with blue anthers crowns the plant in early spring (Plate 99). The narrow-oval to oblanceolate, evergreen leaves have rounded tips and form a flattened, burnished green rosette in the winter.

Swamp pink grows in wet, sandy or peaty acidic soils in full sun to partial shade. Consistent moisture throughout the growing season is best, and dry soil in winter or spring is sure death to this plant, which grows just above the water line in its native haunts. Plants are available as propagated stock from nurseries and establish readily under the right conditions. Plant them with water-loving irises, primroses, astilbes, sedges, and ferns. Rodgersia, ligularia, coltsfoot (*Petasites palmatus*), and western skunk cabbage (*Lysichiton americanum*) are good companions with boldly contrasting leaves.

Mature plants form multiple, tightly packed crowns that can be divided after the foliage hardens, or in autumn. Ripe seeds sown outdoors germinate in one to two years, and seedlings develop slowly.

Hypoxis hirsuta (Linnaeus) Coville

Yellow stargrass (Hypoxidaceae) is a diminutive bulb that has the unusual and desirable trait of blooming over a long season. Claude Barr (1984), author of *Jewels of the Plains,* waxed sentimental about stargrass, saying that "it puts up its miniature reflections of the sun, singly or in clusters, over a long season beginning in spring." In the wild, plants exploit diverse habitats, including dry woodlands, sandy acidic flatwoods, and wet calcareous prairies. Four species, all similar to *Hypoxis hirsuta,* are listed for the Deep South: *H. leptocarpa, H. micrantha, H. rigida,* and *H. sessilis.*

This "sprightly, if modest little perennial," as Louise Beebe Wilder (1990) called it, has narrow, grassy foliage that seldom reaches 30 centimeters in height, and the flower stalk is usually much shorter. The 2-centimeter yellow flowers are indeed starlike and are borne in loose clusters (Plate 100). Only one or two flowers of a cluster open at any given time, so the plant is more of a novelty than a showstopper, but its quiet charm is appreciated by its devotees. A carpet of plants is far showier than a single clump.

In the garden, give stargrass moist, well-drained sandy soil. Scattered clumps are perfect for a rock garden, where they are not overpowered by larger, more vigorous companions. Plants thrive in meadow and prairie gardens among sparse grasses with other diminutive natives like prairie smoke (*Geum triflorum*), heart-leaf Alexander (*Zizia aptera*), pussytoes (*Antennaria* spp.), prairie phlox (*Phlox pilosa*), and violets. In open woods use stargrass in drifts with fire pink (*Silene virginica*), smooth phlox (*Phlox glaberrima*), ebony spleenwort (*Asplenium platyneuron*), and bluets (*Houstonia caerulea*), which are often its companions in the wild. Pot culture in a cool greenhouse is also possible.

Propagation is best accomplished by dividing the corms during the fall or early spring. Sow fresh seed outdoors or inside at 70°F (21°C). Self-sown seedlings appear sporadically.

Manfreda virginica (Linnaeus) Salisbury

The curious false aloe, or rattlesnake master, has been placed by some botanists in the genus *Agave* and by others in *Polianthes*; it is the best-known species of the genus *Manfreda* (Agavaceae), all native to North America. It grows wild on limestone outcrops, in juniper glades, and in open woods from West Virginia and Illinois south to Florida and Texas. It was used medicinally for such diverse ailments as dropsy, diarrhea, and worms; its use for treating snakebite gave rise to the colorful name rattlesnake master, also applied to *Eryngium yuccifolium*.

Though the leaves are leathery and succulent, they are deciduous. Fresh, spiky foliage emerges in early spring from a fleshy, bulblike rootstock. The lance-shaped leaves are rich green, often heavily mottled with dark green and brown. Tall, slender scapes bear brown to greenish flowers with slender, spidery tepals. The inflated seed capsules can be decorative in autumn.

Plant *Manfreda* in average to rich, circumneutral to limy soil in full sun or partial shade. In time plants become robust, with multiple crowns of decorative foliage. Good garden companions include ground covers such as verbena, *Phlox bifida*, and winecups (*Callirhoë* spp.), which surround and accentuate the dramatic foliage. Sow fresh seed with three to four weeks of cold, moist stratification. Young plants may bloom in about three years.

Melanthium hybridum Walter

Melanthium hybridum (Liliaceae [Melanthiaceae]) is shorter (to 100 centimeters) than the similar species *M. virginicum*, and its smaller, ruffled, fragrant flowers often open green; its leaves are broadly lance-shaped. Plants are restricted to the mountains from Connecticut south to Georgia, usually in woods rather than open situations. Though *Melanthium* is native to wet situations, it is forgiving in the garden as long as the soil is moist during flowering. Late summer dryness is tolerated, if true drought conditions do not persist for months on end. Give plants rich soil with consistent moisture in a spot with full sun to partial shade. Flowering is best in sunny situations. Good garden companions for soggy sites include water-loving irises, drooping sedge (*Carex crinita*), swamp milkweed (*Asclepias incarnata*), burnet (*Sanguisorba canadensis*), cardinal flower (*Lobelia cardinalis*), and *Osmunda* ferns. In slightly drier situations use log fern (*Dryopteris celsa*), lady fern (*Athyrium asplenioides*), and blue lobelia (*Lobelia siphilitica*). As with most liliaceous plants, cold moist stratification enhances seed germination.

Melanthium virginicum Linnaeus

Bunchflower graces wet meadows, low open woods, and forested bogs from New York to Indiana, south to Florida and Texas. Tufts of stiff, sedgelike leaves, which may be evergreen, form a basal clump; a few ascend the 120- to 150-centimeter bloom stalk, which is crowned by an open panicle of flattened, starry cream-colored flowers that fade to green. Plants begin flowering in late spring or early summer, but the persistent tepals keep the plant attractive well into summer.

Nothoscordum bivalve (Linnaeus) Britton

This small relative of the alliums, variously called yellow field garlic, false garlic, or crow poison, has a quiet charm in the wild, where it grows in great sweeps in seasonally wet fields and low meadows, as well as old pastures, from Virginia and Nebraska south to Florida and Mexico. In warm temperate gardens, however, it can be a pest which spreads by stolons and seed, coming up in the midst of choicer plants. Though smaller and less hardy than its notorious relative *Nothoscordum inodorum*, *N. bivalve* is best reserved for the wild garden. Flat, unscented, glaucous leaves emerge when soil is moist and are often persistent. The creamy white to pale yellow, starry, upfacing flowers in an uneven umbel arise sporadically in response to rain from late winter through summer, and often in autumn as well, depending on moisture availability.

Sisyrinchium angustifolium P. Miller

The several very similar *Sisyrinchium* species of the eastern United States are commonly called blue-eyed grass; their tepals are usually violet to blue, rarely white. They are generally species of open woodlands, meadows, and cleared areas and are frequently seen on roadsides. Some species, such as *S. fuscatum* Bicknell and *S. capillare* Bicknell, inhabit wet pine savannas and flatwoods of the Southeast. Blue-eyed grass prefers full sun to light shade and a soil that is rich and well drained. The flowers are produced in midspring to early summer, and the seed ripens by midsummer.

One of the more widely distributed species is *Sisyrinchium angustifolium*, which ranges from South Carolina north to southeastern Canada and westward to the Great Plains. It is a robust plant; its grasslike foliage may attain 50 centimeters in length, and its flowers 1 centimeter across. *Sisyrinchium dichotomum* Bicknell has white tepals that are recurved at maturity like those of a turk's-cap lily. It is a rare species (federally endangered) from the mid elevations of the Blue Ridge escarpment. *Sisyrinchium nashii* Bicknell and *Sisyrinchium rosulatum* Bicknell range in the Southeast from North Carolina and Tennessee south to Florida and Texas.

Vegetative propagation of the eastern sisyrinchiums is by division of the clumps (fans) in the summer. Seed can be collected after the pods have turned from green to dark brown or black. One period of cold chilling is needed to induce germination, and most seedlings bloom the first season.

Tofieldia glutinosa (Michaux) Persoon

The diminutive bog asphodel (Liliaceae [Melanthiaceae]) is a real charmer, well suited to rock garden and trough culture where it can be observed at close range. Plants inhabit seepage slopes, bogs, and wet meadows and prairies from Newfoundland and Alaska, south to Minnesota and California, in the Appalachians to North Carolina and in the Rockies to Wyoming. Five subspecies are recognized which vary in size, minor morphological characteristics, and soil requirements, depending on their range.

The botanical nomenclature of this species varies widely. Some authorities report half a dozen species from this region. The discrete eastern North American species seems to be *Tofieldia racemosa* (Walt.) B.S.P., native to coastal pine savannas, pocosins, and bogs; it grows taller, to 1 meter, with a more elongated, open inflorescence, each node of which holds three stalked flowers. *Tofieldia pusilla* (Michaux) Persoon (synonym *T. palustris*) is a plant of the far north, from Labrador to Alaska, south to the Great Lakes and along the Rocky Mountains.

In *Tofieldia glutinosa*, a tuft of flattened, narrow leaves arises in a stiff, upright whorl from a thickened rootstock. A slender, sticky-hairy (glutinous) bloom stalk 15 to 30 centimeters tall is crowned with a tight cluster of small, starry white flowers in summer. Multistemmed clumps are showy in an understated way.

Tofieldia is easy to grow in moist, limy to subacid, sandy or humus-rich soil in full sun or light shade. Eastern plants prefer acid soils; the prairie subspecies (subsp. *occidentalis*) is generally found on circumneutral soils. Bog asphodel is perfect for an artificial bog garden, moist rockery, or container. Combine this diminutive plant with small companions that will not overwhelm it: *Hypoxis hirsuta*, violets, primroses, *Parnassia*, and drooping sedge (*Carex crinita*) are well-behaved partners. The tight rosettes are easily divided in spring or after flowering.

Veratrum viride Aitken

The dramatic false hellebore (also called Indian poke and corn lily) is found in low, wet woods, seeps, bogs, and wet meadows, and along streams, from Quebec and Alaska south to North Carolina, Montana, and Oregon. The distinctive greenish white to lime-green flowers with three narrow petals and three similar, petal-like sepals are borne on drooping pedicels in large terminal clusters in early summer. The lush, pleated 30-centimeter oval leaves overlap on stout stalks 30 to 200 centimeters tall (Plate 101). Plants grow from stout crowns with persistent thick, fleshy roots. Extensive colonies of flowerless plants are often seen, and even when mature, plants in optimal conditions may skip flowering for a year or more; when well flowered, they may fail to set viable seed. All parts of the plant are poisonous if ingested.

Plant *Veratrum* in humus-rich, moist to wet soil in full sun or part shade. Plants bloom sparingly where shade is dense. Bold foliage and unusual flowers make false hellebore a unique garden plant. Use it in bog gardens or in moist woods and along streams. Combine it with marsh marigold (*Caltha palustris*), skunk cabbage (*Symplocarpus foetidus*), cardinal flower (*Lobelia cardinalis*), bog avens (*Geum rivale*), and ferns.

Mature clumps have huge, deep crowns that are difficult to move and divide, but this can be done in fall after the leaves wither. Sow fresh seed outdoors as soon as it is ripe. Seedlings develop slowly and take at least five years to reach blooming size.

Xerophyllum asphodeloides (Linnaeus) Nuttall

Anyone who has visited the Rocky Mountains in summer has fallen under the spell of beargrass (*Xerophyllum tenax*), but few realize that there is an equally showy species native to coastal pine barrens and open, dry mountain woods from New Jersey south to Tennessee and Georgia. This plant, called turkeybeard or mountain asphodel, is unknown to most gardeners because it grows in very specialized habitats and is relatively rare throughout its range.

The generic name means "dry leaf." Plants produce a dense, tufted mound of tough, wiry evergreen leaves from a thickened rootstock. In spring the leafy bloom stalk rises to 120 centimeters, crowned by a dense, mushroom-shaped spike of creamy flowers. As the inflorescence ages, it elongates and ultimately forms a long wand.

Though turkeybeard is touchy in cultivation, in the right spot it makes a showy and long-lived display. The secret to success is well-drained, sandy, acidic soil in full sun or light shade. The deep-seated, stout rootstock is nearly impossible to transplant successfully, so the only way to establish the plant is to set out young seedlings. This is problematic because plants are seldom offered by nurseries. In its native habitat turkeybeard consorts with bayberry (*Myrica pensylvanica*), sweet fern (*Comptonia peregrina*), and bracken (*Pteridium aquilinum*), in the broken shade of pitch pine (*Pinus resinosa*). These plants also make excellent garden companions, along with bowman's root (*Porteranthus trifoliata*), fire pink (*Silene virginica*), wild lupine (*Lupinus perennis*), and bearberry (*Arctostaphylos uva-ursi*).

Norman Deno (1993) reported poor germination of the seed in all indoor treatments, and dead seed after dry storage. He obtained best results by sowing fresh seed outdoors.

Zigadenus densus (Desrousseaux) Fernald

This species is found from southeastern Virginia west to Tennessee and south to Louisiana. It is very similar to *Zigadenus leimanthoides*, save for its smaller size (half that of *Z. leimanthoides*) and spring flowering, and it grows in similar habitats.

Zigadenus glaberrimus Michaux

The smooth bunchflower occurs over a fairly wide area of the southeastern United States, from Virginia and Tennessee south to Florida and Louisiana. It is a plant of moist meadows and grasslands. The basal, ribbed foliage is somewhat glaucous, and the flowers, appearing in mid to late summer, are borne on stems from 50 to 90 centimeters tall. The individual florets are up to 2.5 centimeters in diameter and marked with dark glands at the base, so that this plant is rather striking in flower.

Zigadenus gramineus Rydberg

Zigadenus gramineus has dense, globular clusters of creamy yellow flowers and grows in sloughs, wet ditches, and wet coulees (brushy ravines) in the northern Great Plains. The name *Zigadenus* means "yoke gland" and refers to the green or yellow gland at the base of the petal. Creamy white flowers with jade-green centers are carried on tall, sturdy stems in branched or unbranched inflorescences, appearing in summer. The narrow, glaucous foliage is deciduous.

Give these plants rich, evenly moist soil in full sun. In the wild, the areas where they grow may be inundated in winter and spring, but by blooming time the plants are generally on *terra firma*. Wild plants are often single-stemmed, but they clump up in the garden with time. They share their wetland habitats with blue flag iris (*Iris versicolor*), golden Alexander (*Zizia* spp.), small white ladyslipper (*Cypripedium candidum*), Kansas gayfeather (*Liatris pycnostachya*), prairie loosestrife (*Lysimachia quadriflora*), and bottle gentian (*Gentiana andrewsii*).

Divide the bulbs after flowering. Sow fresh seed outdoors or indoors at 70°F (21°C); germination is rapid and good. Seedlings take three or four years to flower.

Zigadenus leimanthoides Gray

This species ranges from Connecticut south to Florida, and west to eastern Texas, growing in moist meadows and bogs. The often red-pigmented stems are from 30 to 150 centimeters tall, bearing flowers in midsummer (June and July). The tepals are blotched yellow at the base, and the plants grow from an ovoid, tunicated bulb.

Zigadenus nuttallii Gray ex S. Watson

This species inhabits grasslands from the Edwards Plateau in central Texas, north to Kansas and east to Missouri and Arkansas. The attractive, bright green foliage grows from a dark-tunicated bulb. The plants bloom in April and May on stems to 60 centimeters tall. The individual florets are white with yellow blotches at the base of each tepal.

Bibliography

Barr, Claude. 1984. *Jewels of the Plains*. Minneapolis: University of Minnesota Press.

Burrell, C. Colston. 1997. *A Gardener's Encyclopedia of Wildflowers*. Emmaus, Pennsylvania: Rodale.

Burrell, C. Colston. 1999. *Perennial Combinations*. Emmaus, Pennsylvania: Rodale.

Dormon, Caroline. 1958. *Flowers Native to the Deep South*. Baton Rouge: Claitor's Book Store.

Deno, Norman C. 1993. *Seed Germination Theory and Practice*. State College, Pennsylvania: Privately printed.

Dormon, Caroline. 1965. *Natives Preferred*. Baton Rouge: Claitor's Book Store.

Foster, H. Lincoln. 1968. *Rock Gardening*. New York: Bonanza; reprinted, 1995, Portland: Timber Press.

Glattstein, Judy. 1994. *The American Gardener's World of Bulbs*. Boston: Little, Brown.

Miles, Bebe. 1976. *Bulbs for the Home Gardener*. New York: Grosset and Dunlap.

Ogdon, Scott. 1994. *Garden Bulbs of the South*. Dallas: Taylor.

Wilder, Louise Beebe. 1990. *Adventures with Hardy Bulbs*. New York: Collier.

Sources of Bulbs and Seeds

Please note that almost all these suppliers request payment for their catalog if you have not ordered from them previously. The typical fee in 2000 for an initial catalog is $3.00.

Bulbs

The following growers and retailers offered nursery-propagated North American bulbs during the 2000 to 2001 season.

Bluestem Prairie Nursery, Ken Schaal, 13197 E. 13th Road, Hillsboro, IL 62049. Eastern and midwestern species.

Hoog & Dix Export, Heemsteedse Dreef 175, 2101 KD Heemstede, Holland. Wholesale only; source for Dutch-grown calochortus and other specialties.

Pheasant Valley Farms, P.O. Box 886, Woodburn, OR 97071. Oregon native species.

Plant Delights, 9241 Sauls Road, Raleigh, NC 27603. Eastern woodland plants.

Siskiyou Rare Plant Nursery, 2825 Cummings Road, Medford, OR 97501. Bulbs sold primarily through fall supplement.

Telos Rare Bulbs, P.O. Box 4978, Arcata, CA 95518. Extensive list of California and Oregon species.

We-Du Nursery, Route 5, Box 724, Marion, NC 28752. Eastern species.

Seeds

In addition to the following sources, many botanic gardens and local or regional plant societies offer seed to their members.

Alpine Garden Society, AGS Centre, Avon Bank, Pershore, Worcester WR10 3JP, England, United Kingdom. Members only seed exchange.

Alplains, P.O. Box 489, Kiowa, CO 80117. Seed from cultivated plants and from wild populations in the Rocky Mountains and Great Basin.

Jim and Jenny Archibald, Bryn Collen, Ffostrasol, Llandysul, SA44 5SB, Wales, United Kingdom. Extensive list includes many western American items, both wild-collected and garden-grown.

North American Rock Garden Society, P.O. Box 67, Millwood, NY 10546. Largest seed exchange on offer; for members only.

Northwest Native Seed, Ron Ratko, 17595 Vierra Canyon Road #172, Prunedale, CA 93907. Superb selection of wild-collected seed; many bulbs. Address changes frequently, so check specialist journals for advertisement.

Rocky Mountain Rare Plants, 1706 Deerpath Road, Franktown, CO 80116. Website: www.rmrp.com. Garden and wild-collected seed, especially of xerophilic species.

Rogue House Seed, Phyllis Gustafson, 250 Maple Street, Central Point, OR 97502. Wild-collected seed from the Siskiyou Mountains.

Scottish Rock Garden Club, Mrs. J. Thomlinson, Membership Secretary, 1 Hillcrest Road, Bearsden, Glasgow G61 2EB, Scotland, United Kingdom. Members only seed exchange.

Southwest Native Seeds, P.O. Box 50503, Tucson, AZ 85703. Species from the desert Southwest and sometimes northern Mexico.

Theodore Payne Foundation, 10459 Tuxford Street, Sun Valley, CA 91352. Species from southern California and the desert Southwest.

Yucca-Do Nursery, Route 3, Box 103, Hempstead, TX 77445. E-mail: yuccado@ nettexas.net. Species from Mexico and the U.S. Southeast and Southwest; plants also listed.

Metric Conversion Chart

$$°C = 5/9 \ (°F - 32)$$
$$°F = (9/5 \times °C) + 32$$

1 millimeter	0.04 inch
1 centimeter	0.5 inch
1 meter	3.25 feet
1 kilometer	0.6 mile
1 hectare	2.5 acres
1 inch	25 millimeters
1 inch	2.5 centimeters
1 foot	30 centimeters
1 foot	0.3 meter
1 mile	1.6 kilometers
1 acre	0.4 hectare

Contributors

C. Colston Burrell is a garden designer and plantsman as well as the author of *Perennials for Today's Gardens* (Meredith 2000), *Perennial Combinations* (Rodale 1999), and *A Gardener's Encyclopedia of Wildflowers* (Rodale 1997). He is developing his own 10-acre garden in the Blue Ridge Mountains near Charlottesville, Virginia.

Frank Callahan is a contract botanist working for the U.S. Forest Service and Bureau of Land Management. He also collects, prepares, and installs specimens for the herbarium at Southern Oregon University and has contributed material to major herbaria in the United States and abroad since 1977. He distributes tree and shrub seed through his company, Callahan Seeds, and has identified more Big Trees (record-size specimens) than anyone else in the country.

Michael E. Chelednik holds a degree in biology and lives and gardens in Greenville, North Carolina, where his special interests include bulbous plants (particularly rain lilies), Iridaceae, and woody Liliaceae. In 1999 he explored the native plants of northern and eastern Mexico in the field.

Molly M. Grothaus was a leading Pacific Northwest plantswoman and a founder of the Columbia-Willamette chapter of NARGS and of the Berry Botanic Garden in Lake Oswego, Oregon. In addition to maintaining a large collection of bulbs, including many select forms of *Erythronium*, she collected and hybridized rhododendrons. She died in 2000.

Mary Irish is a garden writer and lecturer in Phoenix, Arizona, where until 1999 she was director of public horticulture at the Desert Botanical Garden. Her articles on desert gardening have appeared in many national magazines and horticultural reference books, and she has also done radio and television programs. She is the author of *Agave, Yucca,* *and Related Species: A Gardener's Guide* (with Gary Irish; Timber Press 2000) and *Gardening in the Desert: A Guide to Plant Selection and Care* (University of Arizona Press 2000).

David King is a retired engineering manager who began growing and exhibiting alpine and bulbous plants in England in the late 1970s, accumulating numerous awards. He grows significant collections of *Crocus*, *Erythronium*, and especially *Fritillaria*, in which American species dominate. Since the mid-1980s he has made nearly 30 trips throughout the western United States to observe and photograph wild plants, including all the American species of *Fritillaria*.

Mark McDonough, known in horticultural circles as the "Onion Man," is an avid gardener who has focused on ornamental alliums for the past 30 years. He has published articles on them in botanical society journals, *Pacific Horticulture*, and *Fine Gardening*, as well as a newsletter (now out of publication) called *G.A.R.L.I.C.* He works as CAD manager and information technologist for Sasaki Associates, an architecture, landscape architecture, and planning firm in Watertown, Massachusetts.

Jane McGary works as an editor of scholarly reference books and also of the *Rock Garden Quarterly*, the journal of the North American Rock Garden Society. She grows almost 1000 taxa of bulbous plants in her northwestern Oregon garden and in bulb frames.

Edward Austin McRae is one of the world's leading lily growers. For 40 years he pioneered hybridization methods for lilies at Oregon Bulb Farms, working with eminent hybridizers and earning the highest honors and awards, including the Lyttel Cup of the Royal Horticultural Society and the E. H. Wilson Award from the North American Lily Society. He is the author of *Lilies: A Guide for Growers and Collectors* (Timber Press 1998) and is currently working with the North American Lily Society on a program to preserve the species.

Alan W. Meerow was professor of ornamental horticulture at the University of Florida, Fort Lauderdale Research and Education Center, for 13 years; he is now a research geneticist and plant systematist with the U.S. Department of Agriculture in Miami, Florida. He is a leading expert on the Amaryllidaceae and has authored several dozen scientific papers on the taxonomy of that group, including treatments for several major regional floras. Dr. Meerow is also the editor of *Herbertia*, the journal of the International Bulb Society.

Georgie Robinett, a retired medical social worker, and the late **Jim Robinett**, a software engineer, spent many years traveling to observe native

Contributors

North American bulbs in the wild and operated a small mail-order nursery growing species bulbs from seed. They co-edited *Mariposa*, the newsletter of the American Calochortus Society, and authored articles for the journals of the North American Lily Society and International Bulb Society. They also lectured frequently on California native plants.

Loren Russell is an avid hiker and photographer with a lifelong interest in alpine and subalpine plants in the Pacific Northwest. He has been active in the North American Rock Garden Society for a number of years. In 1998 he organized the field program for the NARGS national meetings in the Western Cascades, and he was also involved in the development of the NARGS-funded Sebring Rock Garden in Eugene, Oregon. A resident of Corvallis, Oregon, he lectures on many aspects of rock gardening.

Parker Sanderson received his degree in botany from the University of California, Davis, and was horticultural manager of the university's arboretum for seven years. He has done extensive fieldwork on Californian bulbous plants. He is presently co-owner of Cistus Nursery and Garden Design in Portland, Oregon.

Index

Note: Current names are in italic type, and synonyms in roman.

Index

Index

Index